MAKING DINOSAUR

TOYS IN

WOOD

DAVID WAKEFIELD

 Sterling Publishing Co., Inc.   New York

To my mother
whose balance of love and
discipline gave me the room to imagine and the
strength to get the job done

Library of Congress Cataloging-in-Publication Data

Wakefield, David.
     Making dinosaur toys in wood / David Wakefield.
         p.   cm.
     ISBN 0-8069-6956-3
     1. Wooden toy making.   2. Dinosaurs in art.   I. Title.
TT174.5.W6W36   1990
745.592'8—dc20   90-9466
                                                        CIP

The toy designs in this book are the copyrighted property of the author. Readers are encouraged to make these toys for gifts or personal use. However, to reproduce these designs in wood or any material for sale or profit, written permission must be obtained from the author. Full-size plans for all of the dinosaurs except The Scooter, The Rocker, and The Swings are available for $5.00. Please send all requests to: David Wakefield, Ancient Beasts, 10646 Sand Ridge Road, Millfield, Ohio 45761.

Copyright © 1990 by David Wakefield
Published by Sterling Publishing Co., Inc.
387 Park Avenue South, New York, N.Y. 10016
Distributed in Canada by Sterling Publishing
c/o Canadian Manda Group, P.O. Box 920, Station U
Toronto, Ontario, Canada M8Z 5P9
Distributed in Great Britain and Europe by Cassell PLC
Artillery House, Artillery Row, London SW1P 1RT, England
Distributed in Australia by Capricorn Ltd.
P.O. Box 665, Lane Cove, NSW 2066
Manufactured in the United States of America
All rights reserved

METRIC EQUIVALENCY CHART

MM—MILLIMETRES   CM—CENTIMETRES

INCHES TO MILLIMETRES AND CENTIMETRES

INCHES	MM	CM	INCHES	CM	INCHES	CM
⅛	3	0.3	9	22.9	30	76.2
¼	6	0.6	10	25.4	31	78.7
⅜	10	1.0	11	27.9	32	81.3
½	13	1.3	12	30.5	33	83.8
⅝	16	1.6	13	33.0	34	86.4
¾	19	1.9	14	35.6	35	88.9
⅞	22	2.2	15	38.1	36	91.4
1	25	2.5	16	40.6	37	94.0
1¼	32	3.2	17	43.2	38	96.5
1½	38	3.8	18	45.7	39	99.1
1¾	44	4.4	19	48.3	40	101.6
2	51	5.1	20	50.8	41	104.1
2½	64	6.4	21	53.3	42	106.7
3	76	7.6	22	55.9	43	109.2
3½	89	8.9	23	58.4	44	111.8
4	102	10.2	24	61.0	45	114.3
4½	114	11.4	25	63.5	46	116.8
5	127	12.7	26	66.0	47	119.4
6	152	15.2	27	68.6	48	121.9
7	178	17.8	28	71.1	49	124.5
8	203	20.3	29	73.7	50	127.0

Introduction

When I was growing up my friends and I went through a period of several years when we were all taken by a complete fascination with dinosaurs. There is so much that is intriguing about these creatures. First, the fact that they disappeared over 150 million years ago, which puts them in the same mythical category as dragons and unicorns, except that dinosaurs actually existed, and we have the bones to prove it! Then there is the incredible size of these creatures. There were hundreds of species of dinosaurs that would have dwarfed the largest creatures alive today. You can't help but be amazed by an animal who had teeth as big as you are.

The strange appearance of these beasts, of course, is another attraction. I think if you asked children to invent bizarre creatures, never having seen a picture of a dinosaur, they would probably come up with something that resembles one.

All of these factors together make for the irresistible attraction of dinosaurs. The further I got into this book, the more intrigued I became. I just couldn't get enough of these amazing animals.

I think that although adults are rarely as obsessed with dinosaurs as their children are, still there is a primal chord struck in all of us by these tremendous beasts. For this reason I designed the smaller versions of some of the animated dinosaurs for adults to put on their desks or coffee tables. I think that the intricate sculptural quality of some of these toys would be enhanced by the use of exotic hardwoods for a more sophisticated look for these display pieces. (Be careful of toxic sawdust.) Some of these toys are somewhat complex, so be patient, and take your time with the assembly steps. I hope there is something here for everyone, and that you experience the same challenge and satisfaction building these that I did in designing them.

Sincerely,
David Wakefield

Contents

Tools, Techniques, and Production Procedures

There are a few hands tools that you'll need to make these toys. (*See Figure 1.*)

The **dovetail saw** is used to cut off protruding dowel ends during assembly. It's also useful for taking toys apart to make corrections. If you can find a small saw without a stiff back, it will work even better than a dovetail saw, because you can flex it slightly and saw flush to your project without your hand being in the way. (*See Figure 2.*)

The **four-in-hand** is a combination flat and curved rasp for coarse work and a flat and curved file for smoothing out rough areas. This is an extremely useful hand tool for a variety of shaping and smoothing tasks. I prefer the smaller size (8″) for most work.

A **rat-tail file** will come in handy to smooth tight curves.

You'll need a standard 16-ounce **claw hammer**. I prefer a metal hammer to a rawhide or wooden mallet for a number of reasons. In hammering wheels on axles, the mass of a metal hammer will drive them through in just one or two hits. Every time you hit a wheel onto an axle, a little glue squeezes out onto the hammer. Glue can be easily wiped off a metal hammer, but it tends to build up on wood or rawhide. After a time, there is an ugly black mess on the end of your mallet. This in turn will leave black marks on the wheels.

In the clamp department, you can get by with two large **C-clamps,** two small **C-clamps,** and two small **bar clamps.** However, if you can afford more clamps, buy them. Often you will have several parts glued up and drying in the clamps when you're ready

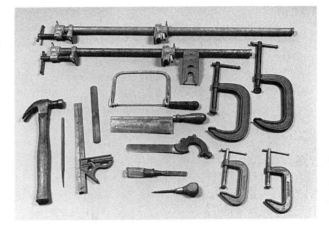

Figure 1. The hand tools that you'll need for toymaking.

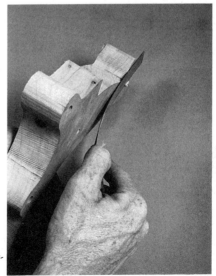

Figure 2. A small saw with a flexible blade will help you saw dowels flush without putting scratches in the surface of your work.

to glue up something else. If all your clamps are in use, you'll find yourself waiting for glue to dry.

You'll need a chisel from time to time, but there's no need to buy an entire set. A ¼" **straight chisel** will work for most situations.

A **coping saw** is needed for a few of the toys in this book, for cutting out small pieces. You can also use it instead of a band saw for cutting out irregularly shaped parts, though this takes a great deal of patience and care.

A small **square** of some sort is essential for marking and for keeping the band saw blades and sanding belts square to their respective work tables.

A **scratch awl** is useful for marking the center of holes before drilling. You can also use it to mark stock for cutting.

A **glue applicator** is indispensable for gluing wheels on axles, applying glue to small parts, and putting glue inside holes. Keep a piece of wire handy to clean out the long nose, or it will become clogged up. If it does clog, soak it in hot water and ream it out with the wire.

Enlarging the Patterns

Most of the patterns for the Animated Dinosaurs are full size. Some of these patterns, however, have been reduced to either 64% or 51.2%. The patterns that are at 64% can be enlarged twice at 125% on a variable copier to bring them up to full size (64% × 125% = 80% × 125% = 100%). The patterns that are at 51.2% can be enlarged by 125% three times to bring them up to full size (51.2% × 125% = 64% × 125% = 80% × 125% = 100%). If you can't find a copier that has the ability to enlarge by 125%, I sell full size patterns for all of these projects except the Huge Dinosaurs for $5.00. These patterns (as with those in the book) are protected by my copyright and can not be used to make any of these designs for resale.

The Huge Dinosaur Rocker, Scooter and Swings are too large to duplicate in this fashion. They can be enlarged by the following method. Make a grid of 1" squares on a piece of paper (36" wide paper is available by the foot at art supply stores). Number the horizontal and vertical lines on the grid you've just drawn *and* the grid behind the pattern in the book. Carefully examine the pattern and note where the pattern line touches each grid line. Make a pencil dot at the corresponding points on the 1" grid that you drew. Repeat for every point where the grid and the pattern touch. Then simply connect the dots using a French curve.

You'll have to extend the grid in the book over the pattern to locate the exact centers of the holes. The placement of the holes is critical, so be extremely careful in locating them.

Transferring the Patterns

Once you have all your full size patterns for a given toy, there are two ways to transfer the patterns to your stock.

The first method is to tape the pattern to your stock with carbon paper between them, and carefully trace the pattern with a stylus. A ballpoint pen that's out of ink will make an excellent stylus, or you can sand the end of a ¼" dowel to a dull point.

The second method is to cut the pattern out carefully and tape it to your stock with clear tape.

Use the tip of a Forstner bit, or a ⅛" bit, to drill (through the pattern) into the wood and mark the exact center of your hole locations. Then cut the piece out on the band saw.

Drilling

In many of the animated dinosaurs, drilling is done before cutting out the silhouettes of the parts. This is done to prevent pieces from splitting if the hole is near the edge.

Whenever you're drilling all the way through a piece, put a scrap under your work to prevent the underside of the work tearing out as the drill bit comes through.

If you're drilling holes that are large enough to require a spade bit, set the depth of the drill so that the tip of the bit just comes through slightly. Then flip the piece over and use the little hole made by the tip of the bit to center the bit as you drill the remainder of the hole. This will prevent tear-out.

The location of holes is extremely important in animated toys, so most of your drilling should be done with Forstner or brad point bits, to prevent the bits from wandering as you start the hole.

When you're drilling the holes through cams and axles, to pin the cam in place, position the toy upside down on the drill press with most of the cam below the axle. This will make it easier to drill through them accurately without the cam shifting. (*See Figure 3.*)

You can make a simple jig to drill the holes in dowels, such as the handlebars of the swings for the rope. Drill a 1″ hole into the end of a block of wood and rip it in half. You'll have a trough to rest the dowel in as you drill. (*See Figure 4.*)

When you are drilling the holes for the brass nails in the miniature animated dinosaurs, the size of the holes will depend on two things: 1. The size of brass (or other material) nails that you find available, 2. Whether the nail pivots in the hole, or is nailed tightly into the hole.

The pivot holes will be slightly larger than the nail and the fastening holes will be slightly smaller. Experiment with scraps before you drill the holes in your actual parts.

Cutting Out the Pieces

Most of the cutting out of pieces is done on the band saw. I recommend a ³⁄₁₆″ skip-tooth blade with a pitch (teeth per inch) of four or six for this type of work, unless specified otherwise. This blade will make very tight turns without binding. It will also follow a straight line fairly well, and will cut quickly. This

Figure 3. It's easier to drill through the cam with the mass of the cam below the axle.

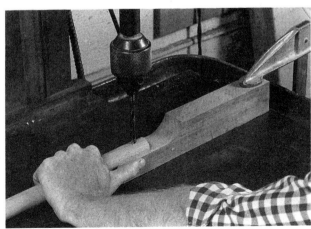

Figure 4. You can make a handy jig for drilling holes in 1″ dowels by simply drilling a 1″ hole in a block of wood and sawing it in half.

helps you keep a smooth fluid line which will speed up your sanding.

Drilling holes in tight corners before sawing will help you make turns that the blade couldn't otherwise.

You'll probably have to do some resawing, as many of the pieces on these toys are quite thin. You can make a resaw guide quite easily by fastening two boards together at perfect right angles and clamping the assembly to the band saw table. (*See Figure 5.*) A ³⁄₈″ or even ½″ blade will be helpful for resawing.

A wedge in between the two pieces after they pass the blade will help to keep the kerf open and prevent the resawn pieces from binding. (*See Figure 6.*)

The band saw can be a dangerous tool if you don't follow good safety practices. Don't wear jewelry or loose clothing that can catch in the blade. Use eye protection, and never have the upper guides more than ¼″ above the work.

Don't get your fingers closer than 1½″ from the blade. Small pieces can be cut out quite easily with a coping saw. If a small piece is cut off your work and gets caught between the blade and the slot in the

Figure 6. A little wedge of wood will keep the kerf open and prevent the resawn pieces from binding the blade.

table, *turn the saw off* to remove the offending scrap.

A final note: always check that the table is square to the blade before cutting pieces out on the band saw. This will save you time and aggravation with your edge sanding, and will help with the accuracy of your assemblies.

Figure 5. To make a resawing fence, simply glue two boards together at *right* angles and clamp them to the band saw table (parallel to the blade).

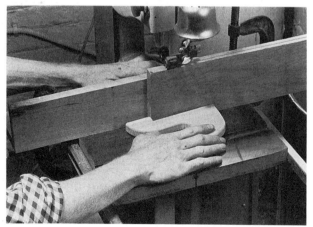

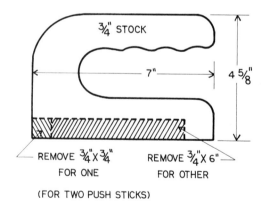

¾″ STOCK

7″

4 ⅝″

REMOVE ¾″ X ¾″ FOR ONE

REMOVE ¾″ X 6″ FOR OTHER

(FOR TWO PUSH STICKS)

Figure 7. Resawing thin pieces can be done safely with the help of a push stick.

Don't Have a Band Saw?

Although the band saw can make work go quickly, it is not essential.

A coping saw will cut out most of these toys with some care, patience and muscle. You will, however, have to mark the pattern out on both sides of your stock. This is done by drilling the holes first and using them to lay out the pattern on the flip side. Then, with the piece in a vise, follow both lines as you cut.

Some of the larger toys can be cut out with a reciprocating saw if you're careful.

Belt Sanding

Always wear a dust mask and eye and ear protection when belt-sanding, and no loose clothing or jewelry.

I use the term *flat sanding* to refer to a stationary belt sander on which the pieces are held to sand flat surfaces. If you don't have one of these, you can mount a hand-held belt sander upside down in a vise and do most of the flat sanding. Caution: Don't use either of these to sand the smaller pieces. It's just too easy to sand off the tips of your fingers. Rub the small pieces on a piece of sandpaper tacked to the workbench or other surface to flat sand them.

I use 80# paper on the stationary sander for initial sanding to remove all the planer marks and clamping dents and get the surface basically flat. I then use either 120# or 150# to finish smoothing the surface. As with all sanding, always flat-sand in the direction of the grain. Belt cleaners can increase the life of belts up to 500%. These are now available in most woodworking catalogs.

When I say *edge-sand*, I am referring to sanding the edge contour or silhouette on a 1″ sander/grinder. As with the flat sanding, I do this twice, once with 80# and once with 120# or 150#. It's a good idea to do the routing *between* the two passes on the sander/grinder. This will remove any burns or marks from the guide or rollerbearing on the router bit.

This tool works fine with a flat platen for outside curves but the edges of the belt tend to dig in on inside curves. You can build a curved platen to take care of this problem. Rip a 1″ dowel in half and screw it to the platen from behind. You'll have to bend the platen so that the front surface (with the ½″ thickness added) is still right behind the belt. (*See Figure 8.*) Some paraffin or graphite paper on the dowel will slow down the heat deterioration. At any rate, the piece of dowel will have to be replaced from time to time. You may want to buy a second platen so you'll have one for each type of sanding.

Figure 8. Half of a 1″ dowel fastened to the platen will give you a curved surface for edge-sanding inside curves. You'll have to bend the original platen to accommodate the added thickness of the dowel.

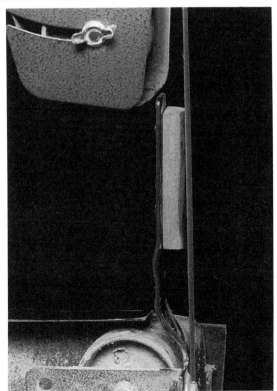

Don't Have a Sander/Grinder?

This tool is fairly inexpensive but you can do without one. A four-in-hand and sandpaper will do the trick.

Routing

The router is, I believe, the most dangerous tool that I use in toy making and requires extreme caution. Wear a dust mask and eye and ear protection when you use the router, and keep your fingers as far as possible from the bit.

Use your common sense when deciding what pieces to shape on the router and what pieces should be done by hand. There are many small parts to these toys, and some of these are too small to shape safely on a machine. I use this rule of thumb: If during any portion of the operation, I have to bring my fingers closer than 2 inches from the bit, then I do the operation by hand. I've found that the edges of small pieces can sometimes be shaped quicker with a four-in-hand or sandpaper than with a router.

The best rule of thumb is this: If you're not absolutely confident of your ability to complete an operation safely, *don't do it!* Doubts can be a powerful force for good when you're woodworking, if you pay attention to them.

Router Bits. I use a quarter-round bit exclusively for shaping the edges of toys.

I recommend purchasing a carbide-tipped bit with a roller bearing. These will stay sharp much longer than steel bits. This saves you sharpening time, costs and down time, and also helps prevent you from burning your work. The roller bearing guide travels slowly along the edge of the work, while the bit is spinning much faster. This prevents burning on the edge of the work.

The Router Table. For smaller toys you'll want to set your router up as a shaper, with the bit held stationary and facing upwards. To do this, you'll need to make or purchase a router table about 18″ square. If

you make your own, use a hard, smooth material (such as Formica®) for the work surface. Silicone spray will keep the surface slick, so pieces slide smoothly along.

To attach your router to the table, first remove the work surface from the router. It usually comes off with a few screws. Then use the screws to attach the router to the underside of the table with the bit poking up through a hole in the center of the table.

If you've made your own table, you'll need to rout out the area under the table about the same diameter as the router's work surface, to make the table, in this area, the same thickness as your router's work surface. Mark and drill the holes for the screws, then attach the router.

Routing Techniques. Keep in mind that when you use your router as a shaper, the bit spins counterclockwise as you look down at it. Pieces must be passed from right to left (clockwise) past the front of the bit (the side closest to you). This will feed the work against the direction of rotation. If you pass the work by the bit in the opposite direction, the bit will want to push the work along. If may even grab the work and fling it out of your hands.

Never start routing on an outside curve or corner. The bit will either chip the wood or fling the piece out of your hands. Start on a straightaway or an inside curve whenever possible. Avoid end grain when starting a cut and always start your cut on the long grain. End grain is much harder to cut and it can catch the bit. As you make your pass, maintain a constant feed rate. Never stop moving the workpiece when it's pressed against the router. If the bit spins in one place on the wood, for even a fraction of a second, it will burn your work. This is especially important to remember on sharp curves, where there is a tendency to slow down as you change directions. It's better to make many short overlapping passes at a constant speed than to slow down at turning points and burn your work.

Feeding the work at a constant rate is a skill, and it will take some practice. If you haven't done much work on the router, you can reduce the risk of ruining your workpiece by making the cut in two passes. Set the bit at half the proper height, so that it removes just half of the desired stock. Make a pass, then raise the bit to the proper height and make another pass to complete the cut.

Don't Have a Router?

Although a router will make short work of your shaping chores, it is also quite easy if more time-consuming to do without one. Simply use a four-in-hand or rat-tail file to break the edges, then smooth them out with hand sanding.

Hand Sanding

This is usually done after all the machine sanding and routing is finished. As with the machine sanding I usually do the hand sanding in two steps. I start out with 80# paper. This will remove any roughness or burns left by the router. It will also take out the cross grain scratches that the edge sanding leaves. Keep in mind that any scratches that the 80# paper doesn't take out certainly won't be cleaned up with 120# so don't go on to 120# till all the cross grain scratches are removed and any roughness on routed edges is smoothed out.

The 120# or 150# will simply smooth the surface and remove the scratches made by the 80# paper. It will not remove any cross grain scratches, roughness, planer marks or band saw marks. Remember, always sand with the grain. When I speak of *breaking the edges* I am referring to lightly sanding the sharp edge left by routing or other cutting, using 120# paper just enough to knock down the sharp corner.

Types of Paper

For smoothing the routed edges a fairly flexible C weight paper is best, a heavier paper is better for breaking the edges, and for serious sanding, such as removing rasp marks, I've found that stiff cloth (J-weight) belt sander belts work great. When they're too worn to use cut them up into 3" × 3" or 4" × 4" squares and they'll last forever for hand sanding.

Gluing and Clamping

Gluing boards edge to edge. Choose the two boards that you want to glue together, and joint the edges. Be sure that the fence on the jointer is perfectly square to the table so that the edges of the boards will be perfectly perpendicular to the faces. Lay out as many bar clamps as you need to keep the entire length of the joint under pressure. Open the clamps up a little wider than the combined width of the board that you will be gluing up. Lay waxed paper on the clamps to keep glue from dripping onto them and onto the work surface.

Stand the boards up on edge, with the edges to be glued facing up. Apply glue evenly to both edges to be glued. I use my fingers to spread the glue, but you may prefer a small brush. Try not to let the glue drip down the face of the board as you spread it. With practice, you'll figure out just how much glue to apply and how to spread it without making a mess.

As soon as you spread the glue, lay the board down in the clamps. Bring the boards together and start to tighten the clamps. Hold the joint between your fingers as you tighten the clamps to make sure that both surfaces end up flush. (*See Figure 9.*) As you clamp the boards, a little glue should squeeze out of the seam along the entire length. If it doesn't, you've done one of the following: You haven't applied enough glue, you haven't tightened the clamps sufficiently, you haven't used enough clamps, or the edges aren't jointed properly.

The first three problems are easily corrected. If your problem is the jointed edges, scrape the glue off and rejoint them. If you're having trouble jointing the edges, check the alignment of your jointer tables and knives. Remember, when you're jointing, once you start the pass you should apply pressure only to the *outfeed* table. Putting pressure on the infeed table will simply duplicate the edge that you already have. If there is a bow on the board, always joint the concave side.

There are two ways to keep boards flat as you clamp them. The first is to use bar clamps above and below the workpieces. *(See Figure 10.)* This method will work for most of the projects in this book. Toy parts are relatively small, and you'll rarely need more than three bar clamps—one above the stock and two below—to glue up wide boards. Alternating the bar clamps in this way counteracts the tendency for the joint to lift in the center.

If you're gluing up very wide or very thin stock, you'll need to do a bit more to keep the boards flat. In this case, wrap a piece of waxed paper around the ends of the boards. Put a rigid piece of stock at least 1″ wide above and below both ends of the boards and clamp them with C-clamps. *(See Figure 11.)*

The best time to remove excess glue squeeze-out

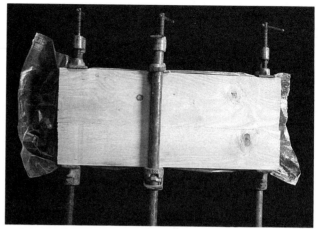

Figure 10. Bar clamps above and below your work will tend to keep the boards flat.

Figure 11. Sticks clamped above and below glue-up will insure a flat surface.

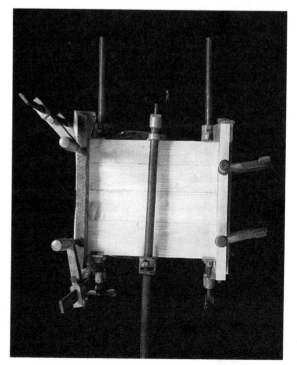

Figure 9. Line the ends of the boards up with your fingers as you apply pressure to the clamps.

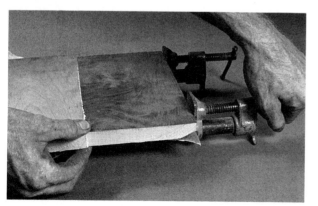

is twenty to thirty minutes after you've clamped the boards. The glue should be the consistency of cottage cheese—just starting to set up. At this point it can be scraped off easily with a chisel without smearing. If you wipe it off earlier, you will press some of the glue into the wood grain. This will make it harder to sand and finish later on. If you wait too long to remove the glue, the glue beads will become brittle and stuck to the wood. There will be a tendency for the glue to pull off tiny chips of wood as you scrape it off.

I usually leave the boards edge clamped for forty-five minutes to an hour. It's best to let the glue set up overnight before you start working with a piece.

Gluing flat surfaces together. The surfaces that are to be glued together should be perfectly flat. Any deep planer mill marks or saw marks should be removed before gluing. 80# sandpaper is sufficient to flatten surfaces that won't be seen after gluing.

Once again, experience will teach you how much glue to use. For areas like the top edge of the Tyrannosaurus head, the squeeze-out doesn't matter. You will either be sanding or sawing that area again, and this will remove the excess glue.

In some areas, the sail of the Dimetrodon, for example, the wood is too thin for much sanding. In places like this, you should put a thin layer of glue on the piece that is to be attached and work it away from the edges toward the center of the piece. This will minimize squeeze-out.

As you bring the pieces together, be careful to position them properly so that you won't have to move them and expose smeared glue. Before clamping, press the pieces together firmly. This will create a suction that will help keep the pieces from shifting when you clamp them.

If the area to be clamped is an exposed part and is not going to be sanded again, use something to prevent the clamps from marring the wood. You can use *cauls* (thin scraps of wood), rubber pads, or you can glue thick pieces of leather to the clamp's faces to avoid the bother of positioning the cauls or pads every time you glue up something.

When you first apply the clamps, rock them back and forth slightly as you snug them up, until the surfaces engage completely. This will help to prevent the workpieces from shifting under the building clamp pressure. It also helps to have the clamps set to the proper opening before you apply the glue. Otherwise, the pieces may fall apart while you're fiddling with the clamps.

Gluing dowels in place. When you are gluing a dowel all the way through a piece, cut the dowel just a little bit long so that it will protrude slightly from both sides. This way you can saw it off and sand it flush to the surface.

To glue the dowel in place, first put down waxed paper under your work. Using a wooden matchstick, a toothpick, or some other long, thin glue applicator, smear the glue evenly on the inside of the hole. Here again, experience will tell you how much glue to apply. Lay the part flat on the waxed paper and drive the dowel in place, making sure that it protrudes from both sides. A sixteen or twenty-ounce hammer will provide the concentrated mass you need to drive the dowel easily, without smashing the end of the dowel or splitting it. Wipe off the glue that's been driven out by the dowel, then let the glue cure. Afterwards, cut and sand the dowels flush. Don't sand the dowel too quickly, or you'll burn the tough end grain of the dowel.

If the hole to be doweled is near the edge of the piece, it's best to drill and plug the hole *before* you cut out the shape of the part. That way, you avoid splitting out a narrow area when you drive the dowel.

When you're gluing dowels in a blind hole, be careful not to put too much glue in the hole. This will prevent the dowel from seating properly, and it may make for a weak joint. Use only enough to cover the end of the dowel, and cut several long grooves running down the side of the dowel. These grooves can be cut with a V-gouge chisel or an awl, or pressed in by crimping the dowel with a pair of pliers, and will allow the excess glue to escape from the hole as you drive the dowel in.

Gluing pegs. Gluing pegs in a toy is similar to gluing dowels in a blind hole, with one important difference. When you peg a part of a toy to another part, you must leave a tiny clearance between the peg head and the toy. If you leave no clearance, the parts will bind. With practice, you'll be able to leave the proper clearance by instinct. But if you're just beginning to make toys, you'll want to make a clearance gauge. This jig guarantees perfect results every time. (*See Figure 12.*) This jig will work for nailing parts together as well.

Remember that pegs need to be different lengths for different situations. The length is measured from the bottom of the peg head to the end of the peg. This dimension is determined by adding the depth of the peg hole, the thickness of the part that the peg goes through, and the clearance between the parts, and then subtracting $1/64''$ to $1/32''$ more (to leave room for glue at the bottom of the hole).

Gluing wheels to axles. When you cut the axles for your toys, double-check the lengths on the bills of materials. The length of an axle is determined by adding the thickness of the wheels, the thickness of the part that the axle goes through, and the clearances needed between the wheels and the part *plus* another $1/16''$ to $1/8''$ so that the axles will protrude slightly from the wheel hubs when you glue them in place. The axle lengths will change slightly depending on how much you sand the toy parts before you assemble the wheels to the axles.

The glue joint between the axle and the wheel has to be as strong as you can make it. To increase the strength, cut several grooves in the ends of the axles where the wheels will fit over them. The grooves will allow more glue to stay in the joint when you press the wheels onto the axles.

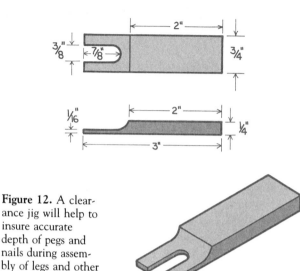

Figure 12. A clearance jig will help to insure accurate depth of pegs and nails during assembly of legs and other moving parts.

Some toymakers recommend rubbing the middle of the axle with paraffin. This will decrease the friction where the axle goes through the toy. This is not necessary if you build your toys from hard, close-grained woods (such as cherry) as I do, but if you use softer, more fibrous woods, treating the axles with paraffin will help the wheels spin freely and decrease the wear of the axle in the hole. Be careful not to get paraffin on the ends of the dowels where the wheels are glued.

To glue the wheels to the axles, first put a piece of waxed paper down on the workbench. Put all the wheels on the paper with the insides facing up. Use a matchstick or a long, thin applicator to smear glue evenly inside the holes. Don't apply glue to more wheels than you can glue up in five minutes, or the glue inside the wheels will start to set up and the joints will be weakened.

Drive an axle into a wheel until you feel it hit the workbench. Turn the wheel/axle assembly over and carefully remove any glue that has been driven out of the hole. Give the axle a twist as you press your finger in toward an imaginary point directly above the center of the axle. Your finger will spiral in, lifting the glue off the wheel without smearing it outward from the hub. (*See Figure 13.*)

Now slip the dowel through the axle hole and set the glued-up wheel on the workbench with the axle pointing straight up. Drive the second wheel onto the axle until the axle protrudes slightly from the hub. Remove the excess glue in the same way you did with the first wheel. Wipe the glue off your hammer head and your finger—I keep a piece of carpet scrap on my workbench just for this purpose. Let the glue cure and sand the axle flush with the hubs of the wheels.

Finishing

I use **Watco Danish Oil** to finish my toys for several reasons. It's easy to use, requiring only a rubdown after each coat. It's nontoxic after it has set up. It gives the toys a deep natural finish without any surface coating. As it soaks in and polymerizes (hardens), it gives the toys a fair amount of protection against abrasion and dirt. It will spot, though, if the toy gets wet.

Remember to always wear gloves while working with Watco as it can be harmful to your skin before it has dried thoroughly.

Finishing one toy at a time. If you're making one toy at a time, the simplest way to finish it is to apply oil with a brush. The instructions on most oil finishes tell you to sand it into the wood, but this is difficult with these toys because there are so many tiny surfaces. A brush will reach into all the cracks and crevices with a minimum of effort. Let the oil soak in for half an hour or so, then rub off any excess before

Figure 13. Spiraling your finger inward and upward will remove the excess glue without smearing it onto the wheel surface.

it gets gummy and hard to remove. Apply a second coat and repeat. Let the finish set up overnight, then apply a final coat. Once again, rub off the excess before it sets up. If you wish, wax the toy with a good carnauba wax.

Finishing many toys at once. If you're making many toys at once, dipping the toys in oil is the way to go. But don't use the five-gallon container that the finish comes in to do the dipping. If you break the seal on the lid, the finish will start to evaporate and will get too thick to soak in properly. Instead, just open the screw-on cap and pour as much finish as you need to cover the toys in a plastic bucket.

I made a simple trough to drain the toys after dipping, so that the excess oil runs back into the bucket. (*See Figure 14.*) Dip the first toy, put it on the trough next to the bucket, dip the second, push the first on a little farther up the trough to make room for the second, and repeat. This way, most of the excess oil will run back to the bucket by the time a toy leaves the trough. When a toy reaches the top of the trough, put it on a clean surface and let the remaining oil soak in.

As you set the toy down to let the oil soak in, separate any surfaces that want to stick together with toothpicks. If the moving parts touch each other, this will prevent the oil from soaking in properly. It will also leave a lot of residue on the surface. It's also a good idea to flip the toy over. If it drained in the trough resting on its wheels, let it soak with the wheels up.

After half an hour, wipe off the excess oil with a rag. You don't have to really rub the toy down. Just wipe off the wet areas. The type of rag you use, however, *is* important. Cotton rags, like old T-shirts, are the best. They are absorbent and lint-free. Synthetic materials don't work well at all. If you wait too long and the toys get gummy, you can use a rag dampened with oil to dissolve the excess. Pay special attention to surfaces where parts might have been touching—between the wheels and body, behind pegged pieces, and so on. Put the oil back in its container and let the toys dry overnight.

The next day, repeat the process. But this time, after you wipe off the toys the first time, let them sit for another half an hour and then really give them a good rubdown.

Painting. Most of the larger toys must be made out of plywood, so painting is essential to protect the wood. You'll want to prime the pieces before laying out the painting lines. Be careful not to get paint inside pivot holes or they will gum up the works.

Apply several coats of paint on end grain as it will really soak it up. A quick sand with 120# is a good idea, between coats, to rough up the surface for good adhesion.

On toys that will be left outside, a little polyurethane inside rope holes and pivot holes will keep water damage down to a minimum.

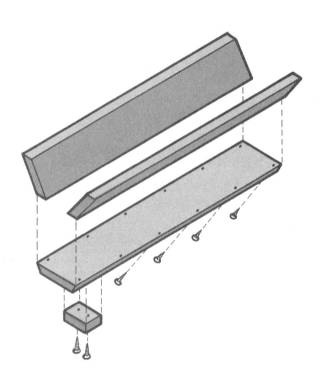

EXPLODED VIEW

Figure 14. A trough will let the excess oil drain off your toys and back into the bucket. It will make the oiling process neater and less wasteful.

SIDE VIEW

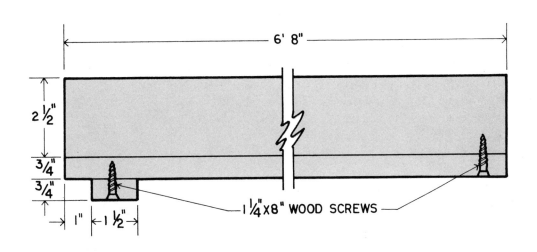

6' 8"

2 ½"

¾"

¾"

1" 1 ½"

1¼"X8" WOOD SCREWS

END VIEW

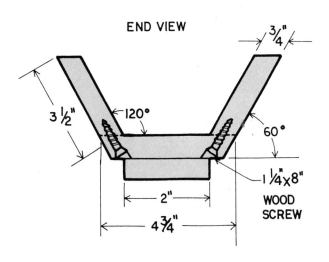

¾"

3 ½"

120°

60°

1¼"X8"
WOOD
SCREW

2"

4¾"

The Pteranodon

This guy's body was covered with fur, not feathers, making him more like a bat than a bird. He didn't so much fly as soar, but he could do this for a very long time.

This was the first of these new dinosaurs that I designed, and its movement is simple but amazing to watch. Holding onto the legs and tail, push the Pteranodon along a flat surface. The wings are lifted by Pitman arms attached to the wheels. The wheels are slightly offset and lift the body up as the wings flap down, and a cam lifts the head at the same time. All of these together give the Pteranodon a very life-like appearance of flight. (*See Figures 1 and 2.*)

The Body Sides

Lay out the body pattern on the inside of the two pieces of stock (B). The reason for this is that the rear pivot holes for the head piece do not go all the way through to the outside and the ½" countersink for the wing pivot pegs must be drilled before the 9/32" holes are drilled all the way through. Notice that the 9/32" holes are not in the center of the ½" hole. There are two holes, one above the other. The remainder is carefully cut away, leaving a vertical slot so that the 7/32" pin can freely pivot up and down when the wings are attached.

Drill the pivot holes in the rear precisely and then lay the two pieces on top of each other to accurately drill the axle holes.

Flat-sand both pieces and edge-sand the silhouettes except the leg cut-aways which will be fitted after the legs are made. Rout the edges where there won't be any spacer and hand-sand these same areas.

The Head

Lay out the head (A), drill and plug the eye hole and drill the 7/16" hole in the rear of the piece. Cut out the silhouette on the band saw. Edge-sand, rout and hand-sand the entire outline. Cut the 3/8" dowel to length (the 1" spacer plus the depth of the pivot minus the clearance). Round off the end and glue it in the hole, making sure it's centered perfectly.

The Spacer

Cut out the spacer (C) and edge-sand a smooth curve on the front edge. Don't flat-sand the sides of the

Figure 1. With one side removed you can see how the cam lifts the head.

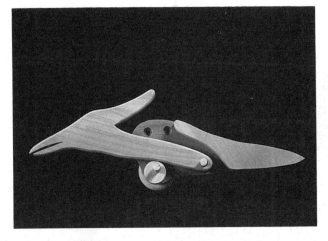

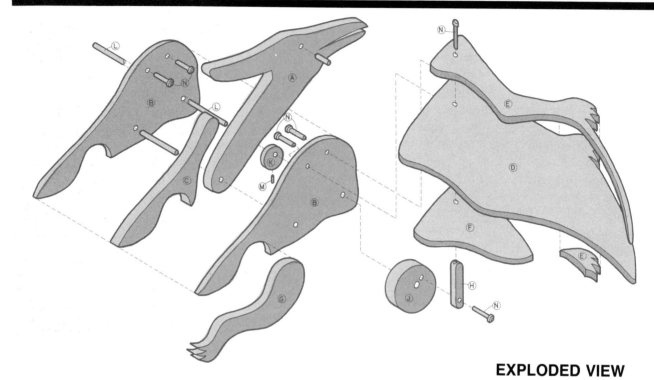

EXPLODED VIEW

MATERIALS

PART	DESCRIPTION	QTY	THICKNESS	WIDTH OR DIAMETER	LENGTH
A	Head	1	¾″	4⅜″	11″
B	Body sides	2	½″	3½″	10⅛″
C	Spacer	1	⅞″	1¾″	7¾″
D	Wings	2	¼″	4¾″	13⅜″
E	Arms	2	¼″	3¾	13
F	Wing Joint Support	2	¼″	2¼″	3½″
G	Legs	2	¾″	1⅞″	6¾″

PART	DESCRIPTION	QTY	THICKNESS	WIDTH OR DIAMETER	LENGTH
H	Pitman arm	2	½″	½″	2¼″
J	Wheels	2	⅝″	2¼″	
K	Cam	1	½″	1¼″	
L	Axle	1		⅜″	3⁵⁄₁₆″
M	Dowel to peg cam	1		⅛″	¾″
N	Pegs	8	⅜″ head	⁷⁄₃₂″	1¹⁄₁₆″ shaft

24

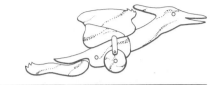

spacer or you may not make the surfaces parallel, which will mess up the assembly.

The Legs

Lay out the legs (G), cut them out on the band saw, flat-sand and edge-sand them. Before routing, fit each leg onto its respective slot in each body side piece. Edge-sand the body sides and check for fit. Edge-sand some more on either the legs or the slots until both legs fit snugly and can be positioned identically with the sides held together. Rout the outer surface of each leg all the way around. Rout the inner surface of each leg, except the upper edge that fits into the slot in the body sides. This will leave more gluing surface when you attach the legs later on. Finally, hand-sand both legs.

The Wing and Arm Assemblies

Lay out the two wing pieces (D) and cut them out. Flat-sand both sides of each wing and edge-sand the entire silhouette except all the claws, including the areas where the long claw will run along the front edge of the wing. These will be sanded after assembly.

Lay out the arm pieces (E) and cut them out carefully, leaving the area around the claws until after assembly. Edge-sand the entire silhouette, except for the hand area and the front edge of the claws which will be sanded after assembly. Hand-sand the edges now, as it will be hard after assembly.

Apply glue to the arm piece. Work the glue away from the edges and away from the rear edge of the long claw section to avoid squeeze-out. Protect the work with scrap wood as you clamp the arm to the wing.

Figure 2. The Pitman arms lift the wings as the wheels turn.

When the assembly is dry, glue and clamp the scrap behind the fingers, using the same wood as the arm and the hand are made of. When this is dry, cut out the claws and edge-sand both the claws and the long front of the wing where the long claw runs. Cut out the pieces that go under the wings (E,F). These give the wing thickness for the peg holes to be drilled into. Edge-sand, flat-sand and hand-sand them. Carefully position them as you glue and clamp them, making sure the flat edge is right up to the edge of the wing. This edge should be end grain.

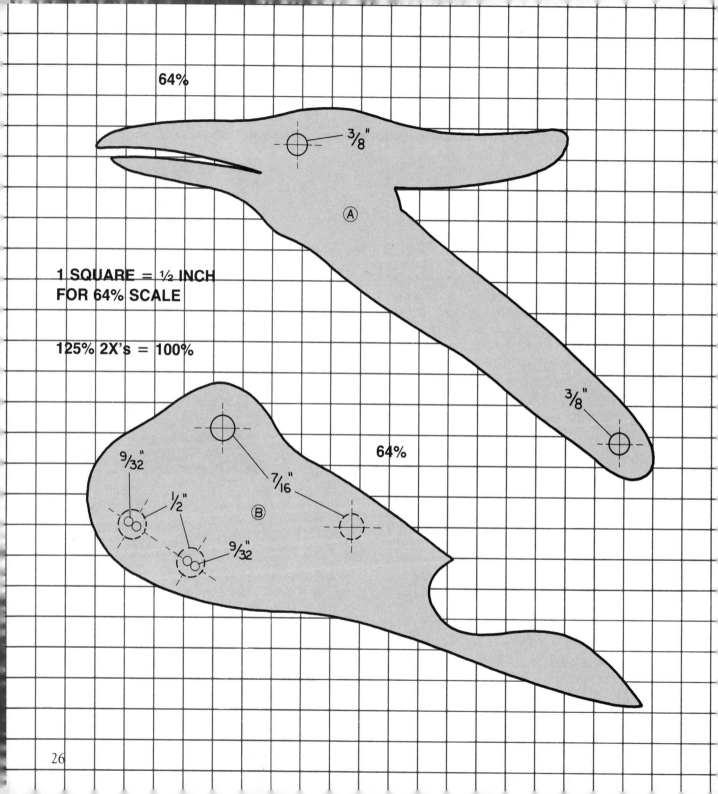

64%

3/8"

Ⓐ

1 SQUARE = ½ INCH
FOR 64% SCALE

125% 2X's = 100%

3/8"

9/32"

1/2"

7/16"

Ⓑ

9/32"

64%

3/8"

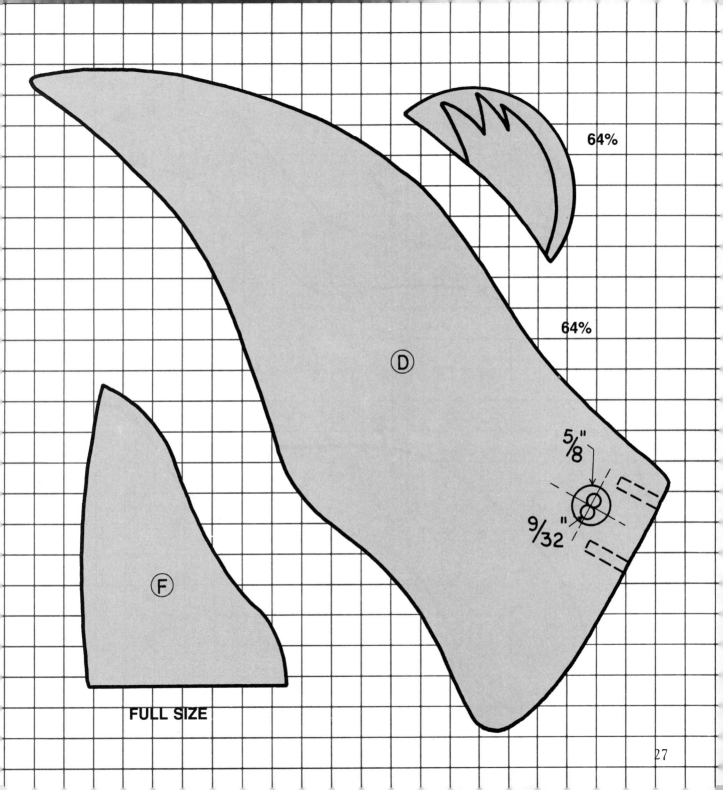

64%

64%

$\frac{5}{8}$"

$\frac{9}{32}$"

D

F

FULL SIZE

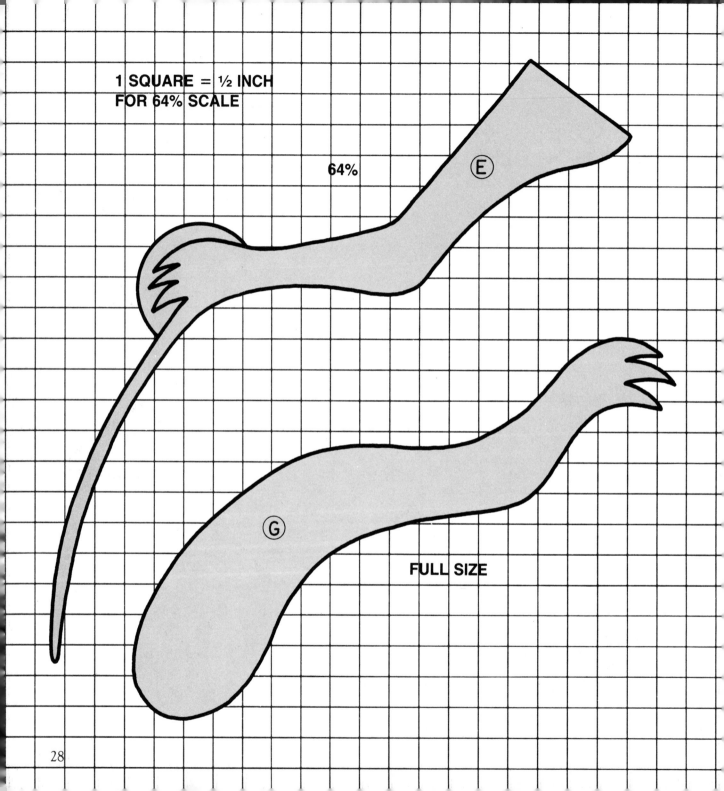

1 SQUARE = ½ INCH
FOR 64% SCALE

64%

E

G

FULL SIZE

28

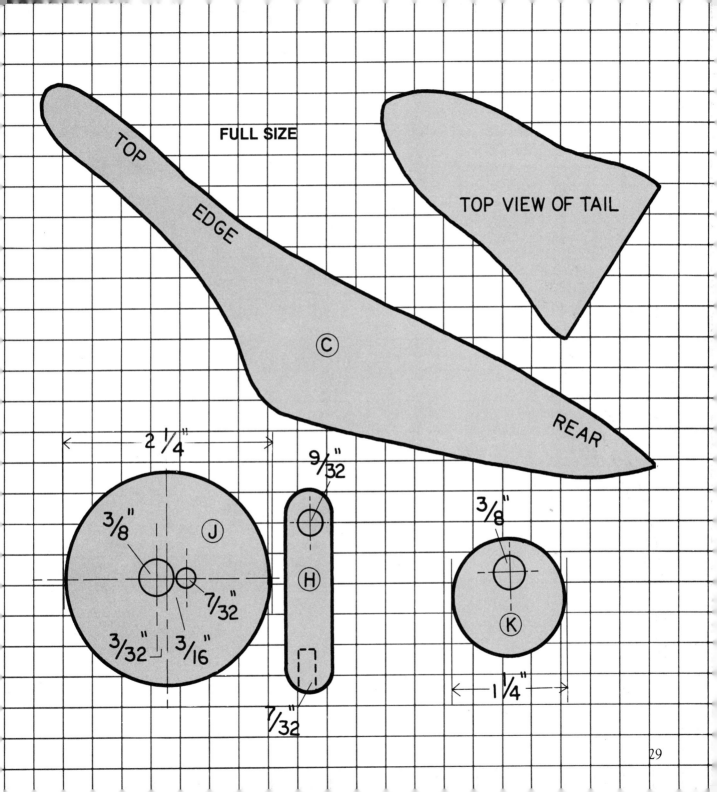

FULL SIZE

TOP

EDGE

Ⓒ

TOP VIEW OF TAIL

REAR

2 1/4"

9/32"

3/8"

Ⓙ

3/8"

7/32"

Ⓗ

3/8"

3/32" 3/16"

Ⓚ

7/32"

1 1/4"

29

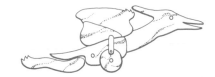

With the wing clamped in a vertical position on the drill press, carefully drill the ⁷⁄₃₂″ peg holes.

Lay out and drill the ½″ countersink in the wings through the arm and the wing to the depth of the under piece. Then drill the ⁹⁄₃₂″ hole through the wing and ream it out by lifting the wing up onto the ⁹⁄₃₂″ bit and carefully tilting it all the way around (See Figure 3). You should end up with a hole ⁹⁄₃₂″ in the middle and larger above and below. Put a 45° bevel on the inner end of the upper and lower surfaces of the wings. This will prevent them from hitting the body as they flap up and down (See figure 4).

The Pitman Arms

Cut out the two long rectangles (H). Clamp them vertically on the drill press and drill the ⁷⁄₃₂″ holes in the ends. Then drill the ⁹⁄₃₂″ holes through the other end and ream them out as you did the pivot holes in the wings. Round off all the four sides on the upper end, and two sides, like a half circle, on the lower end. Sand all the edges and sides. Once you've got all the wheels and wings attached, you can try these out and adjust the length as necessary.

The Wheels and Cams

The axle holes in the wheels (J) should be plugged and redrilled slightly off-center, as in the patterns. The peg hole is off-center also but to the other side of center from the new axle hole. That way the wings go down as the body goes up.

The cam (K) is just a 1¼″ flat wheel with the axle hole plugged and a new axle hole drilled off-center, as in the pattern.

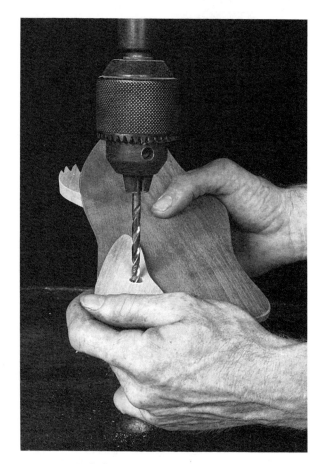

Figure 3. The hole in the wing is flared out top and bottom by tilting it around in a circle while it is held up on the bit.

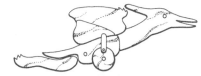

Assembly

Hold the head in position as you carefully position the spacer and glue it between the two sides (don't put glue where the legs will be glued later). After the glue sets up, edge-sand the area where the spacer is. Rout the silhouette, except the leg slots. Transfer the top view onto the rear of the body and cut it out. Edge-sand this area and clamp the body in a vise to round this area with a four-in-hand. Then hand-sand this area with 80# paper to remove all the cross-grain scratches. Finally, hand-sand this area and all routed edges by hand with 120# paper.

Carefully position the legs identically as you glue and clamp them in place. Glue the front wheels on, slipping the cam in place as you pass the axle through the body. The wheels should be positioned identically. Drill a ⅛″ hole through the cam and front axle and glue the ⅛″ dowel in place. Remove any excess dowel and smooth off the cam's surface. Edge-sand the axle ends.

To attach the wings, feed the pegs out from inside the body sides. Then put a *little* glue into the peg holes in the wings and spread it thoroughly. Press the wings, one at a time, onto their respective pegs. The wings should be able to move up and down but should not be sloppy. All four pegs must be inserted to the same depth or the wings will not work smoothly.

Now try your Pitman arms and adjust the length and clearances until the wings work smoothly. Then glue and peg the Pitman arms in place and that's it. When the glue has set up completely, apply the finish and prepare for the amazed expressions as this fellow appears to actually fly across the room.

Figure 4. By carefully holding the wing at 45° to the belt sander you can put a bevel on the upper and lower inside edges of the wing.

The Stegosaurus

The most interesting thing about the Stegosaurus was that he had a built-in air conditioner and could regulate his body temperature by raising and lowering the huge plates on his back.

How Does It Work?

I made this fellow a pull toy because he has so many plates that there is simply no place to hold on to him. The cams on his rear axle make his two-plated spine pieces move up and down. The cam on the front axle makes his little head bob up and down inquisitively.

The offset rear wheels and the large wheels on the side of the forward cam make his voluminous body sway ponderously from side to side, causing his tail to swing back and forth threateningly. The legs are pegged to the wheels and move as well (*See Figure 1*).

This toy incorporates as much movement as any of these toys, and it should be approached with patience and care. It doesn't present any real difficulties, but it does have many small pieces and positioning becomes critical with so many moving parts.

The Body Sides

Since the pivot holes in the front of the body sides (A) are on the inside (and aren't drilled all the way through), lay out the body pattern on the insides of the two pieces. Note that the slot in the rear of the body for the tail attachment is not cut out until after the assembly. Cut out the silhouettes and lay one on top of the other. This will insure perfect alignment of the axles. Drill the axle holes and the peg holes to attach the upper legs, front and rear. (Q,S) Now lay both body sides, one at a time, inside face upward on the drill press. Since the rear pivot slot will be covered

by the leg, you can drill these holes all the way through the pieces. With a scrap under your work, use a $^9/_{16}''$ bit and drill the top and bottom of the slots for the rear of the plate spines (D) to ride up and down in. Carefully chisel out the remainder of these slots.

Now set the depth to drill halfway through the pieces with a $^1/_2''$ bit and drill the holes for the pull cord knots to be hidden in (inside the body sides). Leave the $^1/_2''$ bit in the drill press. Set the depth once

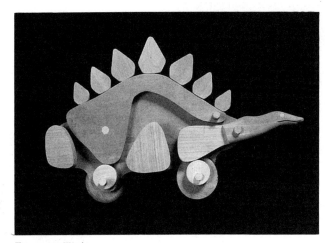

Figure 1. With one side removed you can see how the cams lift the spine ridges and the head (note the pivot wheel behind the head piece).

33

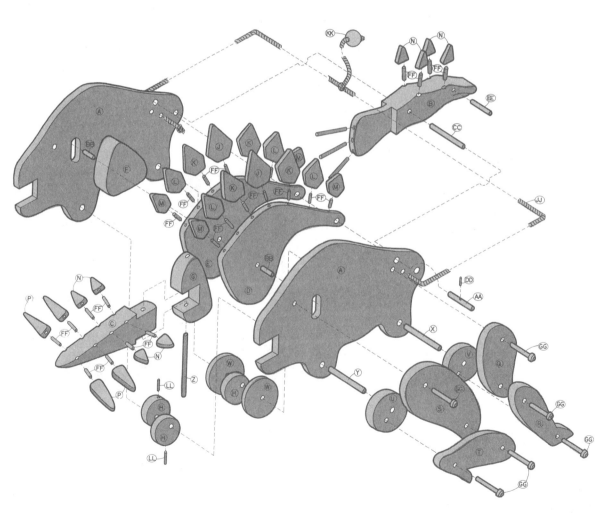

more to go as deep as possible without going through, and drill the holes for the head (B) and the front of the plate spines to pivot in. Finally, with a ¼" bit, drill through the center of the pull cord holes, using a scrap underneath the pieces to avoid tear-out. Flat-sand both sides inside and out. Edge-sand the entire silhouette except where the spacers (F,G) will meet the outside edges (belly and tail area). These will be edge-sanded after assembly. Rout these same edges, again excluding the edge of the spacer areas. Finally, hand-sand the inside edges, once more being careful not to sand the areas where the spacers will meet the edges, or you will have gaps after the assembly. These pieces are now ready for assembly.

The Head Piece

Lay out the head piece (B) on ⅞" stock. Drill the eye hole and the ⅜" hole for the pivot dowel (CC). Glue a ¼" dowel into the eye hole (EE) and sand it flat so that the piece will lay flat on the band saw table as you cut it out. Cut out the silhouette. Flat-sand, edge-sand and rout the silhouette.

Lay out the top and side view of the rear of the head piece, and cut away the waste material so that the back of the head piece will fit between the two thin wheels on the front axle. Use the band saw for the long rip cuts and a back saw for the side cuts to remove the pieces.

There is so much going on inside the body that there isn't enough room to make the rear of the head piece large enough to counterbalance the head, so some weight must be added. For this, 20 penny nails work perfectly. Cut three of them to length with a hack saw, removing the head of the nails. With the head piece clamped in the right position on the drill press, drill the three holes for the nails. Glue the nails in the holes with epoxy or all-purpose cement.

Drill the ¼" holes for the plates (J,K,L,M). These holes should be drilled with a Forstner bit or a brad point bit to avoid wandering. You can use a V-shaped piece of wood to hold the piece at 45° on the drill press and drill right into the center of the routed edge, or you can simply drill the holes with a hand-held electric drill, setting the angle by eye.

The length of the ⅜" pivot dowel will depend on the type of drill bit you used to drill the pivot holes in the sides and how deep the holes are. It will be between 1½" and 1¾". (1¼" between the sides plus the depth of the two holes, minus a little for play.) Cut the dowel to length, round off the ends, and glue it in place in the head piece, perfectly centered.

Finally, hand-sand all the edges, including the mouth slot.

The Tail

Lay out the side view on 1¾" stock (C). Cut it out and edge-sand the silhouette. Then lay out the top view and cut it out, supporting the front edge with a scrap as you cut out the half-circle pivoting area.

Again, support this area as you carefully drill the ⅞₆" hole for the pivot dowel (Z) to pass through. It's important that this hole be perfectly vertical for proper movement of the tail. Next, sand all the surfaces and rout the edges except around the front pivot area where routing would weaken the area

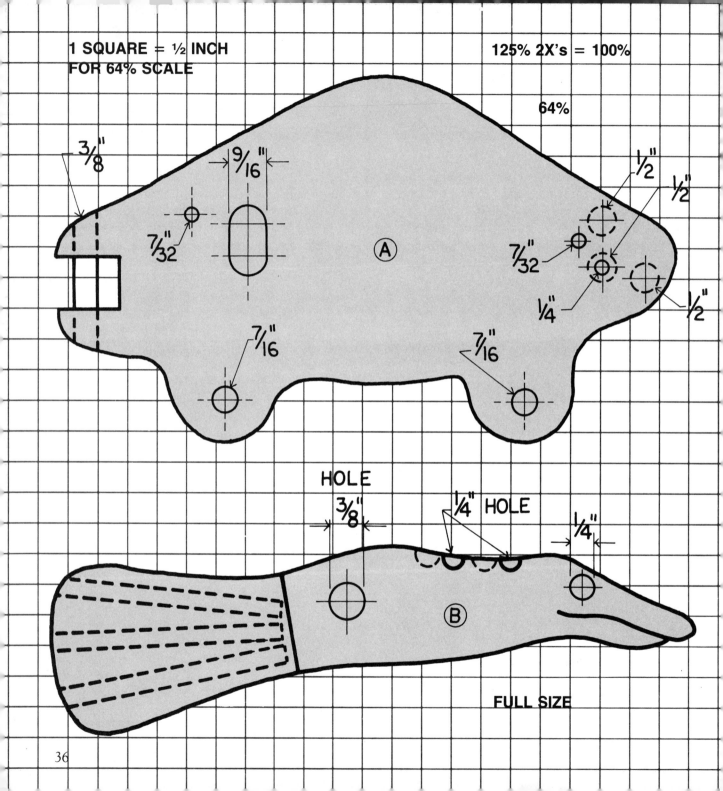

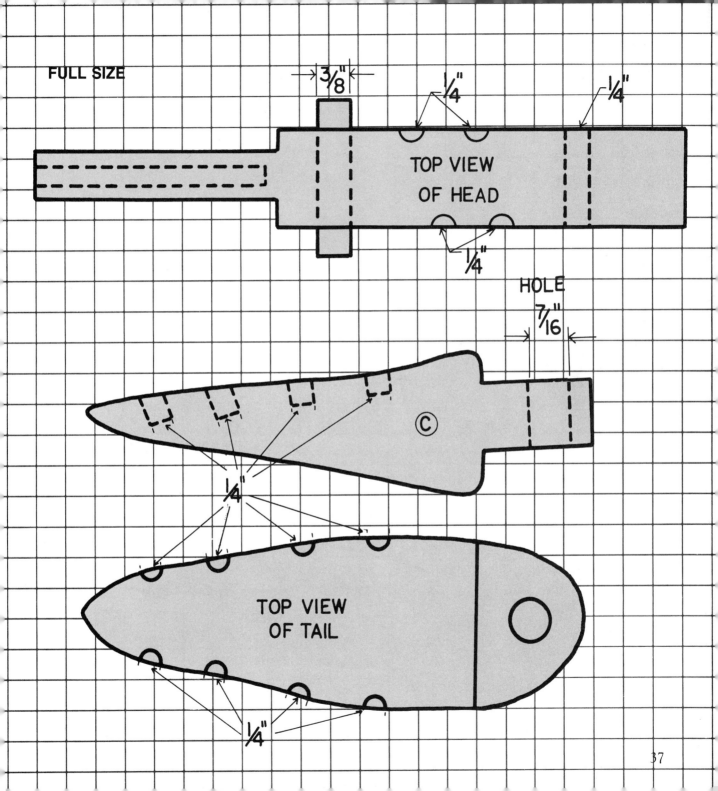

FULL SIZE

3/8"

1/4"

1/4"

TOP VIEW
OF HEAD

1/4"

HOLE

7/16"

©

1/4"

TOP VIEW
OF TAIL

1/4"

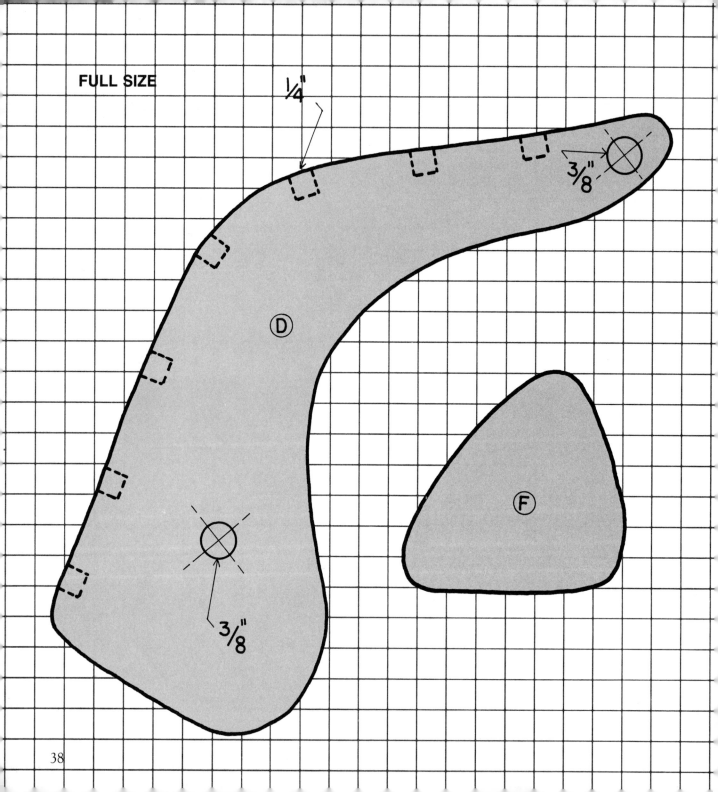

FULL SIZE

1/4"

3/8"

Ⓓ

3/8"

Ⓕ

38

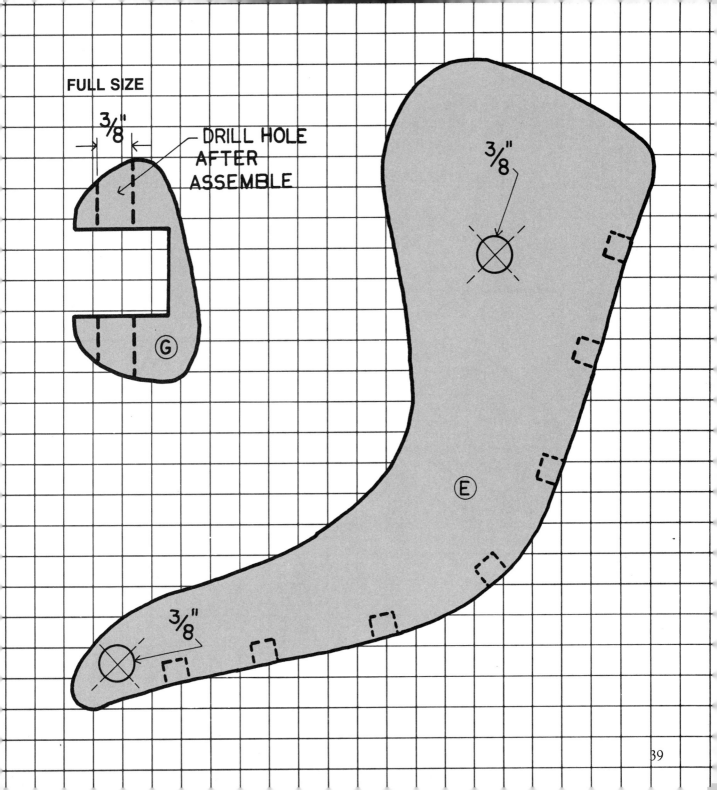

FULL SIZE

$\frac{3}{8}$"

DRILL HOLE
AFTER
ASSEMBLE

G

$\frac{3}{8}$"

E

$\frac{3}{8}$"

39

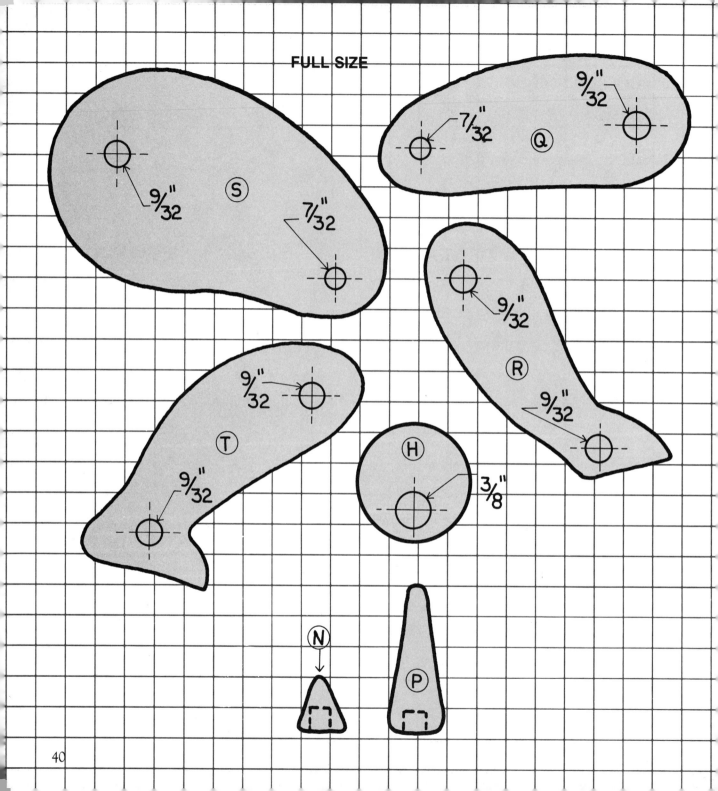

FULL SIZE

40

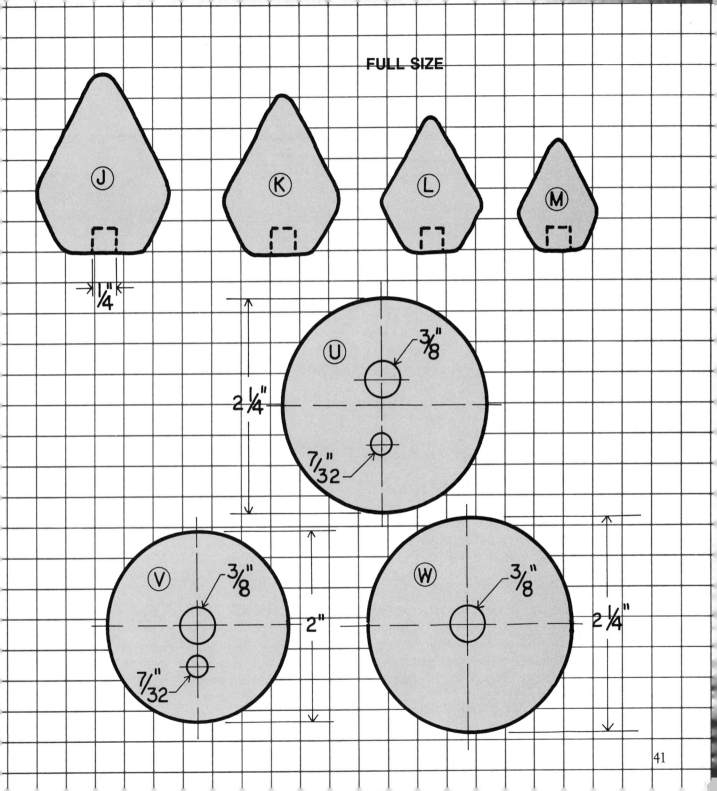

41

around the hole. Then drill the holes for the plates as described under the head piece, noting that the four spikes on the tip of the tail are angled backwards.

The Plated Spines

The right and left plated spine sections (D,E) are not the same, and so attention must be paid to which is which. The spines on top are staggered, and are determined by the position of the spines on the head (*See Figure 1*). The other difference is from which side the pivot dowel protrudes (from the right on the right side piece, and from the left on the left).

Lay out the pieces, drill the pivot holes, and cut out the silhouette. Carefully transfer the plate hole locations from the side to the top of the spine and mark a point in the center with a punch to help position the drill bit.

On the drill press, clamp one of the spine pieces between two boards to drill each plate hole perpendicular to the top of the spine where the plate will be attached. You will have to carefully position the piece for each hole on both pieces. When all the holes are accurately drilled, edge-sand, flat-sand and hand-sand both pieces.

The plates are next. There are 26 plates in all so start by making 30 (a few extra) identical blocks, ½" thick, 1¾" wide and 2" long. Rip a couple of 30" strips of 1¾" × ½" stock and use the crosscut guide on the band saw to cut 2" pieces. Then clamp them together flat on the drill press in groups of 15 with the end grain upward. Mark a line down the center and then locate the centers, thickness wise, of each. Set the

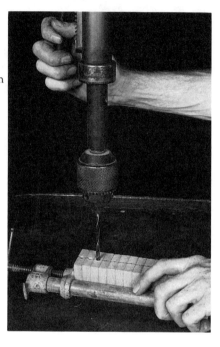

Figure 2. With the spine blanks clamped together on the drill press you can accurately drill the peg holes for attaching them.

drill press to drill to the proper depth and carefully drill all the ¼" holes (*See Figure 2*).

Lay out the side views of all the plates onto these blanks making sure that the bottom of the plate is flat against the end grain edge where the hole is, the plate is perfectly centered on the hole, and the plate is perfectly perpendicular to the end grain edge of the blank.

You can insert a dowel in the ¼" hole to use as a handle. This will make it possible to safely cut the

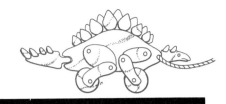

little pieces out on the band saw and to edge-sand them. If this makes you uncomfortable, even with the handle, cut the pieces with a coping saw and edge-sand them by hand.

If your holes are drilled accurately you should be able to use the same length ¼" dowels to attach all the plates. Round the ends of the dowels before assembly and watch for putting too much glue in the holes of both the plates and the body parts.

Attach the plates in the head and tail, position-

BILL OF MATERIALS

PART	DESCRIPTION	QTY	THICKNESS	WIDTH OR DIAMETER	LENGTH
A	Body sides	2	½"	6"	10¼"
B	Head	1	¾"	1⅞"	7"
C	Tail	1	1¾"	1⅝"	5½"
D	Right spine ridge	1	½"	3⅝"	8½"
E	Left spine ridge	1	½"	3⅝"	8½"
F	Belly spacer	1	1¼"	2¼"	2½"
G	Rear spacer	1	1¼"	2⅜"	1⅜"
H	Cams	3	½"	1¼"	
J	Spine plate	2	½"	1¾"	2"
K	Spine plate	4	½"	1¾"	2"
L	Spine plate	4	½"	1¾"	2"
M	Spine plate	4	½"	1¾"	2"

PART	DESCRIPTION	QTY	THICKNESS	WIDTH OR DIAMETER	LENGTH
N	Spine plate	8	½"	½"	1"
P	Spine plate	4	½"	⅝"	2"
Q	Upper foreleg	2	½"	1½"	4½"
R	Lower foreleg	2	½"	1¼"	3½"
S	Upper rear leg	2	½"	2⅜"	3⅞"
T	Lower rear leg	2	½"	1½"	3½"
U	Rear wheels	2	⅝"	2¼"	
V	Outside front wheels	2	½"	2"	
W	Inside front wheels	2	¼"	2¼"	
X	Front axle	1		⅜"	3⅜"
Y	Rear axle	1		⅜"	3⅝"
Z	Tail pivot dowel	1		⅜"	2¼"

PART	DESCRIPTION	QTY	THICKNESS	WIDTH OR DIAMETER	LENGTH
AA	Front spine pivot dowel	1		⅜"	1¾" approx.
BB	Rear spine pivot dowels	2		⅜"	¾" approx.
CC	Head pivot dowel	1		⅜"	1¾" approx.
DD	Dowel to keep spine ridges apart	1		3/16"	½"
EE	Eye	1		¼"	¾"

PART	DESCRIPTION	QTY	THICKNESS	WIDTH OR DIAMETER	LENGTH
FF	Dowels to attach spines	26		¼"	½"
GG	Pegs	12	⅜" head	7/16"	1 1/16" shaft
HH	Cord	1		¼"	16"
JJ	Cord	1		¼"	22"
KK	Handle	1		1"	
LL	Dowels to keep cams from slipping	3		⅛"	¾"

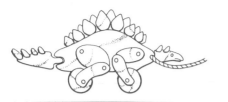

ing them carefully. You may want to lay the spines on a flat surface as you attach the plates, to make sure the entire assemblies are perfectly flat. If any plates are crooked on the spines, they will interfere with the movement.

The pivot dowels in the rear of the spines (BB) can be attached. They should protrude outward a little less than the depth of the pivot hole in the body side. Round off the outer end of the dowels and make sure that the inner side is perfectly flat.

The front pivot dowel will be 1¼″ plus the depth of both pivot holes, minus a little clearance. After you cut it to length, drill a ³⁄₁₆″ hole through the center of it and smooth the ends. Glue a ½″ long ³⁄₁₆″ dowel in the ³⁄₁₆″ hole, perfectly centered with both ends rounded. This serves to keep the two plates apart in the front.

The Legs and Spacers

Lay out all eight leg pieces (Q,R,S,T), and drill the ⁹⁄₃₂″ and ⁷⁄₃₂ holes as shown. Flat-sand and edge-sand the legs and hand-sand the edges. Assemble in opposing sets, making sure to leave clearance for free movement.

Lay out the two spacers (F,G) on 1¼″ stock. Note that the rear spacer does not have the slot cut out until after assembly.

I don't recommend flat sanding the spacer since it's easy to sand them unevenly and mess up the alignment. Edge-sand both pieces.

The Wheels and Cams

The rear wheels (H) are made by plugging the axle holes and redrilling them off-center. Then all four wheels will need the ⁷⁄₃₂″ peg holes drilled in them.

The two big hidden wheels in the front (U) are cut out of ¼″ stock with a hole cutter, fly cutter, or band saw.

The cams, if you don't buy them, are made in the same fashion as the rear wheels. Plug the original axle in a 1¼″ wheel, that you make, and redrill the axle hole off center, as in the pattern.

Assembly

I recommend a dry assembly before gluing to avoid problems. Position the spines and head between the two body sides with the spacers in place. Lightly clamp the assembly together and check for smooth movements.

Problems you might encounter are: 1.) Pivot holes aren't deep enough (drill deeper) 2.) Pilot holes in rear are slightly off (widen channel on the offending side) 3.) Pivot dowel is too long (shorten) 4.) Body sides are not perfectly aligned (re-adjust) 5.) Plates are crooked and rubbing (sorry—make them over).

When you've got all problems ironed out, glue the assembly together, checking for continued smooth movement during clamping.

When the assembly has set up thoroughly, use the pattern to perfectly locate the rear pivot hole for the tail piece. Clamp the work accurately on the drill press and carefully drill the ³⁄₈″ hole.

Next, cut the notch for the tail. Edge-sand and rout this area and the belly where the other spacer is. Hand-sand these areas and then put some glue in the bottom of the tail notch. (Don't put glue in the top of

the hole, or glue will get into the tail hole and bind it up.)

Position the tail and tap the dowel home so that it protrudes a little, top and bottom. After the glue is dry, saw off the excess and sand flush.

Next, glue the one rear wheel on its axle. With the cams between the body sides, twist the axle through both of them as you pass it through the body. Position the cams alternately and glue the second wheel on, making sure they are diagonally opposite (one up, one down). Edge-sand the axle end.

In the front, the cam and two thin wheels will have to be held in place as the axle is slipped through the body. If one outer wheel is glued to the axle, it will give you leverage to twist the axle through the cam and other wheels. Next, glue the second wheel on, making sure that the peg holes are diagonally opposed as with the rear. Sand the ends of the axles, and peg all the leg assemblies in place, leaving clearance for smooth movement.

Drill ⅛″ holes through the center of each cam edge and into the axle. Peg each cam to its axle and smooth the ends of the ⅛″ dowels.

Apply finish and attach the pull cord. The pull cord is two pieces. After melting and twisting both ends of the 14″ piece, feed each end inward from the outside of the body. Tie a square knot right at each end and pull them back through until the knots disappear inside the countersunk holes on the inside of the body sides. It's essential that these don't protrude or they will interfere with the head's movement. Now tie the 18″ piece (with ends melted) to

the center of this loop with a bowline knot (*See Figure 3*) and tie a ball to the end of the cord.

Well, if you made it this far you're probably feeling quite a sense of accomplishment. This fellow is pretty tricky, but the results should be worth it.

Figure 3. A bowline knot is a good way to join the pull cord to the yolk cord so that it won't come undone.

The Dimetrodon

The Dimetrodon was one of the first dinosaurs, living 250 million years ago. Since dinosaurs were cold-blooded, the Dimetrodon's sail gave him quite an advantage over his prey. The sun hitting his sail in the morning would warm up his blood so he could easily kill his prey while they were sluggishly stumbling around.

How Does It Work?

This guy has several movements as he's pushed. The cam on the rear axle pushes the sail up and down, the cam on the front axle opens and closes his nasty mouth, and the legs move by being pegged to the wheels (*See Figure 1*).

The Body Sides

Enlarge the patterns on a photocopying machine, to bring them up to 100%. Join the two halves together carefully and transfer the pattern onto two pieces of ½″ stock. (One being the reverse of the other.) (*See Transferring and Enlarging Patterns under Basic Techniques.*)

Cut out the two body sides (A). Drill the pivot holes most of the way through the sides. Lay the pieces on top of each other precisely, and drill the axle holes and peg holes but not the eye holes. It's better to drill the eye holes after assembly to insure that they're perfectly opposed.

Flat-sand both sides of both pieces. Edge-sand along the top of the body and rout this outside edge (where the sail will emerge). Then hand-sand the inside of the same edge and set the parts aside for assembly.

The Spacers

Cut the three spacers (B,C,E) out of ⅞″ stock. All three pieces have areas that will show, and that can't be edge-sanded after assembly. Edge-sand these areas to make a smooth transition to the edge that will be sanded after assembly (front of tail spacer, top and ends of belly spacer and underside and rear of the head piece.

The Sail

The one sail pattern is used for all three pieces (F, G). As with plywood, it is good to alternate grain direction for strength in a lamination. The spines should have the grain running vertically or they will break right off. You'll probably have to glue up a board wide enough to make the two sides of the lamination. The central piece should have the grain running horizontally.

The best way to make this assembly is to drill and cut out the sides carefully and glue them to the central piece (a contrasting color of wood) before cutting the central piece out. Let me go over this in detail.

To cut out the sides, lay them out on prepared blanks (sanded, with the grain running vertically.) Drill the ⅜″ pivot holes and then drill a 5/16″ hole at the base of each spine. Then carefully cut out the silhouette. If you're very careful, you can hand-sand the edges of the spines and break the fuzz off the edges.

Lay out the center piece and drill the ⅜″ pivot holes. Use these holes to line up all three pieces. A very thin skin of glue will suffice on the spines or

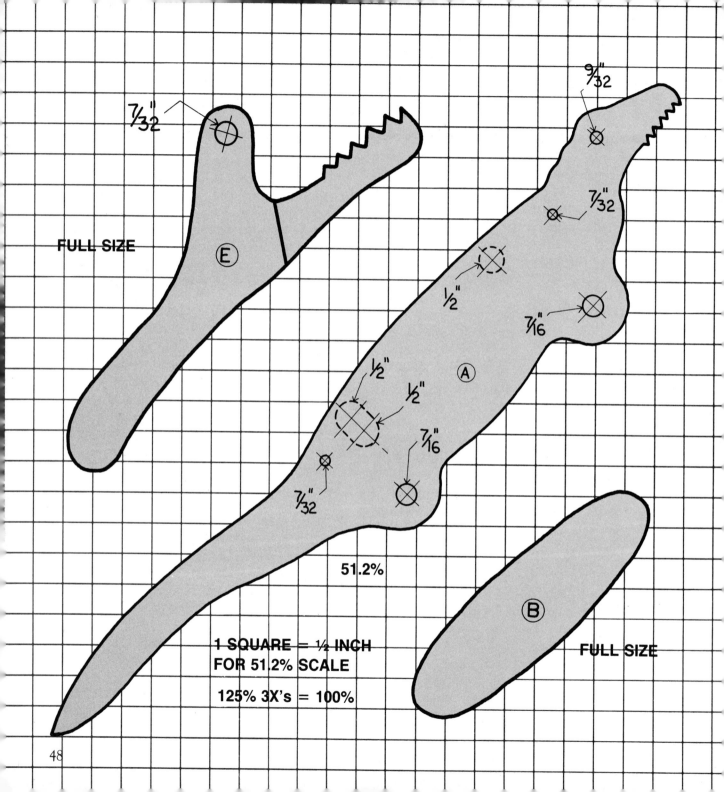

FULL SIZE

7/32"

9/32"

7/32"

1/2"

1/2"

1/2"

7/16"

7/16"

7/32"

Ⓔ

Ⓐ

Ⓑ

51.2%

1 SQUARE = ½ INCH
FOR 51.2% SCALE

125% 3X's = 100%

FULL SIZE

48

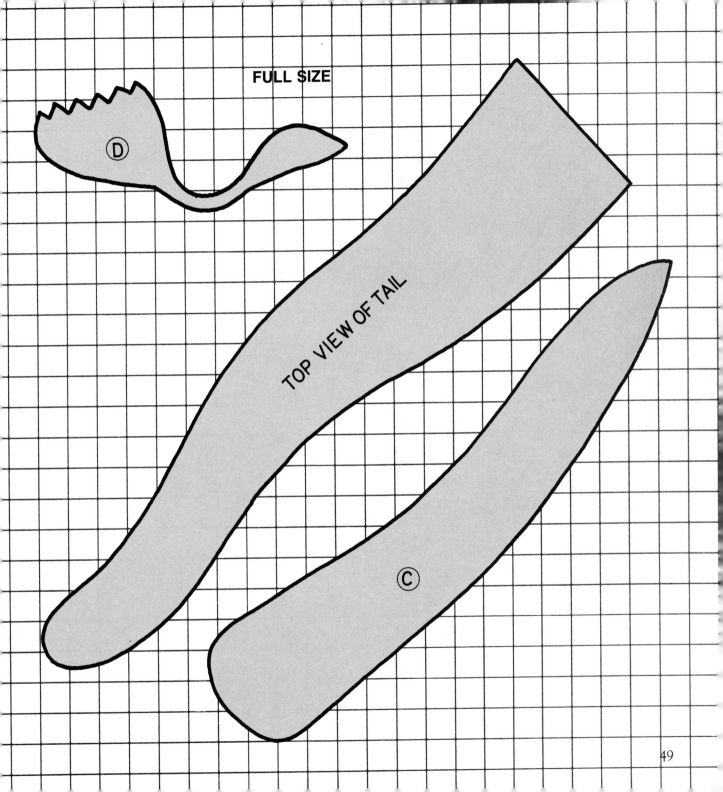

FULL SIZE

D

TOP VIEW OF TAIL

C

49

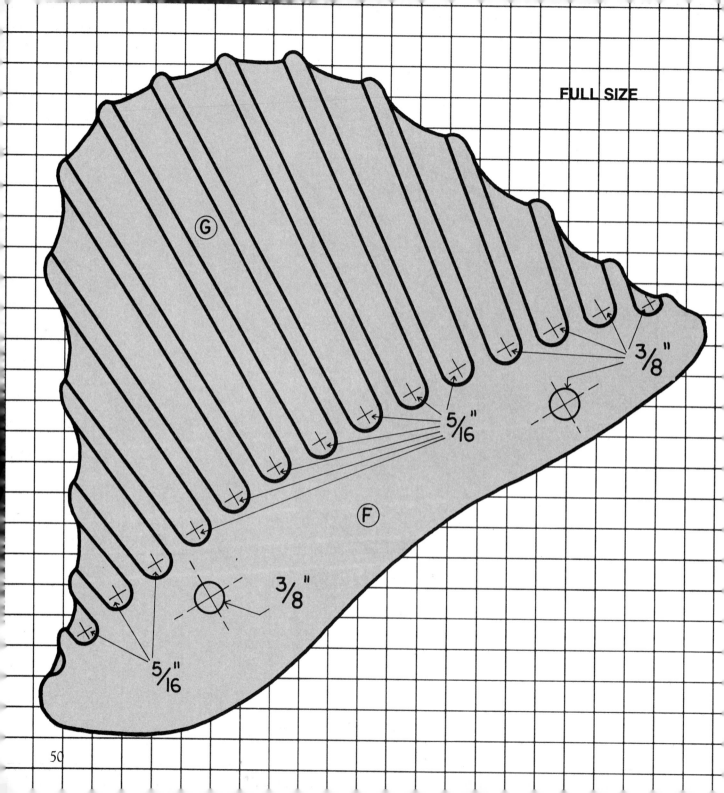

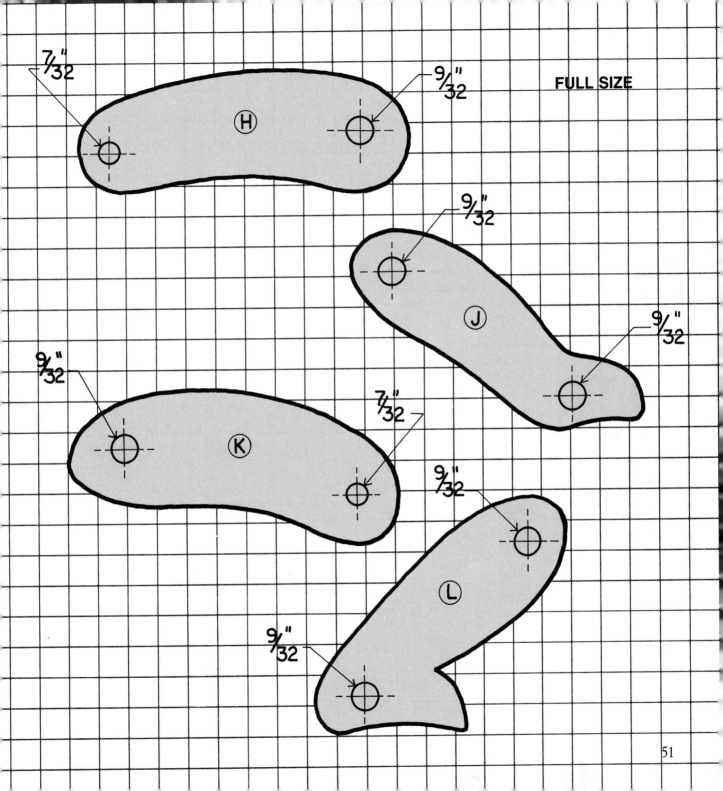

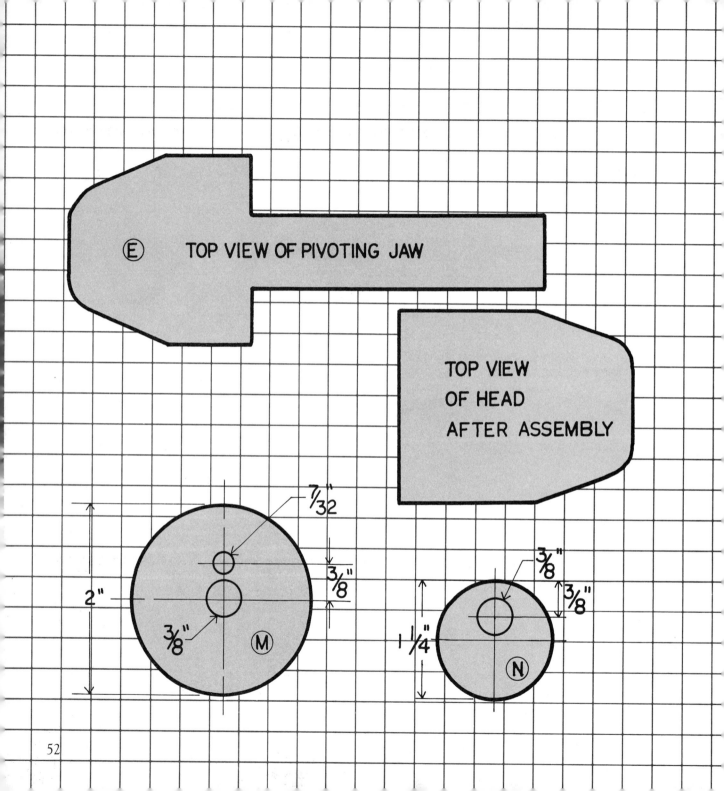

TOP VIEW OF PIVOTING JAW

TOP VIEW
OF HEAD
AFTER ASSEMBLY

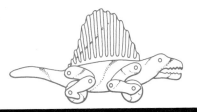
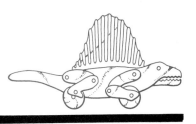
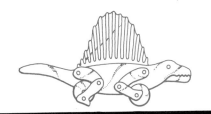

EXPLODED VIEW

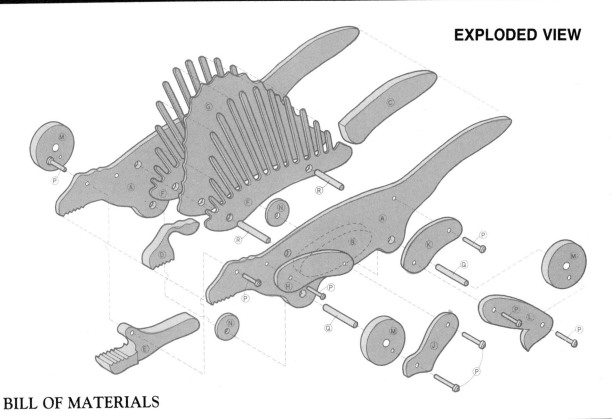

BILL OF MATERIALS

PART	DESCRIPTION	QTY	THICKNESS	WIDTH OR DIAMETER	LENGTH
A	Body sides	2	½″	3½″	18½″
B	Body Spacer (middle)	1	⅞″	1″	3½″
C	Body Spacer (tail)	1	⅞″	1½″	7″
D	Body Spacer (head)	1	⅞″	1½″	3½″
E	Pivoting Jaw	1	2″	1¾″	5¼″
F	Fin Sides	2	¼″	8½″	6½″
G	Fin Center	1	¼″	6½″	8½″
H	Upper Front Leg	2	½″	1½″	3¾″
J	Lower Front Leg	2	½″	1¼″	3¾″
K	Upper Rear Leg	2	½″	1½″	3¾″
L	Lower Rear Leg	2	½″	1¾″	3½″
M	Wheels	4	⅝″	2″	
N	Cam	2	½″	1¼″	
P	Pegs	14	⅜″ head	⁷⁄₃₂″ shaft	1¹⁄₁₆″
Q	Axles	2		⅜″	3¼″
R	Pivot Dowels	2		⅜″	1⅝″

53

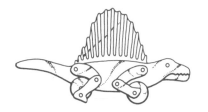 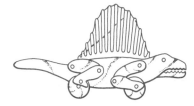 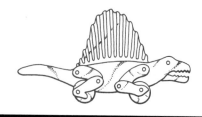

you'll get squeeze-out that will be awfully hard to remove. You'll want a block of 1″ stock above and below the assembly (as large as the entire assembly) to distribute clamping pressure. Use plenty of clamps and be sure nothing moves as you tighten them. $\frac{3}{8}$″ dowels in the pivot holes will keep the assembly from shifting. If glue squeezes in around the dowels, they'll have to be drilled out again after the assembly dries.

Once the whole assembly is dry, you can cut away the rest of the central piece, edge-sand the assembly and hand-sand all the edges. The pivot dowels should be $\frac{7}{8}$″, plus the depth of both pivot holes, minus $\frac{1}{16}$″ clearance. Cut them to length, round the ends and glue them into the assembly, making sure that they are perfectly centered.

The Jaw

Lay out the side view on a piece of $1\frac{3}{4}$″ stock. Drill the $\frac{7}{32}$″ hole and cut out and edge-sand the silhouette. Then, using both top and side views, cut away the rear sides of the jaw piece with a back saw. Then cut away the tapered front sides of the mouth with the piece in a vise, round over the edges with a four-in-hand. Then, hand-sand all of the exposed edges. A file will work well to break the edge on the teeth without rounding them over.

The Legs

Lay out the legs (H,J,K,L) and drill all the holes, noting that four of the holes are $\frac{7}{32}$″, and the rest are $\frac{9}{32}$″. Cut them out, edge-sand and flat-sand them and

break the edges. Assemble in opposing sets, making sure to leave clearance for smooth movement.

The Wheels and Cams

All four wheels simply get a $\frac{7}{32}$″ peg hole drilled in them, as in the pattern. To make the cams (N), plug the axle hole in a $1\frac{1}{4}$″ flat wheel and drill new holes, as in the pattern.

Assembly

You'll want to try the assembly without any glue to make any adjustments necessary. First, just lay the sail on each body side, one at a time, and see how the pivot dowels move in their holes. If there is any binding, enlarge the rear pivot slot in the the body side as necessary. When both sides work smoothly, lay the sail on one side, position the three spacers and lay the second body side on top. Hold the assembly firmly and see that the sail moves smoothly. If it binds, check the length of the pivot dowel as well as the hole locations.

Now lay one body side down, apply glue to both sides of all three spacers and position them carefully. Lay the other side on top, using $\frac{3}{8}$″ dowels through the axle hole to help line up the assembly. Press the assembly firmly together and make sure that the sail still moves freely. Now apply clamps directly over the spacers, using either rubber protectors or scraps to avoid marring the sides. Check the sail's movement as you tighten the clamps.

When the assembly is thoroughly dry, carefully locate and drill the eye hole. A $\frac{7}{8}$″ block of wood

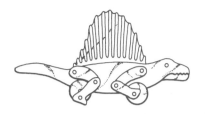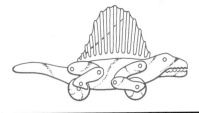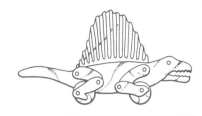

between the eyes will help prevent tear-out, as will a piece of scrap under the work. Cut away any excess material around the head, tail, and belly. Edge-sand the entire silhouette, and rout all the edges except the teeth.

Next, transfer the top view of the tail and head onto the assembly and cut them out with the band saw. Edge-sand, and then put the body in a vise (with scraps to protect it) and use a four-in-hand or rasp and file to round the edges. Hand-sand with 80# paper to get all cross-grain scratches out. Finish up with 120# paper and continue hand-sanding the rest of the body assembly.

Slide the cam on as you glue both sets of axles and wheels on. Make sure that the holes for the pegs are diagonally opposed (one up and one down). Edge-sand the axle ends. Drill a ⅛″ hole through the cam and rear axle, and peg it in place with a ⅛″ dowel and glue (*See Tools, Techniques, and Production Procedures, Figure 3*). Repeat for the front cam and axle. Sand off any excess dowel or roughness on both cams.

Lastly, put a little glue in the peg hole in the jaw piece. Position it carefully and tap the two eye pegs in. Be careful to keep the jaw centered with equal clearance on both sides.

Oil him up, and you're ready to go!

Figure 1. With one side removed you can see how the cams lift the sail and the lower jaw.

The Hadrosaurus

The Parasaurolophus was one of the most striking Hadrosaurs, or Duckbills. It had a crest that extended 3½ feet behind its head. This "horn" was hollow and was connected to its nasal passages. The most widely accepted theory is that this acted as a resonating chamber to amplify the creature's trumpetlike call.

Hadrosaurs also had webbed feet, presumably to help these defenseless creatures escape hungry carninores by swimming out into the water.

How Does It Work?

This toy has an unusual movement. Aside from the lumbering gait, accomplished by the slightly diagonally offset front wheels, the head moves forward and back by means of a cam on the front axle, a fork on the bottom of the head piece, and a pivot dowel in the center of the body (*See Figure 1*).

The Body Sides

Lay out the side pieces (C) and drill the axle holes before cutting the pieces out on the band saw. After they're cut out, lay them one on top of the other, lining up the axle holes, and drill the pivot holes, to make sure they are identically positioned in each half. Drill the 7/32″ holes for attachment of legs and arms.

Flat-sand both sides of both pieces. Edge-sand the neck and the edge around the wheel area (where the spacers will not meet the edges). Rout these edges (outside edge) and hand-sand (inside and out) on these edges. Be careful not to hand-sand the inside edges where the spacers will be, or there will be a gap between the spacers and the sides.

Spacers

Lay out the spacers and cut them out. Lightly flat-sand both sides, just enough to remove planer ridges. Be careful to keep these surfaces perfectly flat or you will have gaps where they meet the sides. Round the top and bottom silhouette of the spacers on the sander/grinder where they will intersect open areas at neck and wheels. This will give them a smoother appearance after assembly.

Head Piece

The lamination of this piece serves two purposes: It makes the head thick enough to sculpt the nose area and give it that "duck bill" appearance, and it enables you to have the grain running vertically to make the main structure of the pivoting piece strong (especially at forks) and to have the grain running horizontally along the head to strengthen the long crest.

Lay out the long head piece (A) and drill the pivot hole before cutting it out. Don't drill the eye hole until after assembly. Flat-sand and then edge-sand the entire silhouette except the head area where other pieces will be laminated. Mark the intersection of the laminated sides and rout the rest of the silhouette, being careful to stop short of your marks. Give the routed edges a quick hand-sand in the neck and fork areas which will be exposed.

Lay out the two head sides (B), with the grain

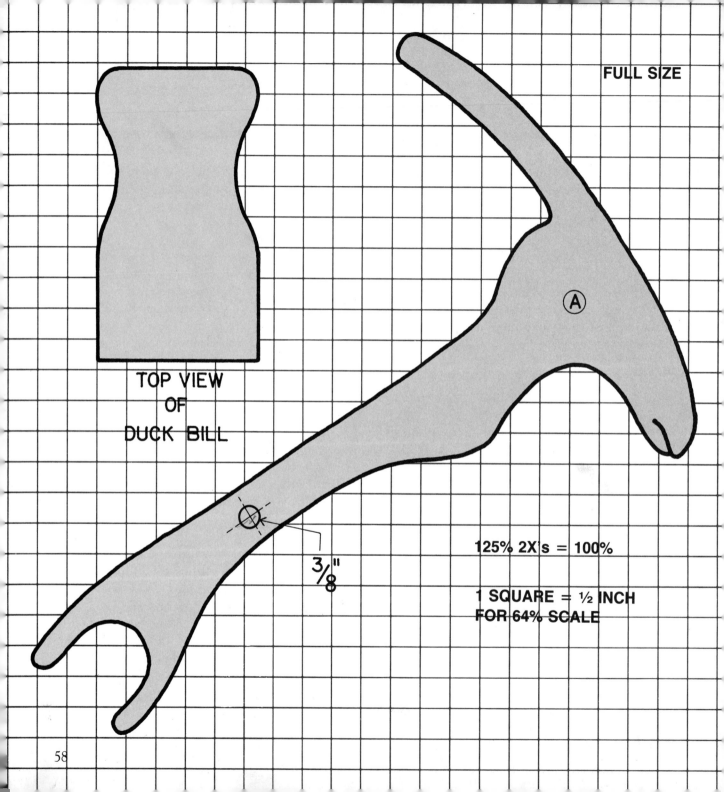

FULL SIZE

TOP VIEW
OF
DUCK BILL

Ⓐ

3/8"

125% 2X's = 100%

1 SQUARE = ½ INCH
FOR 64% SCALE

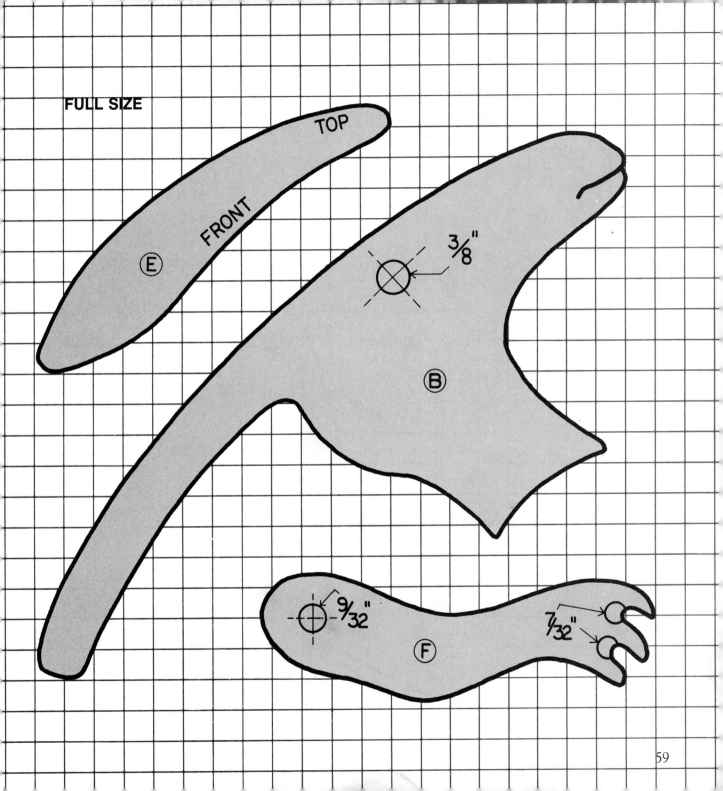

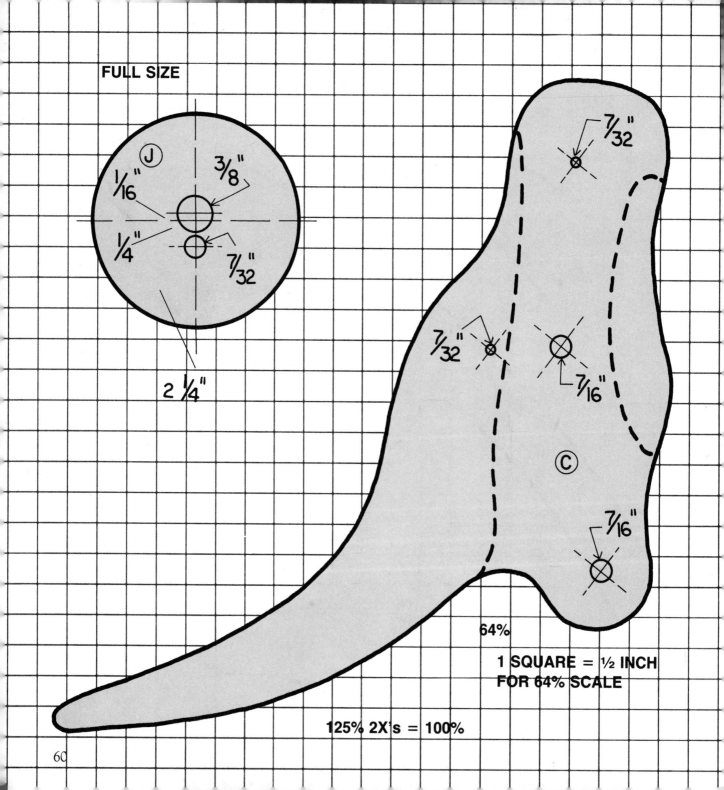

FULL SIZE

J

1/16"
3/8"
1/4"
7/32"
2 1/4"

7/32"
7/32"
7/16"
7/16"

C

64%

1 SQUARE = 1/2 INCH
FOR 64% SCALE

125% 2X's = 100%

60

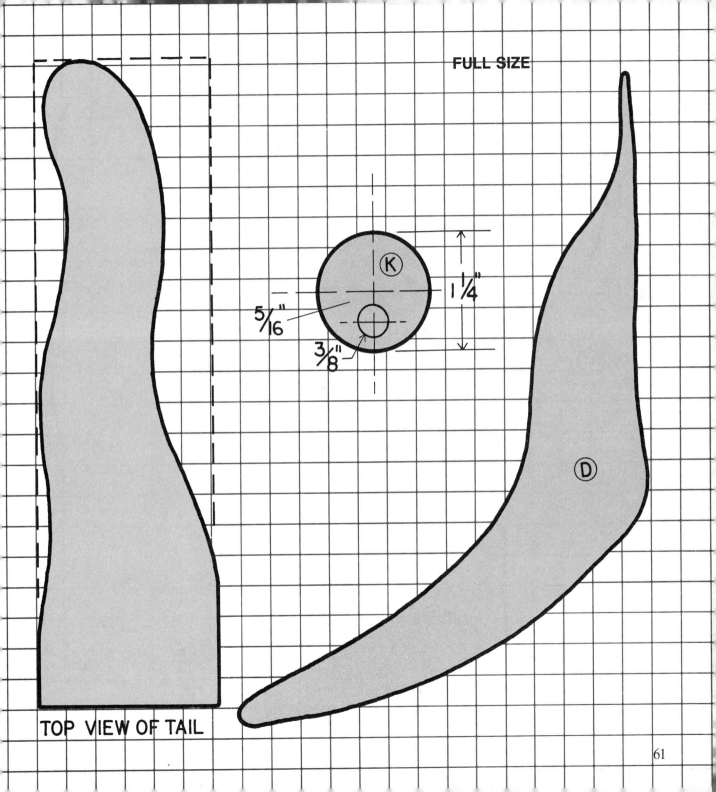

FULL SIZE

$1\frac{1}{4}$"

$5\frac{16}{}$"

$3\frac{8}{}$"

Ⓚ

Ⓓ

TOP VIEW OF TAIL

61

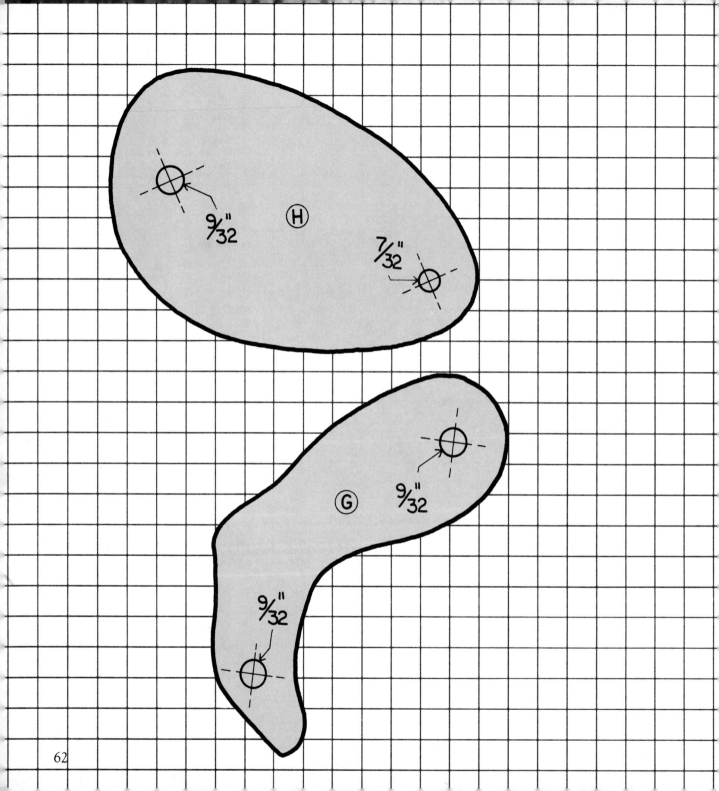

H

9/32"

7/32"

G

9/32"

9/32"

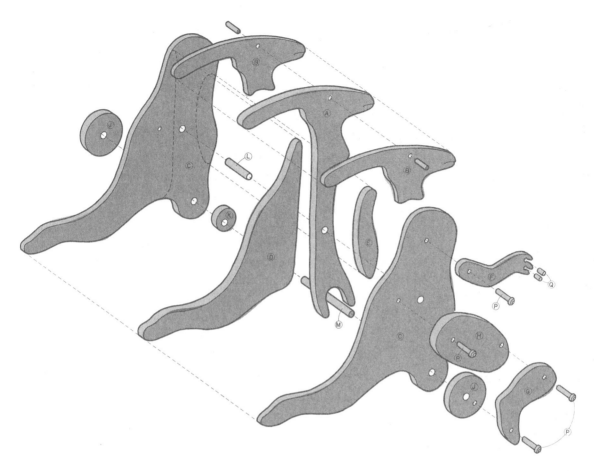

MATERIALS

PART	DESCRIPTION	QTY	THICKNESS	WIDTH OR DIAMETER	LENGTH
A	Pivoting head piece	1	¾"	8¼"	12"
B	Head sides	2	½"	3½"	8¼"
C	Body sides	2	½"	7"	14½"
D	Tail spacer	1	⅞"	2¾"	8"
E	Belly spacer	1	⅞"	1"	4¾"
F	Arms	2	½"	1½"	4½"
G	Lower legs	2	½"	2¼"	4½"
H	Upper legs	2	½"	2¾"	4¼"

PART	DESCRIPTION	QTY	THICKNESS	WIDTH OR DIAMETER	LENGTH
J	Wheels	2	½" or ⅝"	2¼"	
K	Cam	1	⅝"	1¼"	
L	Pivot dowel	1		⅜"	1⅝"
M	Axle	1		⅜"	3½"
N	Eye dowel	1		⅜"	1¾"
P	Pegs	6	Peg head ⅜"	⁷⁄₃₂"	1¹⁄₁₆" shaft
Q	Finger webbing	4	Peg head ⅜	⁷⁄₃₂"	1¹⁄₁₆" (cut off after)

running along the horn. Flat-sand both sides of both pieces. Edge-sand the bottom edge and corners which will be inaccessible after assembly. Rout and hand-sand these same edges.

Carefully position and glue the sides on, keeping glue away from the bottom edge to avoid squeeze-out where it will be hard to remove. Use plenty of clamps (with pads).

After the assembly is dry, drill the eye hole, with a scrap underneath your work to avoid tear-out. Cut out the silhouette again, to get all edges consistent, then edge-sand. Glue the eye dowel in, cut off any excess, and flat sand after the glue has set up.

Mark the top view of the duckbill and use the roller on the end of the belt-sander to make the smooth indent on either side of the snout.

Rout the head silhouette, and with the piece in a vise, use a four-in-hand to round over the edges of the indents, where the router wouldn't reach. Hand-sand the routed edges and rasped areas to smooth the entire head.

Be extremely careful when gluing the pivot dowel (M) in place, or you could split the piece. You may want to sand the ⅜" dowel slightly smaller so that it fits more easily. Carefully support the work around the hole as you tap the dowel in place, and center it.

Legs and Arms

Lay out the arms (F) and legs (G,H) on ½" stock. Drill all the holes for pegs and pivots. The webbing in the hands is accomplished by drilling 7/32" holes at the base of the fingers. Glue and plug the hole with pegs. After the glue is dry, saw off both ends of the pegs and

flat-sand the back of the arms so they will sit flat on the drill press table. Then drill 7/32" holes barely overlapping the pegs that were glued in.

Cut out arms and legs, flat-sand and edge-sand (carefully around the fingers), and hand-sand the edges.

Wheels and Cams

To make the wheels (J), plug the axle holes. The holes are so close that it's better to drill the 7/32" hole first or it will break into the larger hole. Then drill the ⅜" hole with a Forstner bit to avoid wander and breaking into the smaller hole.

If you're making your own cam, drill the ⅜" hole before cutting out the circle to avoid splitting it.

Assembly

It's a good idea to try the movement of the head piece before assembly. Position the spacers and the head piece. Put the cam on a ⅜" dowel and position it with the dowel through the axle hole in body side (See Figure 1).

Now twist the dowel and see if it moves smoothly in the fork. If it's too tight, widen the fork slightly until the cam turns freely, but not too much. See if the head piece can move back and forth without hitting the spacers. If it does, either take a little of the inside edge of the appropriate spacer, or move it away from the head piece during assembly.

Now glue the spacers and position them on one of the side pieces. Lay the head piece in its place and carefully position the other body side. You can put a ⅜" dowel through both axle holes to ensure perfect

alignment. Make sure the central pivot moves freely.

Clamp the entire assembly with plenty of clamps and pads (across spacers), making sure that it doesn't shift as you apply pressure. Check once again that the head piece pivots freely and the axle holes are perfectly aligned. Adjust the sides if necessary.

When the assembly is dry, cut out the silhouette again if necessary. Edge-sand these newly sawn edges. Rout and hand-sand all the edges that haven't been done yet.

Lay out the top view of the tail and cut it out on the band saw, and edge-sand it. A small drum sander on the drill press will help remove cross-grain scratches. Then with the toy in the vise tail upward, round over the edges that can't be routed with a four-in-hand, and hand-sand the whole tail.

Glue one wheel to the axle, twist the cam onto the dowel as you pass it through the axle holes and glue the second wheel on, making sure that the peg holes are diagonally opposed (one up, one down). Edge-sand the axle ends to remove excess glue.

With the toy upside down on the drill press, drill the ⅛″ hole through the cam and the axle and glue a ⅛″ dowel in place. Smooth off the ends.

Assemble the legs in opposing sets, leaving ⅛″ clearance. Hit the backs of the legs on the belt-sander if any glue squeezed out. Glue and peg the legs to the body and the wheels, leaving ⅛″ clearance. Glue and peg the arms tightly to the body.

When you oil this fellow, you'll have to move the arms many times as you wipe off the excess oil, because it doesn't soak in as readily when the parts are touching.

And there he is. Give him a push and watch him move, but you better push fast if the Tyrannosaurus is in the room.

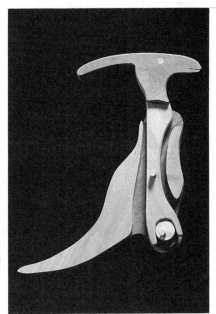

Figure 1. With one side removed you can see how the cam in the fork tips the head forward and back as the wheels turn the cam.

The Stenosaurus

This is one of the few prehistoric creatures that didn't become extinct, but evolved into today's crocodile. In fact, he is quite similar to the present-day *gureal* of India.

How It Works

When you push this fellow along, his mouth yawns open and chomps down in a nasty fashion. This is accomplished by the hidden pegs on the inside of the front wheels *(See Figure 1)*. His low-slung legs give him his 'gator walk.

The Body

After you lay out the body (A), drill all the holes before cutting it out to avoid splitting the thin areas around the eye and axle holes. Then cut out the silhouette, and edge-sand, flat-sand and rout the entire silhouette except the teeth, which should not be routed. Lay out the top view of the tail, cut it out and edge-sand it.

Next, put the body in a vise tail-upward, and rasp, file and sand the edges that can't be routed. Hand-sand all the rough edges, and break the edges of the teeth using a file.

Lay out the head sides (B) and the spacer. (C) Make sure the spacer is 1/8" thicker than the body. Drill the eye holes and then cut out all three pieces. The band saw blade must be perfectly square to the table when you cut out the spacer or the assembly will end up crooked. Edge-sand the edges of the silhouette on all three pieces except the top of the snout, which will be sanded after assembly.

Put glue on both sides of the spacer and carefully position it between the two sides as you press them together. A little hand pressure, at this point, will prevent slippage when you apply the clamps. Make sure everything is lined up perfectly to ensure proper movement, and then apply two or three clamps directly across the spacer area of the assembly.

When the assembly is dry, edge-sand the top of the snout and flat-sand both sides. Rout the silhouette, except the teeth. Break all the edges by hand. A small file will do a nice job on the edges of the teeth.

Figure 1. The dowels inside the front wheels lift the mouth open.

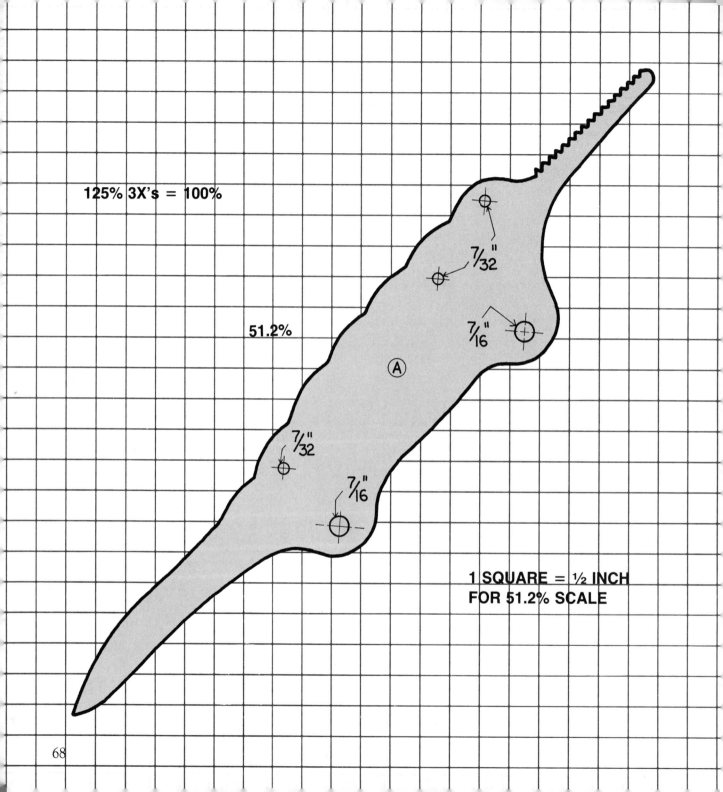

125% 3X's = 100%

51.2%

7/32"

7/16"

Ⓐ

7/32"

7/16"

1 SQUARE = ½ INCH
FOR 51.2% SCALE

68

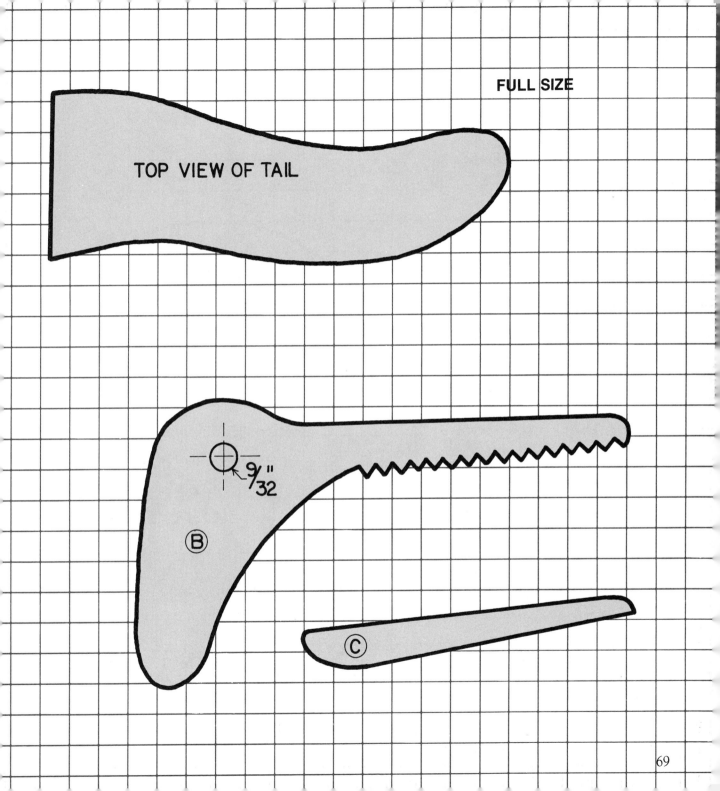

FULL SIZE

TOP VIEW OF TAIL

9/32"

Ⓑ

Ⓒ

69

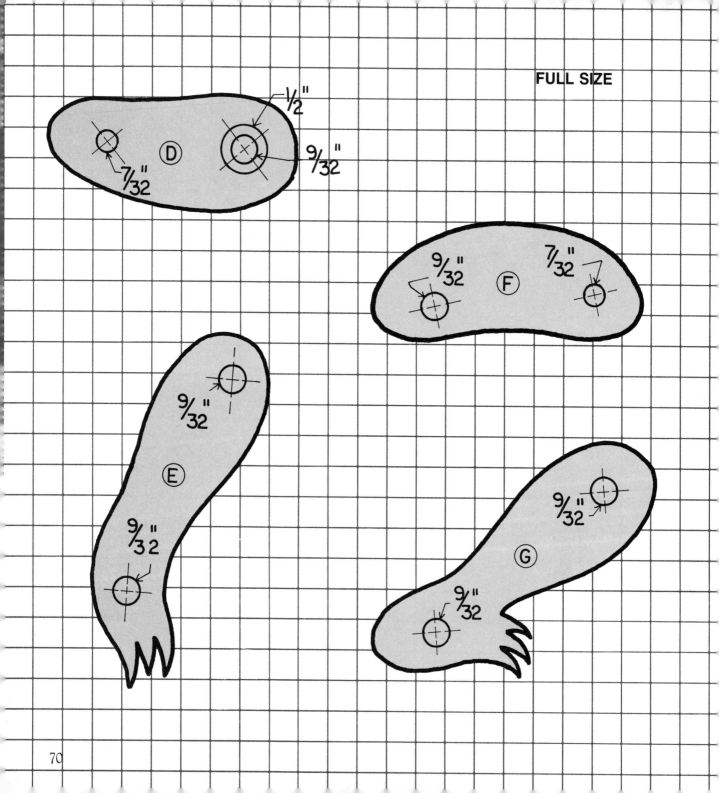

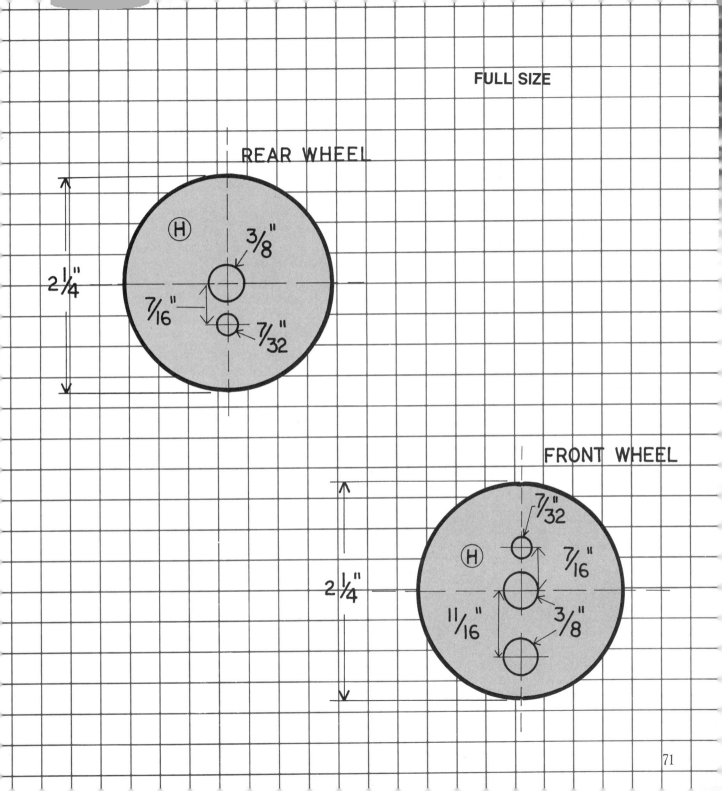

FULL SIZE

REAR WHEEL

FRONT WHEEL

71

The Legs

Lay out the legs (D,E,F,G). Note that the upper forelegs are cut out of ¾″ stock to allow space for the ⅜″ dowels inside the wheels. When you drill the holes, be careful of the sizes. The upper forelegs get a ½″ hole ½″ deep before the 9/32″ hole is drilled the rest of the way through. This will leave enough of the peg sticking through to peg them to the body.

After all the holes are drilled, cut out all the legs, edge-sand and flat-sand them and break the edges by hand.

Wheels and Cams

Set the forward wheels outside-down on the drill press and drill the ⅜″ deep holes for the dowel pegs. Then drill the 7/32″ peg on the opposite side of the axle hole from the ⅜″ hole, and drill the peg holes in the rear wheels.

Cut two ⅜″ dowels to ¾″ (L), round off both ends by hand, and glue them into their respective holes, making sure that they are perfectly perpendicular to the inside of the wheel surface.

Assembly

If you're going to paint this toy, you'll want to do it before assembly. I used a latex paint on the one in the color photos.

Cut the front axle (J) long enough to go through the body and both wheels with their pegs inward, leaving about ⅛″ play. Glue the wheels to the axles (diagonally opposed—with one peg up and one down). After the glue is dry, sand the axle end on the sander/grinder to remove any glue and smooth the axle end.

Glue the pegs together in opposing sets, leaving adequate clearance. Flat-sand the inside of each set to remove any glue forced out by the peg. Glue and peg the legs to the body and the wheels, watching for any glue forced out the inside of the wheels.

Repeat this process for the back wheels (H) and legs, leaving out the dowel pegs.

Lastly, put a little glue in the eye holes in the body and peg the snout assembly in place, making sure that it's centered and the pegs are not so tight that they keep the piece from moving freely.

If you're not painting your Stenosaurus, oil it after the glue is dry and don't go near the water.

BILL OF MATERIALS

PART	DESCRIPTION	QTY	THICKNESS	WIDTH OR DIAMETER	LENGTH
A	Body	1	1¾″		19½″
B	Head sides	2	⅜″	3″	5½″
C	Head spacer	1	1⅞″	½″	3⅝″
D	Upper front legs	2	¾″	1¼″	2¾″
E	Lower front legs	2	½″	1¼″	3⅞″
F	Upper rear legs	2	½″	1⅜″	3″
G	Lower rear legs	2	½″	1⅜″	3⅝″
H	Wheels	4	⅝″	2¼″	
J	Front axle	1		⅜″	3⅞″
K	Rear axle	1		⅜″	3⅛″
L	Dowels in front wheels	2		⅜″	¾″
M	Pegs	14	⅜″ head	7/32″	1 1/16″ shaft

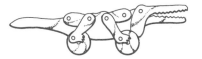
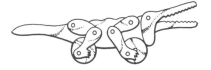

EXPLODED VIEW

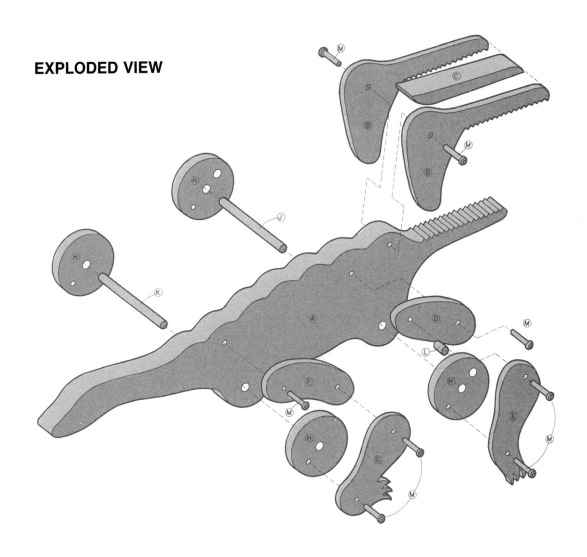

The Icthyosaurus

One of the earliest fishes, the Icthyosaurus looked like a combination of a dolphin and a shark. It was a vicious predator and ate almost anything in the water.

How Does It Work?

If you hold this fellow behind the dorsal fin and push him, his tail and dorsal fin go up and down by means of the cam on the rear axle. The parallel offset wheels in the front give him a swimming motion by lifting the body up as the flippers drop, and lifting the flippers as the body drops. Altogether, the mechanisms give him a smooth, fluid movement (See Figure 1).

The Body Sides

Lay out the body sides (A) and drill the axle holes before cutting them out with a band saw to avoid splitting. (Do not cut out the mouth slot until assembly.) When the sides are cut out, lay them on top of each other (with the axle holes lined up perfectly) and drill the eye holes to ensure perfect alignment.

Mark the forward flipper peg holes on the inside of each piece and drill the ⅛" holes ¼" deep. Then drill the 9/32" holes all the way through. Notice that these holes are not centered. They are at the top and the bottom of the ½" hole making a slot that the peg can pivot in as the flippers rise and fall. Clean away the scrap to make a neat vertical slot. Don't drill the ¼" holes for attaching the rear flippers until the holes are drilled in the flippers themselves. This way you can line them up perfectly.

Flat-sand both sides of each piece. Edge-sand both pieces, except where the spacers will meet the edge. This area will be sawn and sanded after assembly.

Rout all the outside edges you sanded, again skipping the area where the spacers will meet the edges. Finally, hand-sand the routed edges and the inside edges where you routed. Don't sand the edges where the spacers will be glued or there will be gaps after assembly.

The Spacers

Cut out the three spacer pieces (B,C,D). Edge-sand the corners that approach the edge of the glued-up silhouette. This way the edges that show after assembly will look smoother.

The Tail and Dorsal Fin

Lay out the dorsal fin pieces (E), leaving it long in the rear (as in the pattern piece) until the tail is attached. Note the marks where the tail will attach. Drill the eye peg hole and then cut the piece out.

Flat-sand both sides of the piece and edge-sand the silhouette, being careful to leave the top of the rear section straight so that it will fit perfectly into the dado slot in the tail. Rout both sides of the dorsal fin that will be exposed. Hand-sand the routed edges.

The tail (F) can be made in two different ways. The first way will enable you to cut the dado on the table saw. The second way wastes less wood, but the dado slot will have to be cut by hand.

For the first method, glue up a block of wood 5" wide, 3½" thick and 7" long. Cut a ¾" dado slot 1⅛" deep in the center of the bottom, the long way. Lay

out the side view on the block and cut it out, and then lay out the top view and cut it out.

For the second method, lay out the side view on a 2″ thick piece of stock, 5″ wide, by 7″ long. Cut out the side view. Lay out the top view and cut it out. Lastly, lay out the dado slot. Cut the sides of the slot with a dovetail saw and chisel out the waste material.

All the surfaces of the tail can be sanded on the roller end of the belt-sander with a sweeping motion. Then round over the edges with the four-in-hand, and hand-sand all these edges.

Position the fin piece on one of the body sides so that the eye holes line up and the end of the pieces extend off the end of the workbench. Position the tail piece so that it is as close to the body as possible without hitting it when it pivots up and down. Mark their juncture with a pencil, glue both pieces together and clamp in a vise (with softwood faces). This will mar the surface less than clamps.

When the assembly has dried thoroughly, saw off excess material with a coping saw and briefly sand this area on the stationary belt-sander.

The Flippers

It is easier to drill the holes in both sets of flippers (G) if you do it before you cut them out. Lay them out on square pieces of stock with the inside edge (the one that will be next to the body) flush to an end grain edge of the block. If you make all four pieces the same length and width, you can clamp them together and drill the holes for $7/32″$ pegs and $1/4″$ dowels perpendicular simply by setting them on the drill press table. A center punch will help keep the drill bit from drifting.

Next, cut out the flippers on the band saw, and flat-sand and edge-sand them. The thicker front flippers an be routed if you set the $1/4″$ quarter-round bit to about one-half its normal cutting height. Don't try routing such small pieces unless you are completely competent and confident. The edges can be rounded over easily with a four-in-hand, then hand-sand these rounded edges.

The smaller flippers need only have the edges broken by hand with sandpaper. Use these finished flippers to exactly locate and drill the $1/4″$ holes in the rear of the body where they will be attached.

The Cams and Wheels

If you're making your cam, drill the hole before you cut out the circle.

The front wheels are made by plugging the axle holes and redrilling them, as in the pattern.

The front wheels need to be held about $1/2″$ away from the body to work the flippers. This is done by two $1 1/4″$ wheels on the axle, inside either side of the body. Manufactured wheels of this size generally have a $1/4″$ axle hole. These will have to be enlarged to $3/8″$ by redrilling them with a twist drill.

Assembly

Glue and position the three spacers. Position the fin and the tail piece with the tail extended off the end of the workbench. Place the other side piece on top and line up the eye and axle holes. Clamp the entire assembly together with plenty of clamps (with pads to protect surfaces). You can put a $3/8″$ dowel through each pair of axle holes to make sure that they are lined

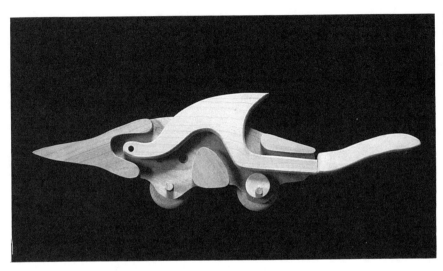

Figure 1. With the side missing you can see how the cam in the rear lifts the entire dorsal fin and tail assembly.

up properly. You should be able to look straight through the eye holes and the hole in the fin and tail piece. It's critical that all these holes are lined up perfectly.

When the assembly is dry, saw off the excess material in the spacer areas. You'll have to put the assembly up on a block to saw the rear spacer without the tail interfering. Edge-sand these areas, again using a block to sand the rear spacer. Rout these areas. You won't be able to rout the rear spacer because of the tail, so round over this area with a four-in-hand and hand-sand. Hand-sand the other routed edges.

Cut the eye pegs to length so that they will come just short of meeting in the middle of the eye hole in the fin and tail piece, with about 1/16" space on either side of the body. Put glue inside the eye hole in the fin and tail piece, being careful not to get any glue in the eye holes in the side pieces. Tap the eye pegs into place. The tail and fin piece should end up perfectly centered with a 1/16" space on either side of the body between the sides and peg head.

The front wheels will have to be put on inside-out for the offset axle to end up flush to the outer wheel surface, so you may as well put the rear wheels on inside-out so that they look the same. (Don't put the front wheels on yet, though.)

Glue the rear wheels, axle and cam in place, sliding the cam onto the axle as you pass it through

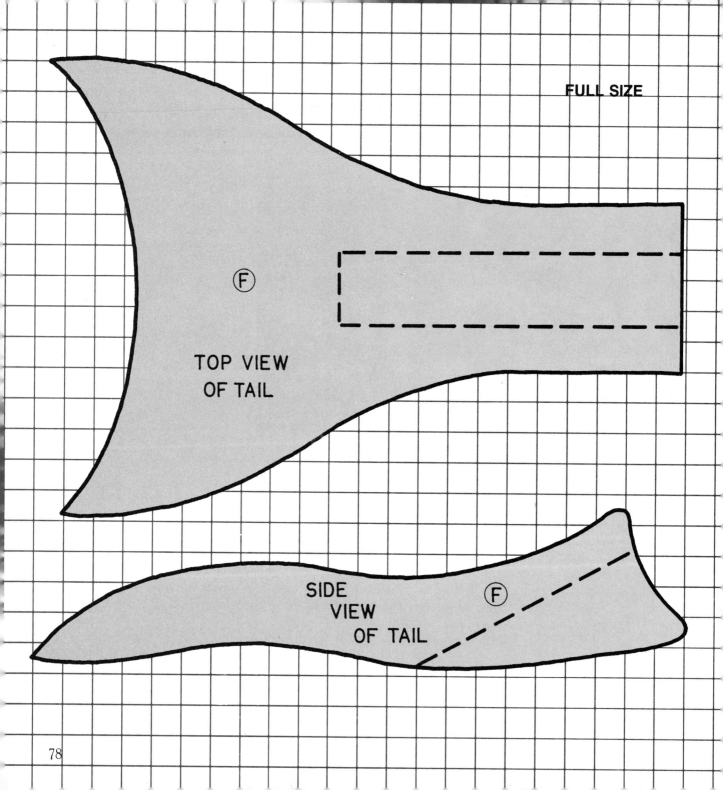

FULL SIZE

F

TOP VIEW
OF TAIL

SIDE
VIEW
OF TAIL

F

78

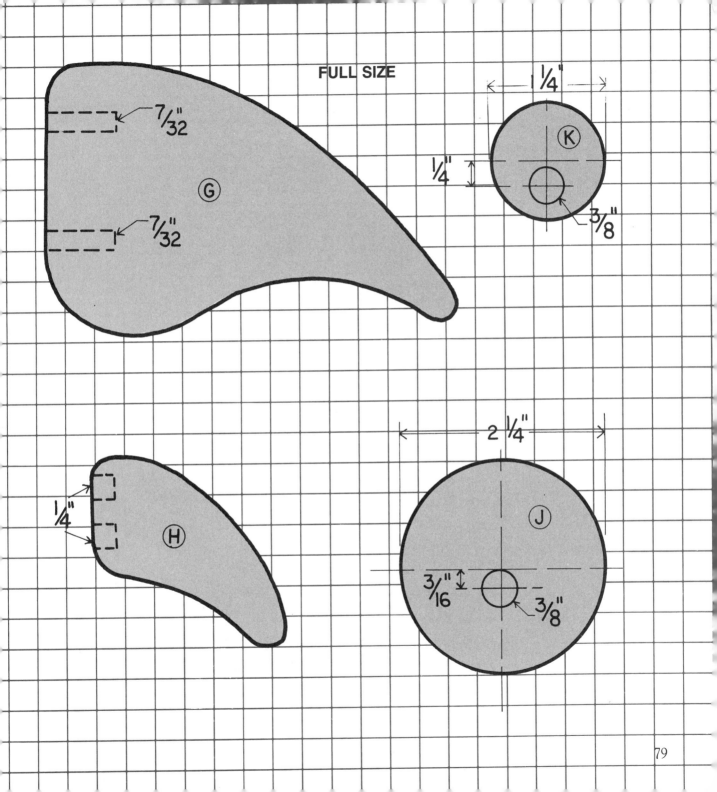

FULL SIZE

G

7/32"

7/32"

K

1/4"

1/4"

3/8"

H

1/4"

J

2 1/4"

3/16"

3/8"

79

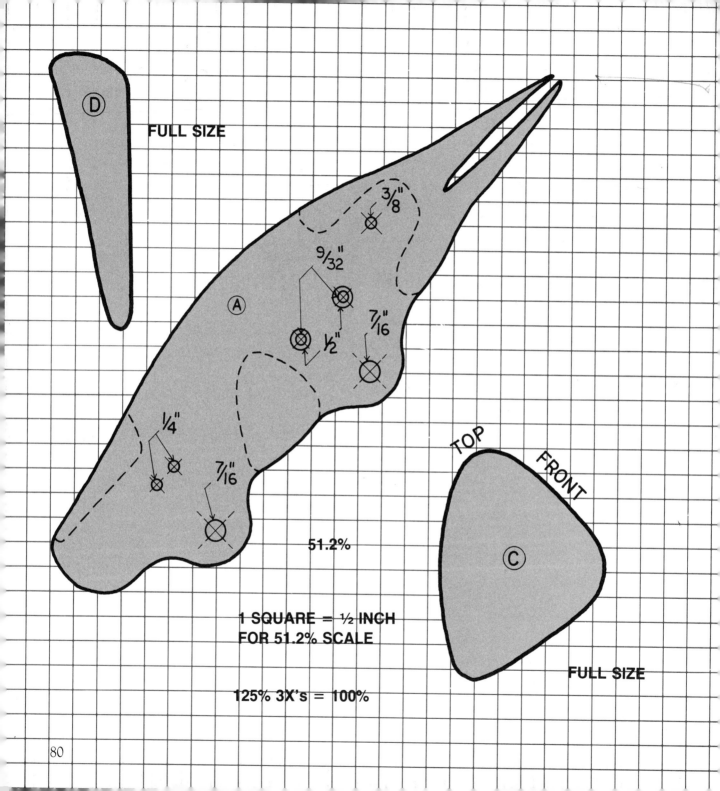

FULL SIZE

Ⓓ

3/8"

9/32"

Ⓐ

1/2"

7/16"

7/16"

1/4"

51.2%

TOP

FRONT

Ⓒ

FULL SIZE

1 SQUARE = ½ INCH
FOR 51.2% SCALE

125% 3X's = 100%

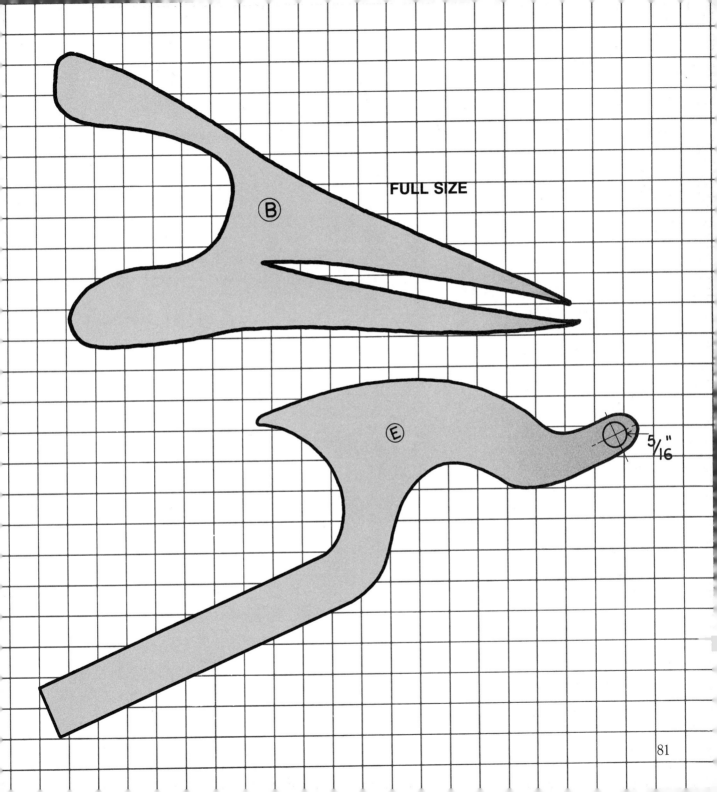

FULL SIZE

Ⓑ

Ⓔ

5/16"

81

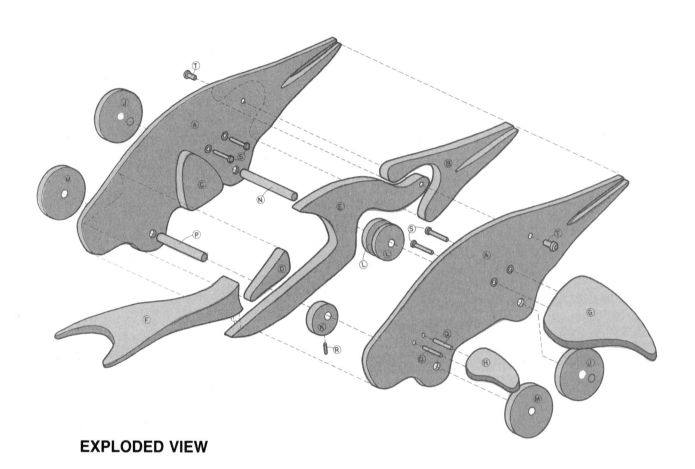

EXPLODED VIEW

the body. Drill an ⅛″ hole through the cam and the axle and glue the ⅛″ dowel in place and smooth off any excess. Edge-sand the axle ends.

The front flippers are next (before the front wheels, since the axle would block access to the flipper peg holes). Put a little glue inside the peg holes in the front flippers (too much glue will keep the flippers from sliding on far enough). Slip the pegs through the holes in the sides from the inside. Press the flippers onto the pegs, making sure that the inside edge of the flipper ends up parallel to the body side and that the flipper is on as far as possible while still being able to move up and down freely.

Glue one wheel onto the front axle (inside-out) and twist the two 1¼″ wheels onto the axle as you pass it through the body. Glue the second wheel onto the other end of the axle. Try not to use too much glue, since the axle ends will have to be sanded by hand. Position the 1¼″ wheels so they come just short of either inside edge of the body, and the outer wheels extend equally on either side of the body. Hand-sand the ends of the axles. Drill the ⅛″ hole through both of the 1¼″ wheels and axles, and glue the ⅛″ dowels in place, smoothing off any excess.

The rear flippers can now be glued and pegged in place.

When all the glue is thoroughly set up, you can oil your "vicious fishous," and stand clear of this voracious predator.

BILL OF MATERIALS

PART	DESCRIPTION	QTY	THICKNESS	WIDTH OR DIAMETER	LENGTH
A	Body sides	2	⅜″	4¼″	14½″
B	Head spacer	1	⅞″	3⅛″	6″
C	Belly spacer	1	⅞″	2⅛″	2⅛″
D	Tail spacer	1	⅞″	⅞″	3″
E	Dorsal fin	1	¾″	2¾″	9″
F	Tail	1	2″	5″	7″
G	Front flippers	2	½″	3″	4½″
H	Rear flippers	2	⅜″	2⅛″	2″
J	(Outer) front wheels	2	⅝″	2¼″	
K	Cam	1	½″	1¼″	
L	(Inner) front wheels	2	⅜″	1¼″	
M	Rear wheels	2	⅝″	2¼″	
N	Front axle	1		⅜″	4″
P	Rear axle	1		⅜″	3⅛″
Q	Rear flipper dowels	4		¼″	½″
R	Cam pin	1		¼″	¾″
S	Front flipper pegs	4	⅜″ head	⁷⁄₃₂″	1¹⁄₁₆″ shaft
T	Eye pegs	2	½″ head	⁵⁄₁₆″	1⁹⁄₁₆″ shaft

The Plesiosaurus

The Plesiosaurus was a huge sea creature. One fossil was found in Australia with a head measuring eight feet long. Loch Ness Monster watchers believe that perhaps it is a Plesiosaur that haunts the Loch, showing its huge head, neck, and tail from time to time.

How Does It Work?

This toy presented more difficulties than any other I've designed, so approach it with patience. There are several particularly tricky areas.

The head moves from side to side by means of two oval wheels tipped sideways on the front axle. The head piece pivots in the neck area and a ¼″ dowel extending down between the two diagonal oval wheels moves the rear of the head back and forth making the head snake to the right and left. There is also a 1″ wheel at the rear of the piece to reduce friction and let it pivot freely (*See Figure 1*).

The flippers are moved up and down by short Pitman arms attached to the wheels (*See Figure 2*).

The Body

Lay the body pattern (A,B) out on a 1″ piece of stock. The axles must be perfectly perpendicular to the parallel edges of the board. Transfer the axle positions to one edge of the board. The axle holes should be a little below center to accommodate the small wheels and still hold the body off the ground. With the board clamped to the drill press table, drill the two axle holes.

Remove the rectangular area over the front axle by drilling holes in all four corners of the rectangle

Figure 1. As the axle turns, the ovals tip one way and then the other, moving the head and neck back and forth by means of the peg that rides between the ovals. (Note the 1″ wheel that reduces the friction and makes the head and neck move more easily.)

and cutting out the waste with a jig saw or a coping saw. With the band saw table at 45°, cut out the silhouette of the body base.

Now lay out the reverse pattern (upper body half) on 1¾″ stock. With the band saw table perfectly square to the blade, cut out this silhouette, removing the cavity where the head enters the body and pivots.

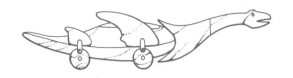

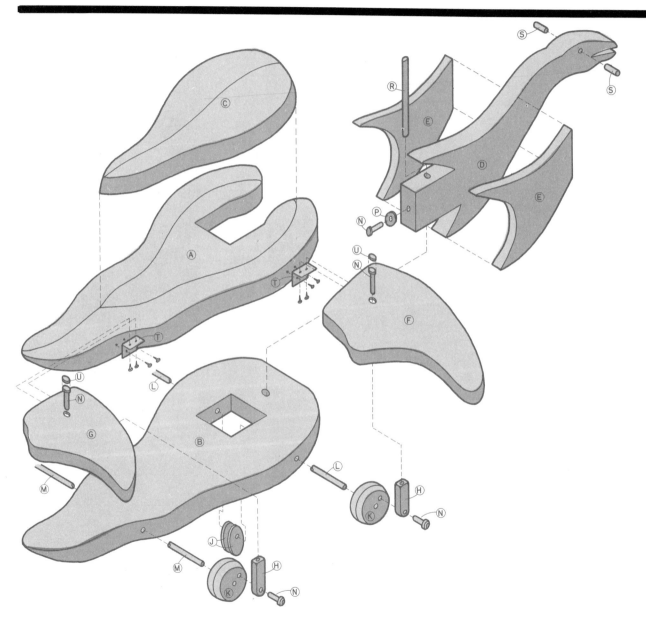

Make a pencil line all the way around the silhouette, ⅜″ from the bottom edge. You can lay the piece on the body base to make sure which surface on which to mark your ⅜″. This ⅜″ will make the flat surface to attach the flipper hinges. This cut does not enter the cavity but ends just before the cut turns to go back in the cavity.

With the band saw table at 45°, cut along this pencil line, leaving a ⅜″ flat ridge all the way around the bottom of the upper body piece.

Lay the upper body piece upside down on a 1¼″ piece of stock, and mark a line where the pieces meet. This is the outline of the ridge piece. Cut this out on the band saw with the table at 45°. There will be little

support under the piece as you finish the cut. This will make it next to impossible to correct sloppy cuts, so make sure your cut is good before you cut the final edge and release the piece.

You'll want to sand the sides of the neck cavity in the front with the sand grinder, since this area will be visible after assembly.

Now you can glue the body together. Start by gluing the two large pieces together between two pieces of wood as a clamping surface (*See Figure 3*). When this has set up, you can glue the top piece on using the same method.

Sand the ridge around the entire body with the table on the sander/grinder set at 90° (flat). Then

BILL OF MATERIALS

PART	DESCRIPTION	QTY	THICKNESS	WIDTH OR DIAMETER	LENGTH
A	Top of body	1	1¾″	5½″	15″
B	Bottom of body	1	1″	5½″	15″
C	Small back ridge	1	1¼″	3″	9½″
D	Head	1	⅞″	3½″	13¼″
E	Neck sides	2	½″	3½″	5⅝″
F	Front flippers	2	⅜″	2⅝″	5¼″
G	Rear flippers	2	⅜″	2⅛″	4″
H	Pitman arms	2	⅜″	⅝″	2⅛″
J	Oval wheels	2	¼″	¾″	1⅜″ approx.
K	Wheels	4	⅜″	1½″	

PART	DESCRIPTION	QTY	THICKNESS	WIDTH OR DIAMETER	LENGTH
L	Front axle	1		⅜″	6½″
M	Rear axle	1		⅜″	4½″
N	Pegs	5	⅜″ head	⁷⁄₃₂″	1¹⁄₁₆ shaft
P	Pivot wheel on head piece	1	⅜″	1″	
Q	Dowel riding between ovals	1		¼″	½″
R	Pivot dowel for head	1		⅜″	2⅝″
S	Eye	1		¼″	⅞″
T	Hinges & screws	4		⅜″	1″
U	Plugs in flipper holes	4	¹⁄₁₆″	½″	

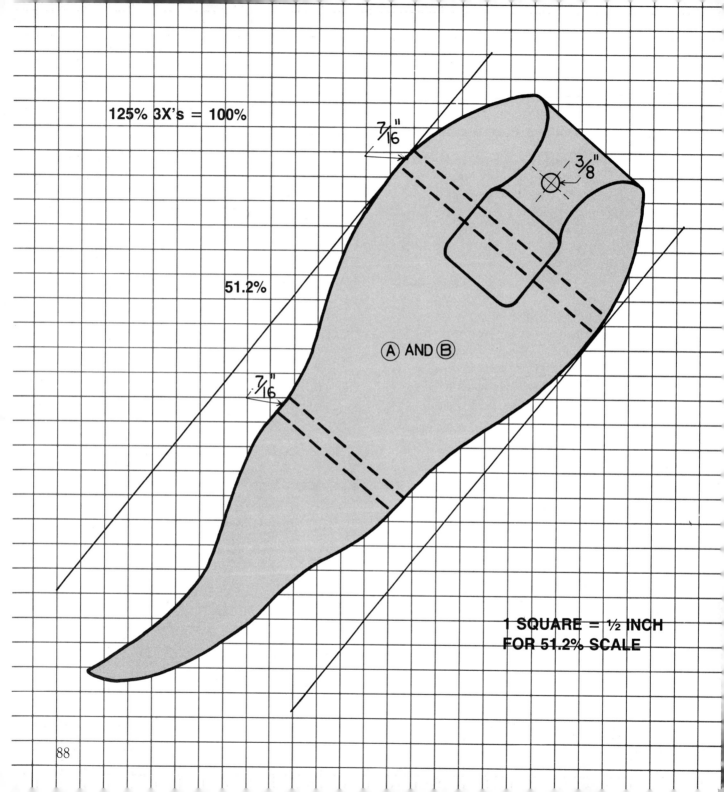

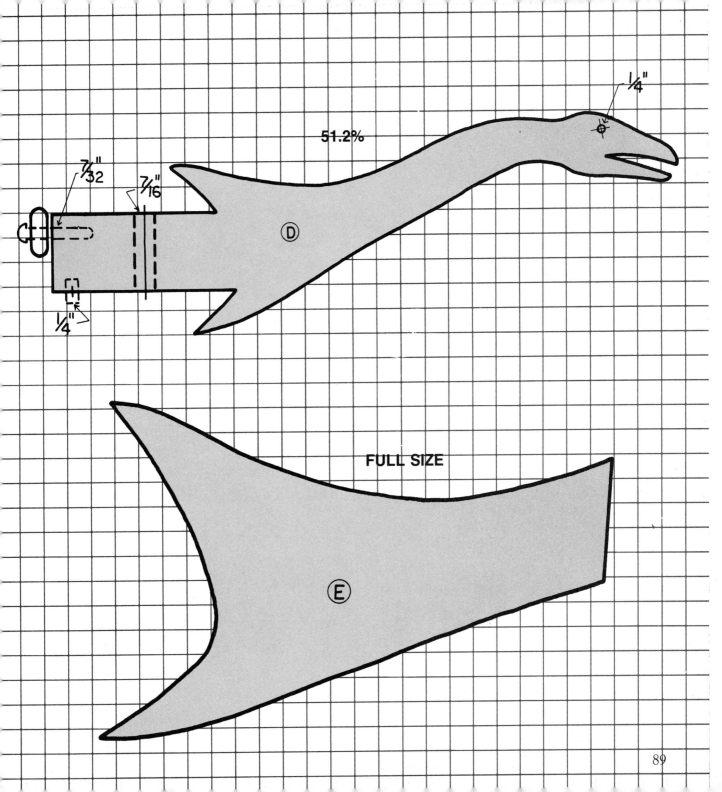

51.2%

$\frac{7}{32}$"

$\frac{7}{16}$"

$\frac{1}{4}$"

D

$\frac{1}{4}$"

FULL SIZE

E

89

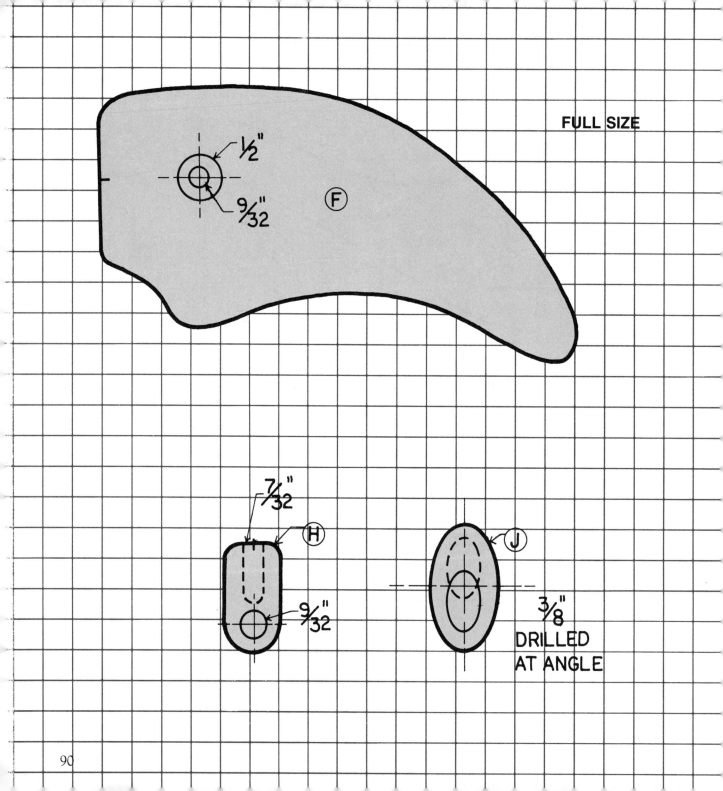

FULL SIZE

½"

9/32"

Ⓕ

7/32"

Ⓗ

9/32"

Ⓙ

3/8"
DRILLED
AT ANGLE

90

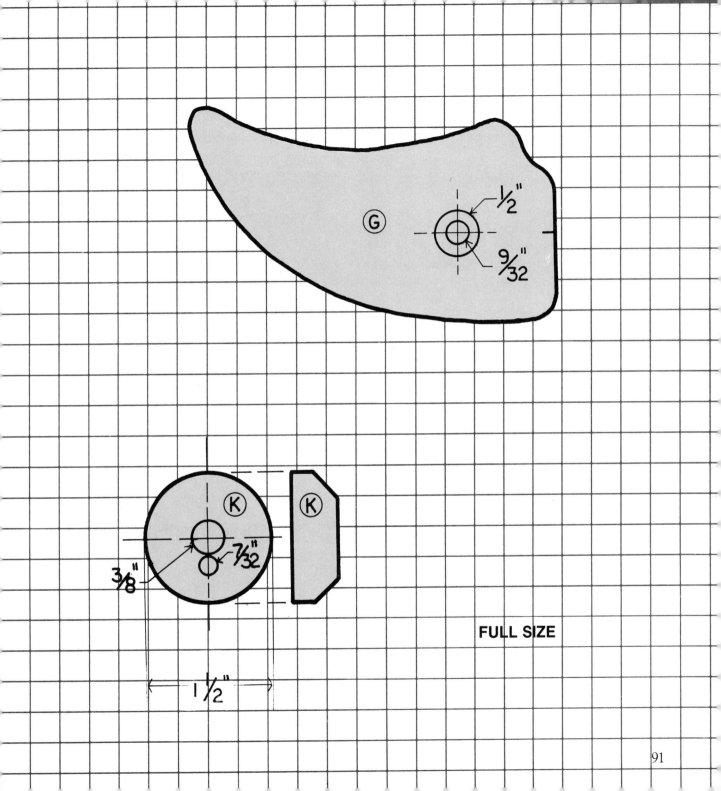

Ⓖ

½"

9/32"

Ⓚ

Ⓚ

3/8"

7/32"

1½"

FULL SIZE

with the table at 45°, sand the underside edge of the body.

The easiest way to sand the top surfaces of the body is to use the sander/grinder freehand. You can feel when the entire surface is touching the belt. Move the piece in smooth fluid strokes around the curves. You should be able to remove all the saw marks this way too.

Round over the top edge of the top piece to about 60° on the sander/grinder, since the band saw won't tilt beyond 45°. To take the same amount off both sides, keep an eye on the ridge; it should end up in the center.

Lastly, a good deal of hand-sanding in the direction of the grain will take off all of the cross-grain sander marks and soften the edges.

The pivot hole can now be drilled from underneath. Put axles through the body temporarily. You can rest the axles, upside down, on two boards (of equal thickness) to hold the body parallel to the drill press table by means of the axles *(See Figure 4)*. Set the throw so that the drill will go through the bottom piece and enter the upper ridge piece without going through. Drill to that depth with a ⅜″ bit. This must be accurate, so you might use a Forstner or brad point bit to prevent the bit from wandering.

The Head and the Neck

When you transfer the head (D) pattern onto your stock, carefully mark the centers of the holes onto the sides of the piece. Drill and plug the eye hole and flat-sand the unmarked side of the piece so that it lays flat on the band saw table. Cut out the silhouette on the

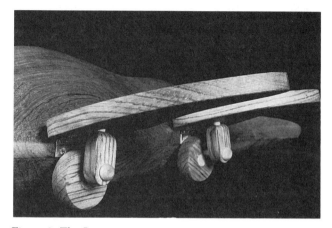

Figure 2. The Pitman arms are attached to the side of the wheel (off-center) so they lift the flippers on their hinges as the wheels turn.

Figure 3. You can use a board to spread the pressure out as you glue the body together.

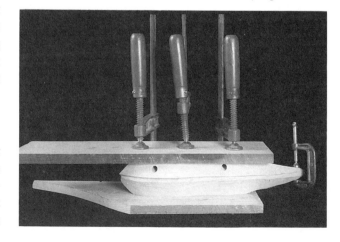

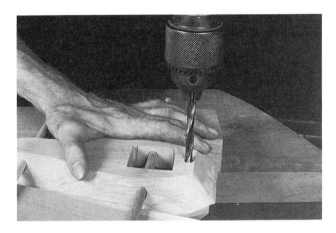

Figure 4. If you rest the wheels on thick scraps (equal thickness) the pivot hole can be drilled accurately on the drill press.

band saw. Use a square to transfer the hole locations from the side to the top, bottom and rear of the piece for the pivot hole, the wheel peg hole and the hole for the ¼″ dowel that sits in between the oval wheels. Before you drill these holes, put the head piece in place with the body upside down and see that when the pivot hole mark is sighted down through the ⅜″ hole, the ¼″ hole will be directly over the front axle. Check to see that there will be room for the ⅜″ thick wheel behind the piece.

Drill all these holes carefully, making sure that they are all square to the surface that they're drilled into.

Cut out the two sides of the neck, trying to match the grain direction. Flat-sand and edge-sand the head piece. Mark the juncture of the two side pieces on the neck and rout the rest of the silhouette, stopping short on where the side pieces will be joined. Flat-sand both side pieces and edge-sand the curve in the rear of these pieces. Round over this area with a four-in-hand and sandpaper now since this will be harder to do after gluing them to the neck.

Glue the sides to the neck, and when this has set up, edge-sand the outline where the edges meet. With the piece upside down on the band saw, cut the gentle curve on either side of the neck to taper the head out to the sides of the added pieces.

Turn the piece over and mark a ⅜″ wide strip down the middle of the top of the neck (two pencil lines). With the band saw table at 45°, cut along this line. Start at the outside edge, and curve into this line, follow it, and then curve smoothly out at the other end. Look at the photo to see how it should look.

These angled cuts can be sanded on the sander/grinder. Then hand-sand with the grain to remove all the cross-grain sander marks and soften the edges. Don't glue any of the dowels or pegs until assembly.

The Flippers

Lay out the flippers (F,S) and cut them out with the band saw. Locate and drill the holes for the attachment of the Pitman arms. First, drill a ½″ hole, leaving ⅓″ or less at the bottom of the hole. Then drill the ⁹⁄₃₂″ holes the rest of the way through. To increase the ability of the peg to pivot, slide the hole up onto the drill bit (while it's turning, and pivot the piece around the bit held at a 45° angle (*See Figure 5*). This will leave the ⁹⁄₃₂″ hole the same in the middle but larger at the top and the bottom. Be careful not to mar the edges of the ½″ hole as a ½″ plug will have to fill the hole cleanly.

Next, flat-sand, edge-sand and hand-sand the flippers. The pegs that go through the flippers (N) will have to be able to pivot freely, so plugging the holes is tricky. Make ½″ × ¼″ plugs with a plug cutter or pieces of dowel. With the peg in position, glue the plugs carefully in place, being careful not to get glue on peg heads. They should only stick about ⅟₁₆″ into the hole. When the glue has thoroughly set up, sand the excess plug material flush to the surface of the flipper.

Transfer the mark on the inside bottom edge of the flipper, from the pattern. This is the center of the hinge. When you lay out the hinge, leave the barrel off the edge of the flipper and make sure the hinge is perfectly square to the edge of the flippers. Drill the holes, being careful not to go through the flipper.

Mark a line directly over the axle holes on the body. Use these lines to locate the hinges on the ⅜″ ridge that goes around the body. Mark and drill the holes. The size of these holes is critical. If they are too big they won't hold firmly, but even more importantly, if they are too small the soft brass screws will break off in the hole and you'll be in real trouble. I recommend trying a sample hole in a scrap and screwing the hinge to it. Then, drill all your holes this size.

Wheels, Oval Drive and Pitman Arms

Manufactured wheels will not work on this toy because they need to have a bevel on the edge to fit under the flipper on the down stroke.

You can cut the wheels out (K) with a hole saw, a fly cutter (or circle cutter), or on the jig saw. If you use the jig saw, be sure to drill the axle hole first, as the wheel is so small it may split if you drill the hole afterward.

Then, with the table on the jig saw at 45°, cut around the wheel ½″ up the side making a 45° level all the way around each wheel.

If you're very careful you can sand the square edge and the bevel on the sander/grinder with the table at 45° for the bevel. Be careful to sand gently and quickly to avoid taking the wheel out of round, or simply sand edges by hand.

To drill the peg holes in the wheel, put a plug in the axle hole (without glue) to prevent the hole from collapsing as you drill the peg hole right next to it.

To make the tipped oval wheels (J), cut a 2″ scrap at 30 on the band saw. Use this for support as you drill the axle hole at that same angle with a Forstner bit. Hold the piece firmly to the scrap, especially as the bit passes through the wood.

Figure 5. The hole in the flipper is flared outward (top and bottom) by tilting it around in a circle while it is up on the drill bit.

Now, lay out the oval around these holes, noting that the edges will be the same distance from the hole two thirds of the way around, and then will be farther away for the rest of the circumference. Once it's cut out, if you flip the wheel over it should be identical in reverse, with the edge equidistant from the hole ⅔" of the way around. Don't hesitate to make them over as it is essential that they be perfect.

The Pitman arms (H) must also be precise. It's a good idea to attach them to the toy without glue and adjust the length as necessary.

Cut a strip of wood ½" × ½" by 14". You'll want to make a couple of extras in case one or two get messed up in the drilling process. Lay out six of the Pitman arms with a space between each one and drill the peg holes before cutting to length, to avoid

splitting and to let you accommodate any drill bit wander when cutting to length.

Cut the pieces off square to length. Clamp them in an upright position on the drill press and drill the peg holes into the end grain (perfectly centered).

This next operation takes some care. In order for the Pitman arm to pivot freely on the peg the lower hole must be reamed out a bit (not in the center but on the inside and outside).

With the drill press on, slip the piece up onto the 9/32" bit and carefully tip it fore and aft and from side to side, just as you did with the flippers.

This will result in a hole that is 9/32" in the middle with a slight flare on the inside and outside.

Now for a little careful work on the sander/grinder. The bottom of the Pitman arms is simply rounded, leaving the same amount of material around the bottom half of the hole.

The top of the arm gets a rounded bevel on all four sides. Be careful to end the rounded edge at the edge of the hole, not in the center of the piece. You don't want to shorten the piece at all in this process.

Finally, hand-sand to break all the edges, especially the four edges that meet at the top peg hole.

Assembly

All stages of assembly should be done without glue first.

Peg the friction wheel on the rear of the head piece and slip the piece into the body. Put the 1/4" dowel in the underside of the head piece and then put the 3/8" dowel through the body and head piece (leaving the dowel long so that you can remove it after the trial assembly). Note any adjustments necessary and remove the head piece and make corrections.

Now for the front axle, cut the axle 2" long and slip the ovals on as you pass it through the body. Hold a 1/4" dowel straight down between the two ovals and twist the axle to see how far apart the ovals must be set so that they don't bind up on the 1/4" dowel. You want the ovals as close as possible without binding the dowel that will stick down from the rear of the head piece.

Once you've figured out the optimum position for these ovals, glue them in place by putting glue on the axle and sliding the oval on. Then using a toothpick or other glue applicator, put a bead of glue around the axle on either side of each oval. Make sure that they are identically tilted, positioned as you want, and perfectly centered on the dowel.

When the glue is thoroughly dry, position the head piece as in the first trial run and try twisting the axle to see if the movement is smooth. Make any adjustments necessary. Now glue and peg the pivot wheel in place. With a toothpick or glue applicator, put glue in the 3/8" hole in the top of the body for the 3/8" pivot dowel. Slip the head piece into the body, and glue the 1/4" peg in place. Then slide the 3/8" dowel up through the body and head piece. Tap it into the glued hole and cut off the excess.

This next operation is quite critical, so take your time and make sure it's perfectly done. With the body upside down, twist the axle until the ovals are tilting

side to side (fore and aft, not up and down). This will be where the head points straight forward, so move the axle side to side until the head is pointing directly forward. If you pinch the axle with your thumb and forefinger right next to the body on either side and twist it back and forth, the head should move to one side and then the other and return to the center.

Once you have the ovals perfectly centered, mark the axle ends for cut off. Leave a gap next to the body the thickness of the wheels plus $\frac{1}{16}$″; cut off the ends of the dowels.

The flippers will have to be screwed in place before the wheels are put on, because of the position of the hinges. Carefully put the pegs in the wheels without glue as you glue on the wheels. This will prevent the hole from collapsing. Make sure that the pegs are identically positioned (either both up or both down). Remove the pegs.

Cut the rear axle to length, again leaving $\frac{1}{16}$″ space on either side of the body. Glue the rear wheels on in the same fashion as the front wheels and remove the pegs. When the glue has set up, sand the outside of the wheels by hand, to remove the glue and smooth the ends of the axles.

This last operation can be frustrating. If everything has been cut and drilled precisely, and you're lucky, the Pitman arms may work perfectly on the first try. Or you may have to make them over to get the length perfect. At any rate, a dry assembly is essential. Be careful not to push the flipper peg too far into the top of the Pitman arm as this will inhibit the pivoting action. The same is true for the pegs through the Pitman arms into the wheels.

Note also that if the Pitman arm is too short the flipper will hit the surface that the toy is rolled on; if it is too long it will bind at the top of the cycle. The flipper should come just short of hitting the rolling surface.

Now that they're perfect, glue all the pegs into the wheels and Pitman arms. When the glue is thoroughly dry, oil him up and away you go. The Loch Ness Monster lives!

The Miniature Brontosaurus

Actually *Brontosaurus* is a misnomer for *Apatosaurus*, one of the larger Sauropods. They were vegetarians and their feeble peglike teeth and the presence of polished stones in their skeletons has led to the belief that they had a gizzard-like pre-stomach that helped them to digest the massive quantities of poorly chewed vegetable matter that they needed to feed such a huge body.

How Does It Work?

A cam on the front axle makes his head and tail bob up and down in a pleasing fashion as he's pushed along. The feet are pinned to the wheels, which give his legs the walking movement *(See Figure 1)*.

The Head and Tail Piece

Lay out the head and tail piece (A) on ⅝″ stock. Drill the 5⁄16″ pivot hole and the 3⁄16″ eye hole with a scrap under your work to prevent tear-out. Cut out the silhouette on the band saw, flat-sand both sides, edge-sand the entire silhouette, and hand-sand the edges.

The Body Sides

Lay out the body sides (B) on ½″ stock. Cut out the two pieces, and lay them on top of each other with the best sides outward. Keeping them perfectly aligned, drill the axle holes, the pivot hole and the leg attachment holes, bearing in mind that the leg attachment holes should be slightly smaller than the diameter of the brads or nails that you're going to use.

Flat-sand the inside surfaces of both pieces. Edge-sand the silhouette, except along the back where the spacer will be positioned during assembly.

Now hand-sand the inside edges of the silhouette again, skipping the area where the spacer will be glued, or there will be a gap after assembly.

The Spacer

Lay out the spacer (C) on ¾″ stock and cut it out. Edge-sand the front and rear edge, which cannot be edge-sanded after assembly but will show. Do not flat-sand the spacer as the flat surfaces must remain perfectly parallel for axle and pivot holes to remain true.

The Legs

Lay out the legs (D,E,F,G) on ⅜″ stock and drill the holes for the brads, keeping in mind both the size of your brads and which holes are to be snug and which ones will allow movement.

Cut the legs out. Edge-sand them, flat-sand them, and break the edges by hand.

Assembly and Finishing

Apply glue to either side of the spacer. Put a ¼″ dowel through the pivot hole in both sides as you position them and clamp the assembly. This will help you to align the sides perfectly. Check that the wheel holes line up as you clamp the assembly.

When the assembly has set up, edge-sand the back area with 80# paper and flat-sand both sides with 80# and 120#. Rout the entire silhouette and then edge-sand it with 120# to remove any marks from the router bearing surface. Hand-sand to remove

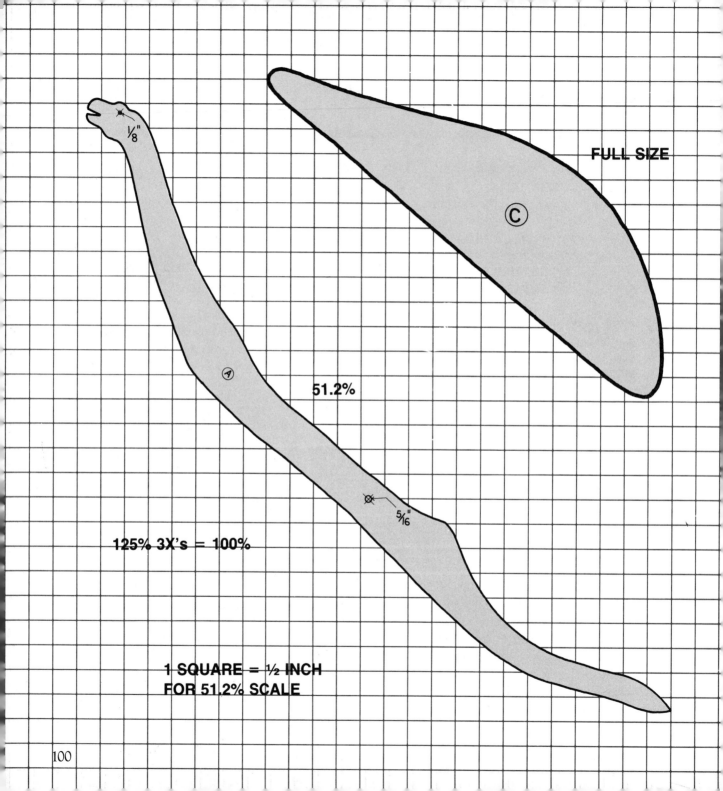

FULL SIZE

Ⓒ

⅛"

Ⓐ

51.2%

5⁄16"

125% 3X's = 100%

1 SQUARE = ½ INCH
FOR 51.2% SCALE

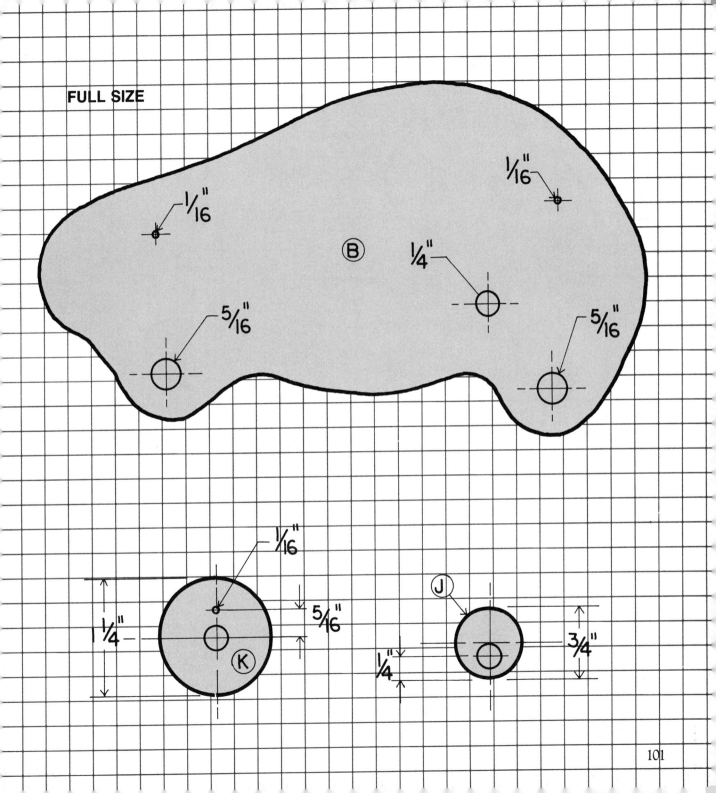

FULL SIZE

101

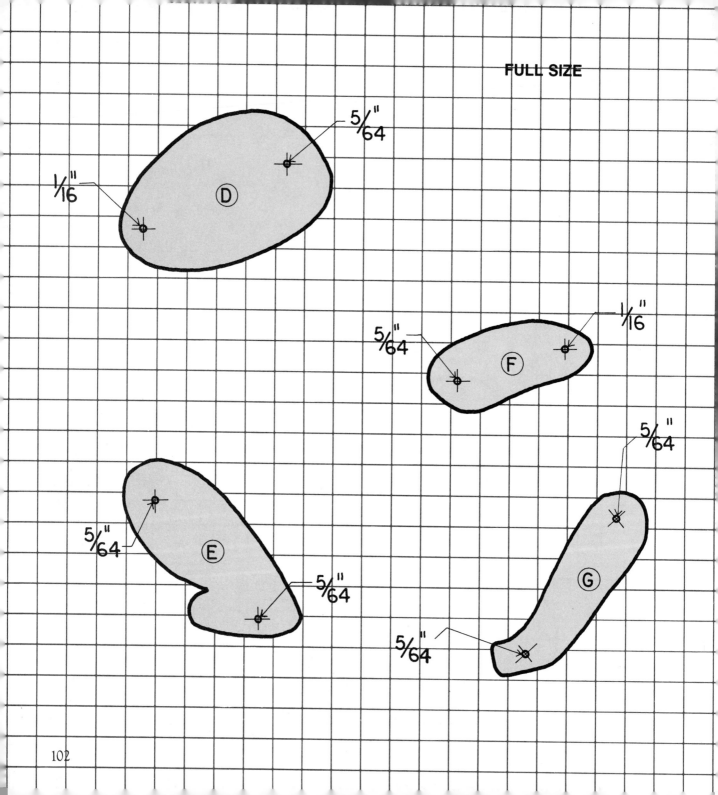

FULL SIZE

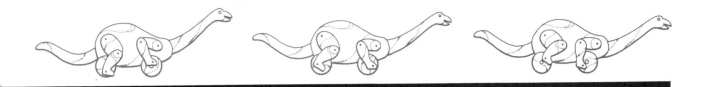

any roughness or burns from the router and cross-grain scratches from the sander/grinder.

Position the head and tail piece and drive the pivot dowel through the body until it just enters the other side. Then put some glue in the second pivot hole and drive the dowel the rest of the way through. Flat-sand the body sides with 120# again after the glue has set up to remove rough ends of the dowel and any squeeze-out.

To make the cam, see "Wheels & Cams" in the Tyrannosaurus section. Drill the nail holes in the wheels. Glue the front axle to one of the wheels. Slip the cam on as you pass the axle through the body. Glue the second wheel on, making sure that the holes for the brads are diagonally opposed (one up, one down). Repeat for the rear axle and wheels, leaving

Figure 1. With the side removed you can see how the cam lifts and drops the front of the head and tail piece as the wheels turn.

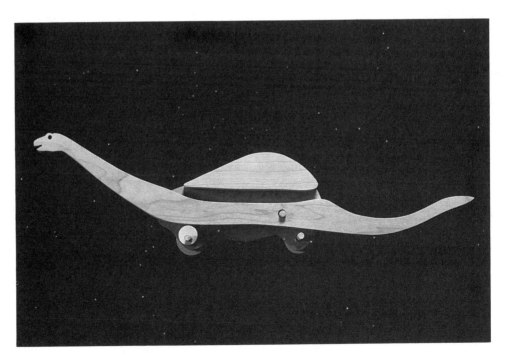

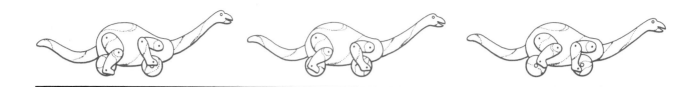

the cam out. Drill a small hole through the cam and axle and glue a toothpick in place. Smooth off the ends after the glue has dried. Edge-sand the surfaces of the wheels when the glue has set up.

I recommend oiling at this point, as it's hard to rub all the hidden areas after final assembly. When your finish has set up, nail the legs together in opposing sets, leaving enough clearance for smooth movement.

Nail the legs to the body and the wheels, again watching your clearance.

There are you: one of the smallest of one of the largest of the dinosaurs.

MATERIALS

PART	DESCRIPTION	QTY	THICKNESS	WIDTH OR DIAMETER	LENGTH
A	Head & tail piece	1	⅝″	3″	17½″
B	Body sides	2	½″	4″	6¾″
C	Spacer	1	¾″	1½″	5⅜″
D	Upper rear leg	2	⅜″	1½″	2½″
E	Lower rear leg	2	⅜″	1¼″	2½″
F	Upper front leg	2	⅜″	⅞″	1⅞″
G	Lower front leg	2	⅜″	⅞″	2½″
H	Axles	2		¼″	2⅝″
J	Cam	1	½″	¾″	
K	Wheels	4	⅜″	1¼″	
L	Pivot dowel	1		¼″	1¾″
M	Brass nails	12		16 gauge	¾″

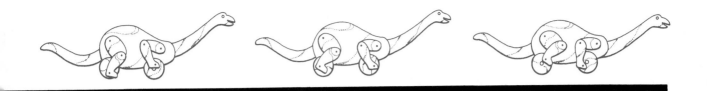

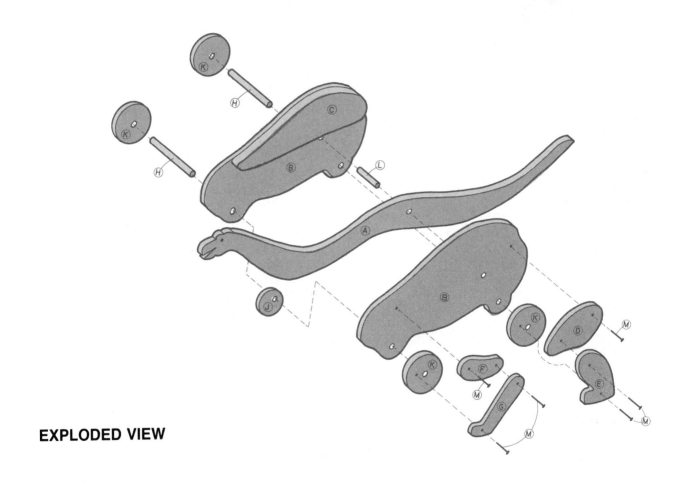

EXPLODED VIEW

The Miniature Tyrannosaurus

The Tyrannosaurus is perhaps the most familiar of all the dinosaurs. He is well known as a ferocious predator, but did you know that he is thought to have been a scavenger, drawn to the smell of carcasses?

How Does It Work?

As you push this fellow along, holding on to his tail, his mouth opens and closes threateningly by means of a cam and drive dowel *(See Figure 1)*, while the offset wheels and attached legs give him an ominous swaying gait.

The only difficulty in making the Tyrannosaurus is the small size of the pieces. I recommend using a scroll saw or coping saw to cut out the arms, legs, and head if you are at all uneasy about using the band saw on such small pieces.

The Body

After you lay out the body pattern (A), drill the axle hole before cutting the piece out to prevent splitting. You should drill the holes for the pins at this point (eyes and leg attachment). These holes should be slightly smaller than the diameter of the nails that you are going to use.

As you cut out the silhouette, cut straight across the top of the teeth instead of cutting them out. This will make it easier to drill the hole for the ¼″ drive dowel.

Next clamp the body piece between two boards on the drill press table so that the drive dowel hole is perfectly vertical. Use a square to make sure that it's not tipped to either side and drill the ⁵⁄₁₆″ drive hole.

You can now cut out the teeth. Then transfer the top view of the tail onto the body piece with a piece

Figure 1. From the front you can see how the cam between the front wheels lifts the ¼″ dowel which, in turn, opens the mouth. (Note the tilt in the body because of the offset front wheels.)

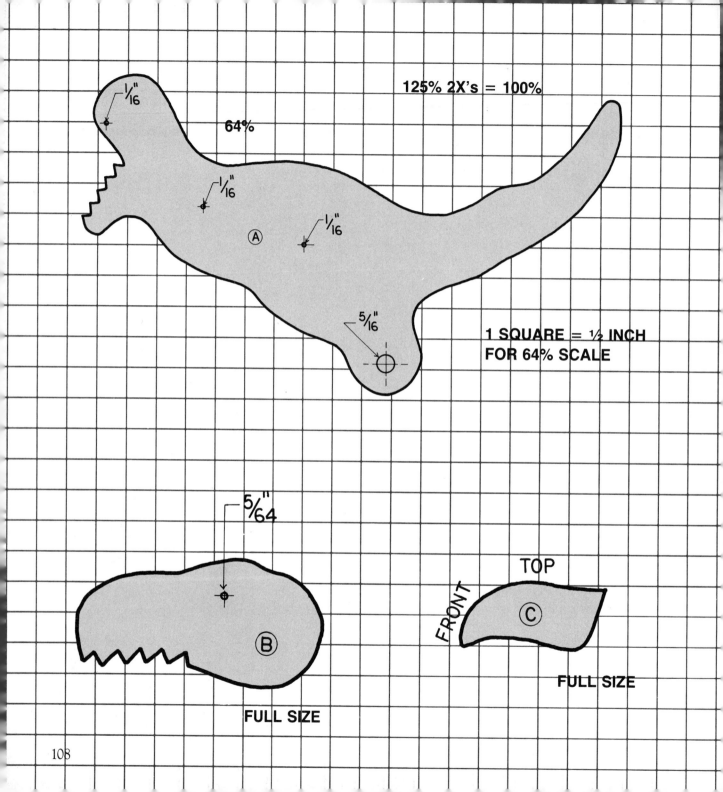

125% 2X's = 100%

64%

1/16"

1/16"

1/16"

Ⓐ

5/16"

1 SQUARE = ½ INCH
FOR 64% SCALE

5/64"

Ⓑ

FULL SIZE

FRONT

TOP

Ⓒ

FULL SIZE

108

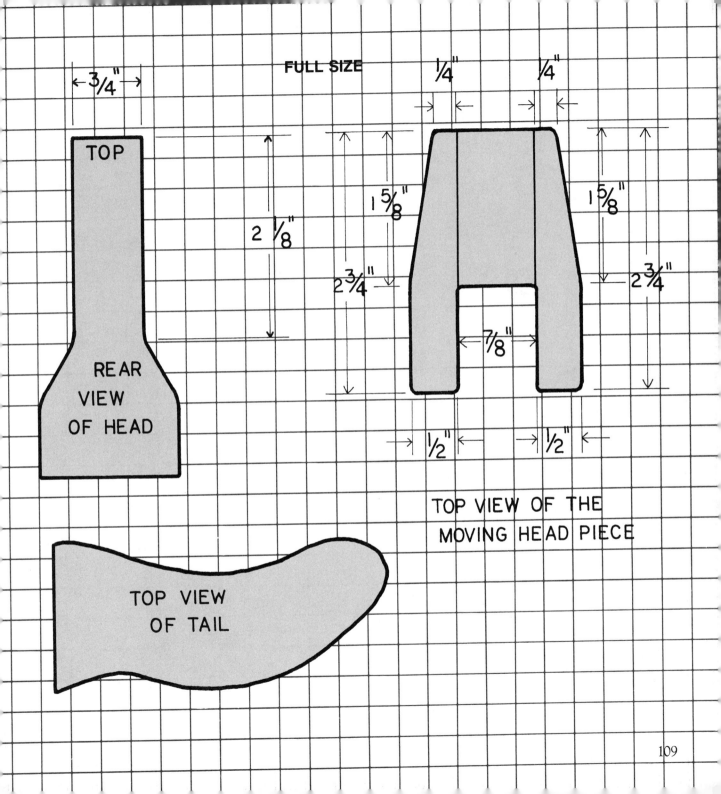

FULL SIZE

3/4"

1/4" 1/4"

TOP

1 5/8"

1 5/8"

2 1/8"

2 3/4"

2 3/4"

REAR
VIEW
OF HEAD

7/8"

1/2" 1/2"

TOP VIEW OF THE
MOVING HEAD PIECE

TOP VIEW
OF TAIL

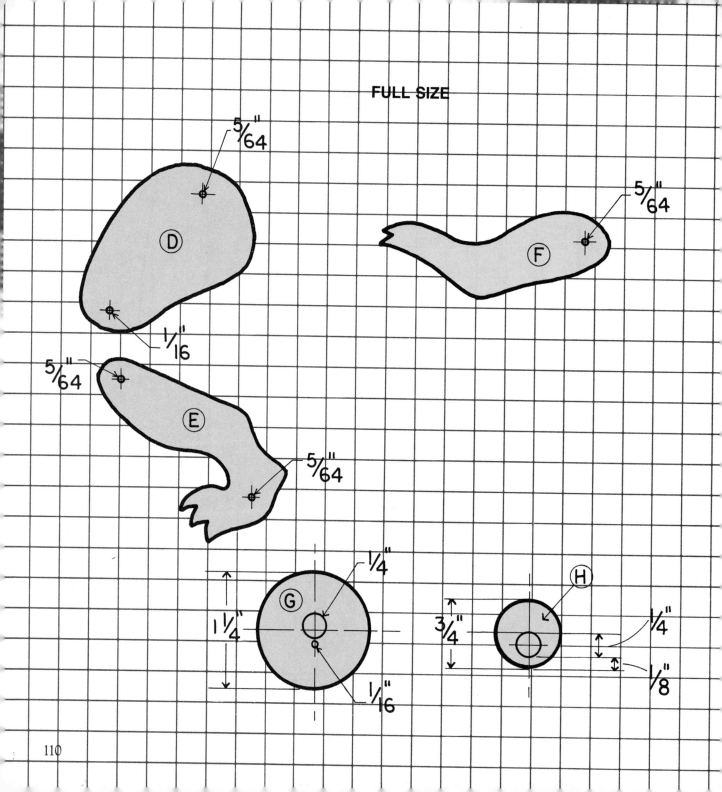

FULL SIZE

5/64"

D

1/16"

5/64"

F

5/64"

E

5/64"

1/4"

G

1 1/4"

1/16"

H

3/4"

1/4"

1/8"

of paper that will lay flat on the contoured tail. Holding it firmly, standing up, cut out the sculpted sides of the tail.

Clamp the body upside down in a vise. You may want to scribe the sides of the notch to be removed, for the cam, to make sure you cut them perfectly. You can either cut the notch out with a dado blade (in three passes), or use a dovetail saw or a backsaw to cut either side of the notch to the depth of the dotted line on the pattern. Then use a sharp chisel and carefully cut away the waste material.

Flat-sand both sides of the body and edge-sand the entire silhouette. Rout the outline, except the head, the tail, and around the axle hole. Then clamp the body in a vise upside down and round over edges of the tail with a four-in-hand. You may as well hand-sand the tail while it's in the vise.

Now, with the body face down make two marks on top of the head to show where to cut away the sides of the head. Set the rip fence first to cut one side and then the other, to a distance of 2⅛″ from the top of the head. Make sure that you end up with a little more than ¾″ thickness so that edge sanding will take it down to ¾″ thick. Then, with the rip fence removed, continue these cuts, angling outward to the edge of the piece. The angle of the cut is not as critical as making both cuts identical.

Now, with the face still downward, edge-sand these areas. Hand-sand the whole body to remove any roughness or cross-grain scratches and smooth all the routed and unrouted edges. Use a file on the edges of the teeth.

The Head

To make the headpiece, lay out both of the sides (B) on ¼″ stock and spacer (C) on 1⅛″ stock. Drill the eye holes to insure perfect alignment. Carefully glue and clamp the sides to the spacer, using a wire pulled tight through the eye holes to insure alignment (See Figure 2). Lay out the top view of the head. With the teeth resting on the band saw table, cut away the tapered sides. Flat-sand these sawn areas and then rock the piece on the belt sander to flat-sand the rest of the side and smooth the transition between the two surfaces. Round the edges over with sandpaper. A file will help to break the sharp edges on the teeth.

Figure 2. A wire held taught, through the eye holes, will line them up as you glue the head assembly together. (Note that the front teeth line up perfectly.)

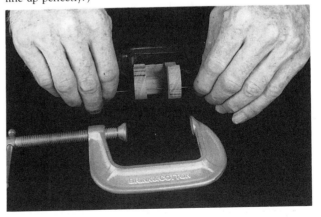

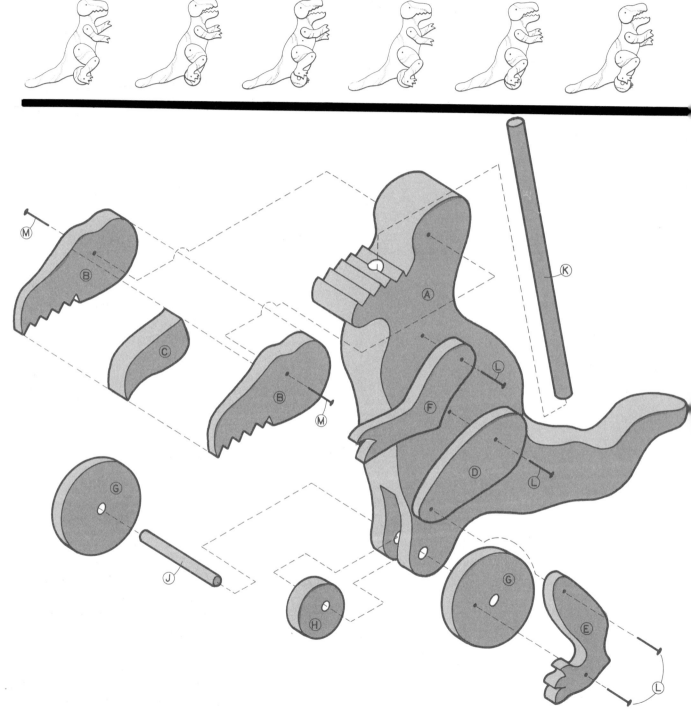

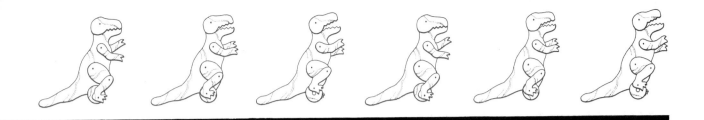

The Legs

Lay out, drill, and cut out the leg pieces (D,E,F). Be sure to drill the knee holes so that the brads fit snugly, and the other holes so that the brads will move freely without the head slipping through.

Cut out the leg pieces on the band saw. Flat-sand and edge-sand them all, either by hand, or on the machine sanders if you're totally confident.

The Wheels and Cam

Glue short sections of ¼" dowel in the wheel holes and redrill the axle holes slightly off center. Then drill the holes to attach the feet to the wheels. (Note the wheel pattern: The brad is on the other side of the center of the wheel from the offset axle hole.)

To make the cam (H), lay it out, drill the axle hole first, and very carefully cut out the cam with a coping saw. Smooth any roughness by hand and round over the edges.

Assembly and Finishing

Cut the axle (J) to length, glue it to one of the wheels and slip the cam on the axle as you pass it through the body. Glue the other wheel on, making sure one brad hole is up and the other down.

When the glue is dry, sand the ends of the axle on the sander/grinder or by hand.

Drill a small hole through the cam and into the axle and pin it in place with a toothpick and some glue. Cut off the excess and sand it smooth.

It's a good idea to oil this creature before assembly, as the pieces are so small it's hard to rub down after assembly.

After the finish has set up, nail the leg assemblies together in opposing sets, leaving clearance for smooth movement. Then nail the leg assemblies to the body and the wheels. The arms get nailed tightly in place. Start the nail, and when the arm touches the body, bend it slightly and keep hammering until it is snug against the sloping shoulder. Insert the drive dowel (with both ends slightly rounded over) and lightly pin the head in place. Adjust the length of the dowel if necessary and nail the head securely, again making sure to leave equal clearance on either side to insure free movement. There you have him: the king of the carnivores in a somewhat less threatening size.

BILL OF MATERIALS

PART	DESCRIPTION	QTY	THICKNESS	WIDTH OR DIAMETER	LENGTH
A	Body	1	1½"	6"	9½"
B	Head sides	2	½"	1½"	2¾"
C	Head spacer	1	⅞"	⅞"	1¾"
D	Upper leg	2	⅜"	1½"	2¼"
E	Lower leg	2	⅜"	1⅜"	2½"
F	Arms	2	⅜"	1"	2½"
G	Wheels	2	⅜"	1¼"	
H	Cam	1	½"	¾"	
J	Axle	1		¼"	2⅜"
K	Drive dowel	1		¼"	4⅞" approx.
L	Brass brads (or nails)	8		16 ga.	⅞"
M	Brass brads (or nails)	2		16 ga.	¾"

The Miniature Triceratops

The Triceratops is one of the *ceratopsian* dinosaurs. These had an amazing variety of horny plates protecting their head and neck. They were herd animals and behaved much like the musk ox when threatened by predators, gathering in a circle facing outward. They could also be quite aggressive, and would even attack the carnivorous Tyrannosaurus.

How Does It Work?

This sculpted beauty has a simple but pleasing movement. The legs move with the wheels and the cam and dowel smoothly lift the horny plate (*See Figure 1*).

The Body

Lay out the body pattern (A) on 1¾″ stock. Drill the wheel holes, the eye holes and the leg attachment holes. Cut out the silhouette on the band saw. Edge-sand the silhouette and flat-sand both sides. Lay out the top view and cut out. Edge-sand the sawn areas. Use a drum sander on the drill press to remove any cross-grain scratches.

With the band saw table at 45°, cut the bevel on the back and belly areas (*See photo of finished toy*). This belly cut should come down the front of the rear leg on the right side and start there on the left side.

Smooth all these bevel cuts on the 1″ sander/grinder with the table at 45°. Use a drum sander to get the inside curves in front of the rear legs.

Carefully lay out and drill the ⁵⁄₁₆″ hole directly down through the front axle. Cut the slot out for the cam with a dado blade, or lay out the slot with a

pencil and carefully saw the sides with a dovetail saw, and chisel out the waste material, coming from both sides, to avoid splitting along the grain below the desired depth.

A lot of hand sanding is necessary, but well worth the effort, to bring out the interesting grain patterns on this sculpted body.

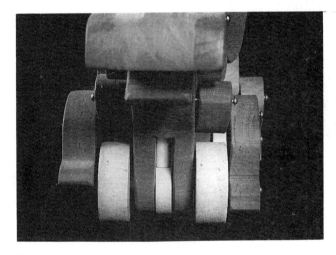

Figure 1. Looking from the front you can see that the cam on the front axle lifts a dowel which in turn lifts the rear of the head plate, making the mouth close.

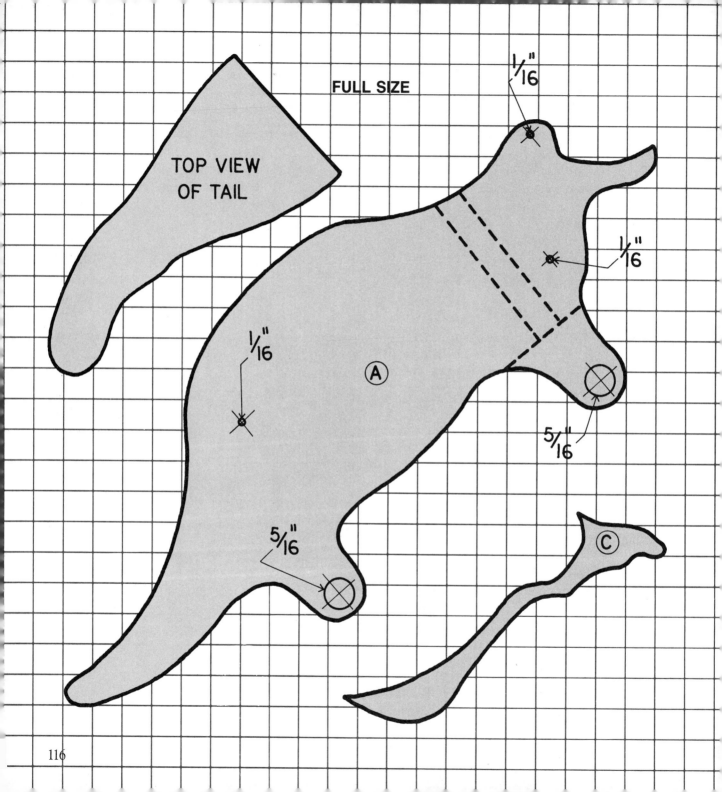

FULL SIZE

TOP VIEW OF TAIL

1/16"

1/16"

1/16"

Ⓐ

5/16"

5/16"

Ⓒ

FULL SIZE

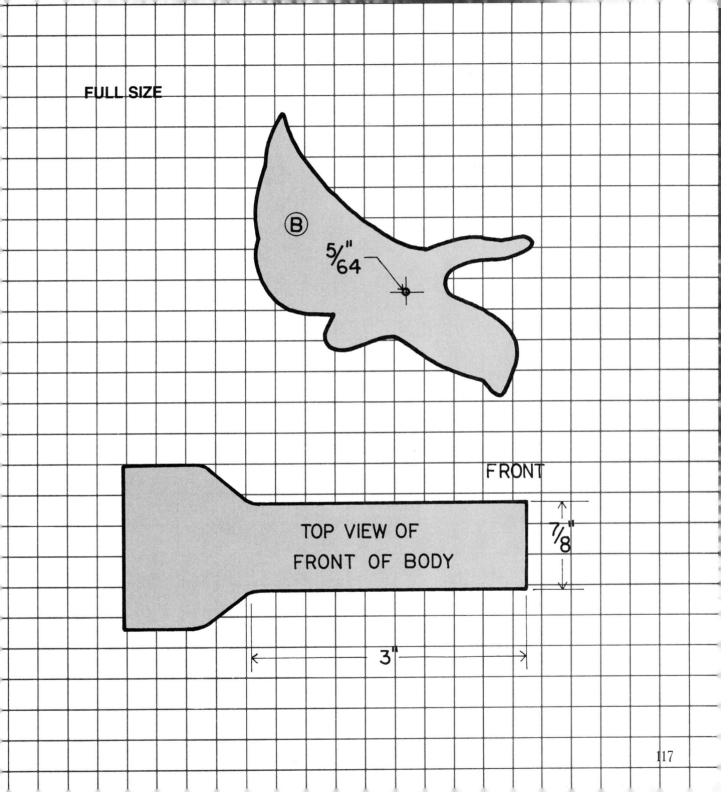

B

$\frac{5}{64}''$

FRONT

TOP VIEW OF
FRONT OF BODY

$\frac{7}{8}''$

3"

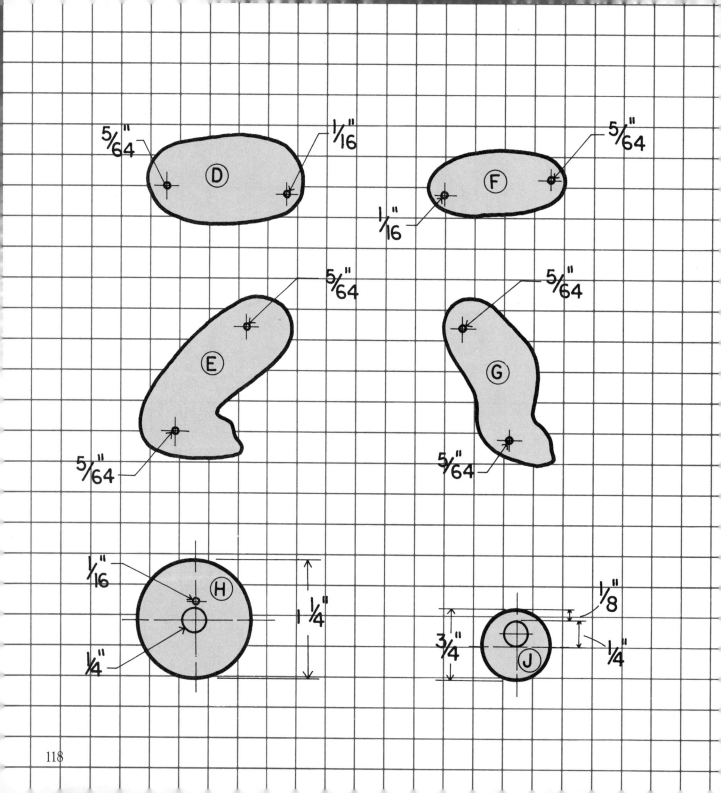

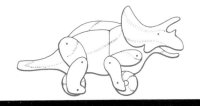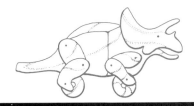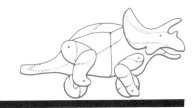

The Head

Lay out the spacer (C) on ⅞″ stock, with the grain running the long way for strength. Be very careful to keep to the lines when you cut it out, as smooth movement relies on accuracy.

Use the sander/grinder and a small drum sander to smooth the silhouette. The top and the back of the plate will be sanded after assembly, but the nose area will be inaccessible.

Use a dovetail saw to remove waste on either side of the central horn and round the area over with a rasp, to conform the silhouette edges to the silhouette of the sides in this area.

Lay out the side pieces (B) on ¾″ stock, drill the eye holes, and cut out extremely carefully. Use the sander/grinder and a drum sander to smooth the edges, except the top of the plate from the horns back, as this will be sanded after assembly.

Glue the sides to the spacer, lining them up perfectly. A piece of wire pulled tight through the eyes will help to insure perfect alignment (*See Figure 3*). When the assembly is dry, edge-sand the top and the rear of the plate and the front of the nose.

Lay out the top view and use the rip fence on the band saw to cut the sides of the front up to where they flare outward. Remove the rip fence and cut the flares.

Use the sander/grinder or the drum on the end of the belt sander to carefully sand the sides of the head and the flares on the sides of the plate.

Break all the edges by hand and hand-sand the entire head to remove all the scratches from the sander.

The Legs

Lay out the legs (D,E,F,G) on ⅜″ stock. Drill the holes according to the nails you use, keeping in mind which holes are pivots (larger than the nail) and which are secure (slightly smaller than the nail). Cut the pieces out on the band saw if you are comfortable with small pieces. If not, use the jig saw or scroll saw. Hand-sand the edges, and put aside, to oil before assembly.

Figure 2. A wire held taught through the eyes will help line up the head sides as the spacer is glued carefully between them.

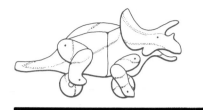
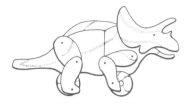
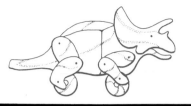

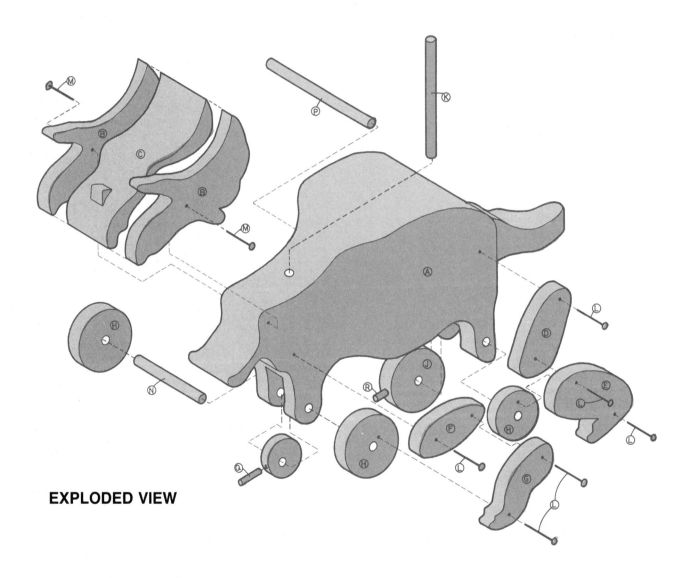

EXPLODED VIEW

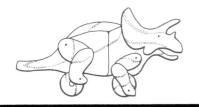  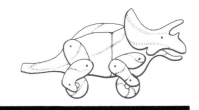

The Wheels and Cams

To make the cam (H), lay it out on ¼″ stock and drill the ¼″ hole before carefully cutting it out with the jig saw, scroll saw, or coping saw. Smooth the edges by hand. Drill the peg holes in the wheels slightly smaller than the nail diameter that you're using.

Assembly

It's a good idea to attach the head to the body with the nails lightly pressed into place (with ¼″ drive dowel and cam in place). Adjust length of ¼″ drive dowel until assembly works smoothly.

Then, glue the front wheels to axle, with cam positioned, as you slip the axle through the body.

Make sure that the nail holes in the wheels are diagonally opposed (one up and one down).

Glue the rear wheels on (one nail hole up and one down). Edge-sand all the axle ends. Drill a tiny hole through the cam and the axle and glue the toothpick in place to keep the cam from slipping around the axle. Smooth the edges of the cam again.

It's a good idea to oil this toy before final assembly as it's very hard to wipe off afterward. After oiling and drying, nail the legs together in opposing sets and then nail them to the body and the wheels, leaving enough clearance for smooth movement.

Next, nail the head to the body (with the drive dowel in place), again leaving clearance.

If you liked making this creature, you may want to try the large version in my first book, *How to Make Animated Toys.*

BILL OF MATERIALS

PART	DESCRIPTION	QTY	THICKNESS	WIDTH OR DIAMETER	LENGTH
A	Body	1	1¾″	3½″	8¾″
B	Head sides	2	¾″	2″	4″
C	Head spacer	1	1″	1″	4″
D	Upper rear leg	2	⅜″	1″	1⅞″
E	Lower rear leg	2	⅜″	1¼″	2⅛″
F	Upper front leg	2	⅜″	¾″	1½″
G	Lower front leg	2	⅜″	1″	2″

PART	DESCRIPTION	QTY	THICKNESS	WIDTH OR DIAMETER	LENGTH
H	Wheels	4	⅜″	1¼″	
J	Cam	1	¼″	¾″	
K	Drive dowel	1		¼″	2½″ approx.
L	Brass brads	12		16 ga.	⅞″
M	Brass brads	2		16 ga.	¾″
N	Front axle	1		¼″	1¾″
P	Rear axle	1		¼″	2⅝″

The Miniature Stegosaurus

The Stegosaurus could raise its huge plates to absorb the warmth of the early morning sun, and then lower the plates in the heat of the day.

How Does It Work?

This miniature is similar to the larger version but quite a bit simpler. The head, tail, and plates are all one piece which pivots by means of a cam on the rear axle and a pivot dowel in the front of the body (*See Figure 1*).

The Body Sides

Lay out the body sides (A) on ⅜″ stock. Cut out the silhouettes, lay them carefully on top of one another and drill the rear axle holes and pivot holes at the same time. (Don't drill the front axle holes at this time.) Drill the holes for the leg attachment as well, making these holes slightly smaller than the brads you're going to use.

Edge-sand the silhouettes and flat-sand both sides with 80# paper. Hand-sand the *inside* edges except where the spacer will be glued.

The Head, Tail and Plates

Lay this piece (B) out on ½″ stock, marking the hole locations at the base of the plates. Drill these holes and the eye and pivot holes with a scrap under your work to prevent tear-out. Chisel out the remaining material between the two rear pivot holes to make a smooth channel for the pivot dowel to ride up and down in.

Cut out the silhouette on the band saw. Flat-sand both sides and edge-sand it. Break all the edges by hand with sandpaper or a file.

The Spacer

Lay out the spacer (C) on ⅝″ stock and cut it out on the band saw. Edge-sand the front and back so they will look smooth after assembly.

The Legs

Lay out the legs (D,E,F,G) on ⅜″ stock. As you drill the holes, bear in mind which holes the nails should fit tightly in and which should let them pivot.

Cut out the legs on the band saw. Flat-sand and edge-sand them, and then break all the edges by hand with 120# paper.

The Wheels and Cams

Drill the leg attachment holes in the wheels as in the patterns.

Lay the cam out on ½ inch stock. Drill the ¼″ hole and then cut it out with a coping saw. Smooth the silhouette by hand and break the edges.

Assembly and Finishing

Use a 3″ long ¼″ dowel through the front pivot hole of the body sides to position them as you bring them together with the spacer between them (with glue on both sides of it). Another dowel through the rear axle holes will help with alignment. Clamp the assembly across the spacer with pads to protect your work. When the glue has set up, remove the ¼″ dowel and edge-sand the belly and front axle areas. Drill the front axle hole with a scrap under your work to

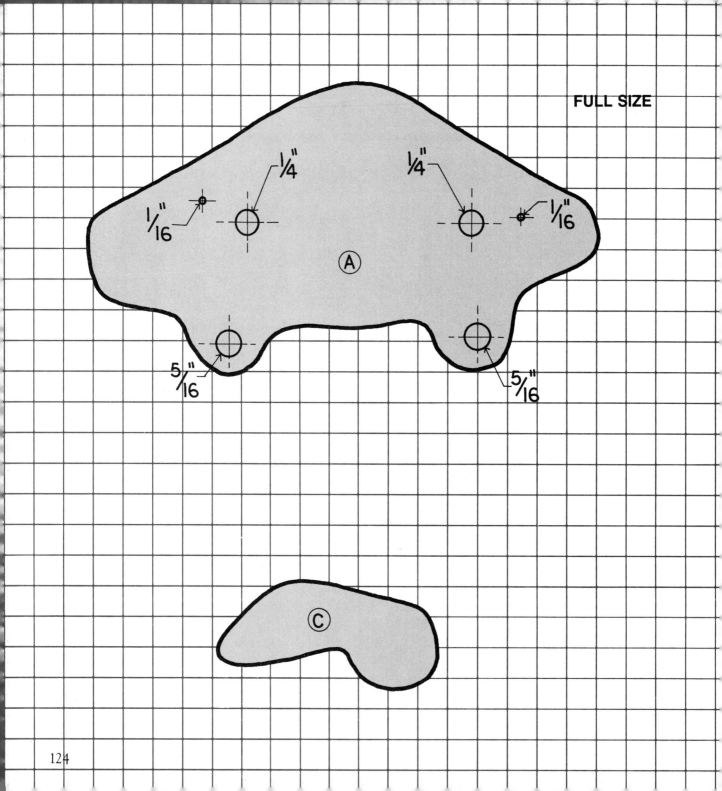

FULL SIZE

124

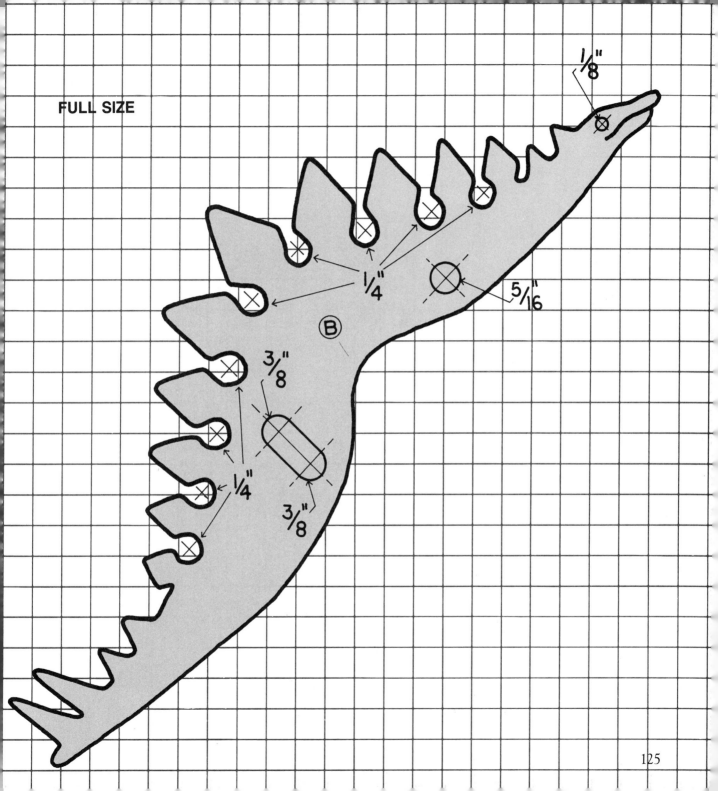

FULL SIZE

125

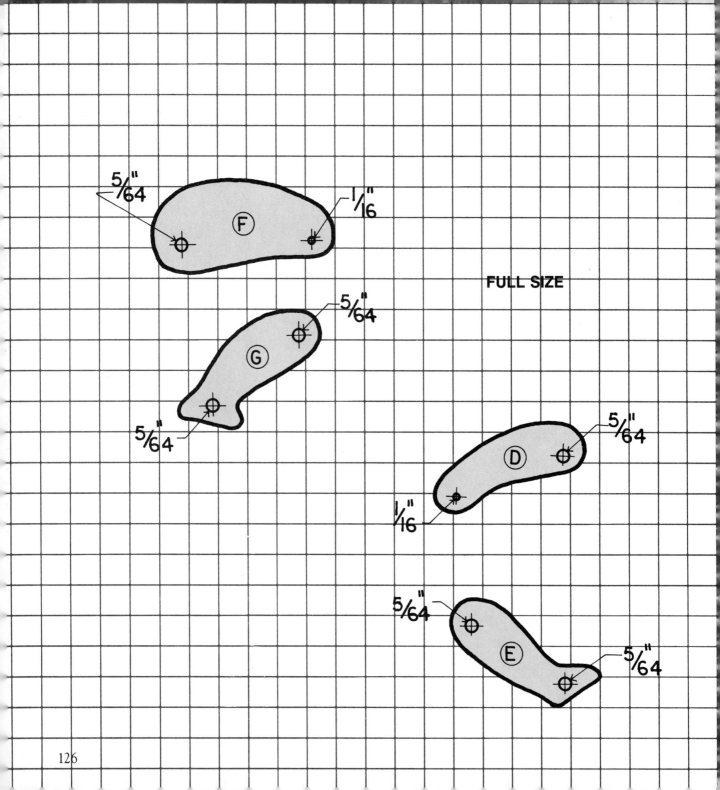

FULL SIZE

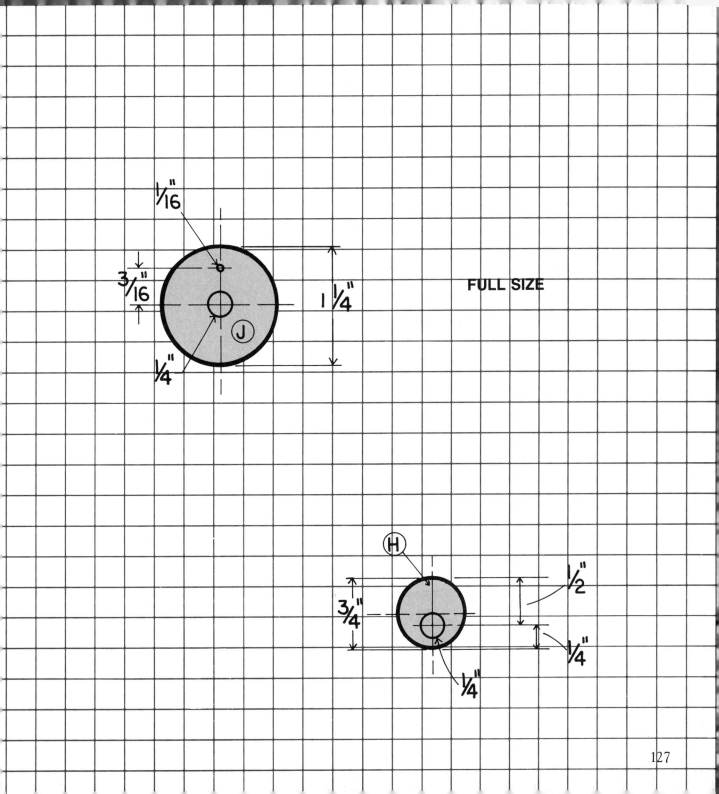

EXPLODED VIEW

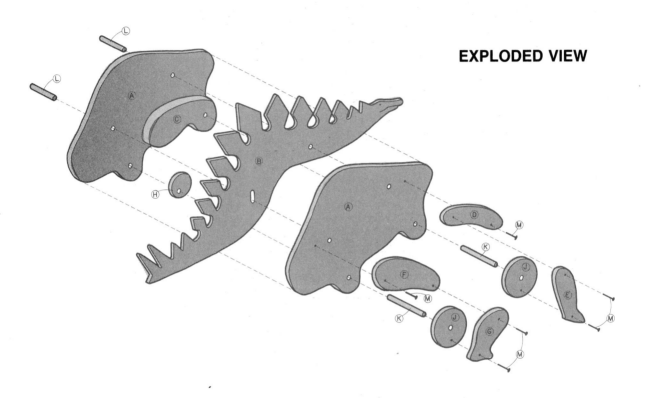

BILL OF MATERIALS

PART	DESCRIPTION	QTY	THICKNESS	WIDTH OR DIAMETER	LENGTH
A	Body sides	2	3/8″	3¼″	5¾″
B	Head, tail & plates	1	½″	3″	9¾″
C	Spacer	1	5/8″	1¼″	2½″
D	Upper front legs	2	3/8″	¾″	1⅞″
E	Lower front legs	2	3/8″	¾″	1⅞″
F	Upper rear legs	2	3/8″	1″	2″
G	Lower rear legs	2	3/8″	¾″	1⅞″
H	Cam	1	½″	¾″	
J	Wheels	4	3/8″	1¼″	
K	Axles	2		¼″	2″
L	Pivot dowels			¼″	1⅜″
M	Brass brads	12		16 ga.	⅞″

128

Large Animated Dinosaurs. Top row: Stegosaurus, Pteranodon. Middle row: Icthyosaurus, Hadrosaurus, Dimetrodon. Bottom: Plesiosaurus.

The Variable Swing Rack and Dinosaur Swings,
from left: Brontosaurus, Tyrannosaurus, Stenosaurus,
Dinosaur Egg.

Miniature Animated Dinosaurs. Top row, from left: Pteranodon, Hadrosaurus, Dimetrodon, Tyrannosaurus. Bottom row: Stegosaurus, Triceratops, Brontosaurus.

D

On wall, from left: Dimetrodon Clothes rack, Triceratops Clothes rack, Brontosaurus Hangers. On bureau top: Stenosaurus. On bureau side: Dinosaur Plaques. On floor: Brontosaurus Rocker, Plesiosaurus Scooter. On bed-frame: Dinosaur Magnets.

prevent tear-out. Rout the entire silhouette on both sides. Hand-sand the routed edges.

Cut the pivot dowel slightly long and round off the ends. With the head and tail piece in position, tap the ¼" dowel through the body until it starts to enter the hole in the other side. Put glue in this hole and tap the dowel through so that it protrudes slightly from either side. When it is dry, flat-sand the sides with 120# to remove dowel ends and glue.

Put one wheel on the rear axle and slip it through the cam as you pass the axle through both axle holes. Glue the second wheel on with the nail holes diago-

nally opposed (one up, one down). Repeat the process for the front axle, without the cam. Drill a small hole through the cam and the axle and glue a toothpick into the hole. Break off any excess and sand it smooth.

It is a good idea to oil the body and the legs before final assembly (after the glue is dry) since it is hard to wipe off excess oil between such tiny parts.

Finally, nail the legs together in opposing sets and nail them to the body and wheels, leaving enough clearance for smooth movement.

One more miniature-scale vegetarian.

Figure 1. With the side missing you can see how the cam on the rear axle lifts the whole head, tail and spine piece up and down. (Note the pivot dowel in the rear riding in the slot in the head, tail and spine piece.)

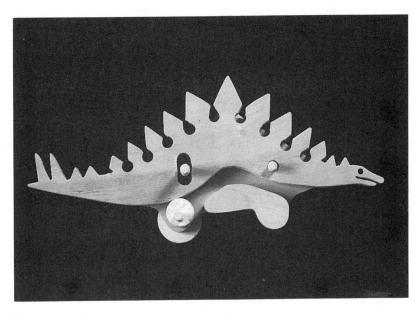

The Miniature Hadrosaurus

One man has spent nearly twenty years measuring the nasal cavities of these creatures and creating what he thinks are the actual sounds that they produced by blowing air through their huge crests.

How Does It Work?

This miniature is identical to the larger version in movement, with the cam on the axle rocking the head forward and back as the offset wheels made him sway from side to side (*See Figure 1*).

The Body Sides

Lay out the body sides (A) on ⅜" stock. Cut out the silhouettes, lay them on top of each other, and drill all the holes at the same time.

Flat-sand both sides of each piece. Edge-sand the silhouette, except where the spacers meet the edge of the body. These edges will be sanded after assembly. Round over the outside edges of the neck and the wheel areas, because the head piece will be in the way after assembly. Hand-sand the inside edges of these areas as well. Don't sand the inside edges where the spacers will be attached or there will be a gap after assembly.

The Pivoting Head Piece

Lay out the central head piece (B) with the grain running the long way. Drill the pivot hole (not the eye hole) and cut out the silhouette, skipping the mouth line, and leaving ⅛" around the head silhouette. This will be cut to the line after the head sides are attached. Edge-sand from the neck down. Try fitting a ¾" dowel in the fork area, as if it were the cam. It should fit easily but not sloppily. Break all the edges by hand except the neck and head.

Lay out the two head sides (C) on ¼" stock, with the grain running along the horn or crest. This will reinforce the cross grain of the head pivot piece. Cut these pieces out slightly large, like the pivot piece, without cutting the mouth line. The line across the neck (on the bottom edge) should be cut accurately on both pieces, as you won't be able to get at it after assembly. Edge-sand this line and round over the outer edge of this area (keeping in mind which side of each piece will face outward).

Apply glue to the inside surface of both pieces, working glue away from the bottom edge, to avoid glue squeeze-out on the neck of the pivot piece. Position the pieces carefully and clamp them thoroughly. When the glue has set up, drill the ¼" eye hole, with a scrap under your work to avoid tear-out. Glue the eye dowel in place. Cut out the silhouette, including the mouth line. Flat-sand both sides and edge-sand the silhouette. Rout the silhouette.

Use the roller on the belt sander, or a drum sander on the drill press, to form the indents that define the duckbill. With the piece in a vise, round over this area to match the routed edge. Hand-sand all the routed edges, etc. Cut the pivot dowel to length, round over both ends, and glue it in place (perfectly centered).

The Spacers

Lay out both spacers (D,E) and cut them out on the band saw. Edge-sand the areas of the silhouette that

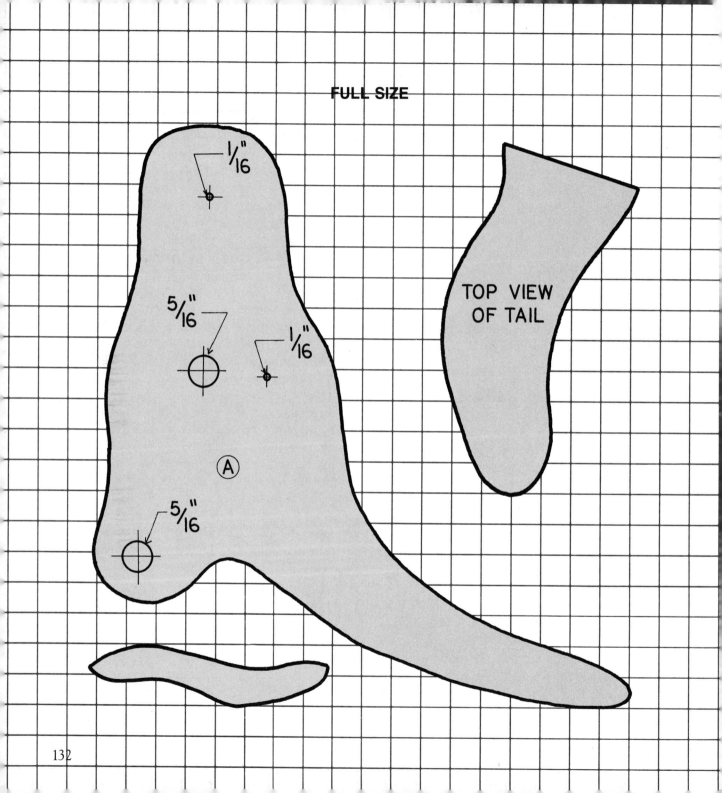

FULL SIZE

1/16"

5/16"

1/16"

(A)

5/16"

TOP VIEW
OF TAIL

132

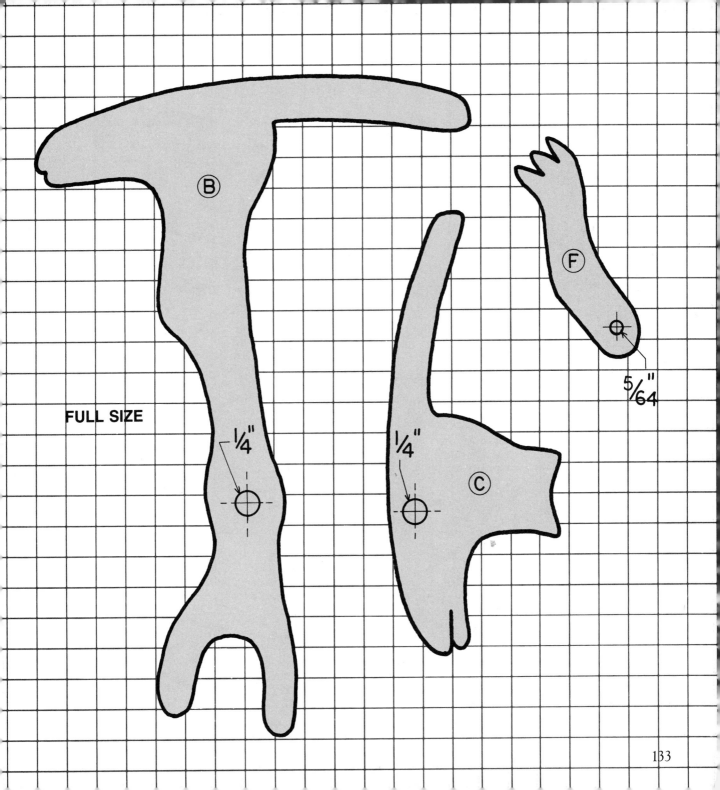

FULL SIZE

Ⓑ

¼"

Ⓒ

¼"

Ⓕ

⁵⁄₆₄"

FULL SIZE

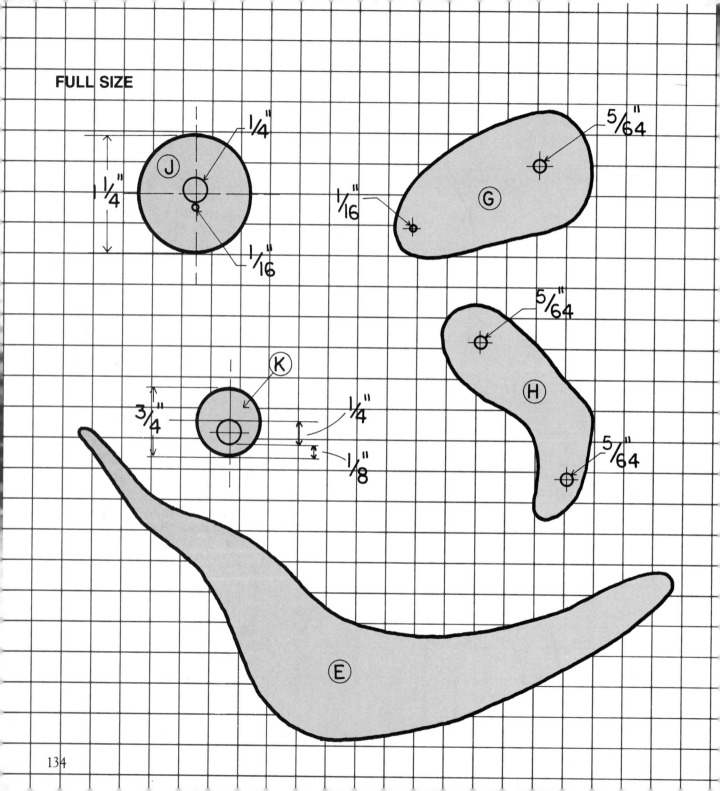

1/4"

J

1/4"

1/16"

5/64"

G

1/16"

5/64"

H

K

3/4"

1/4"

1/8"

5/64"

E

134

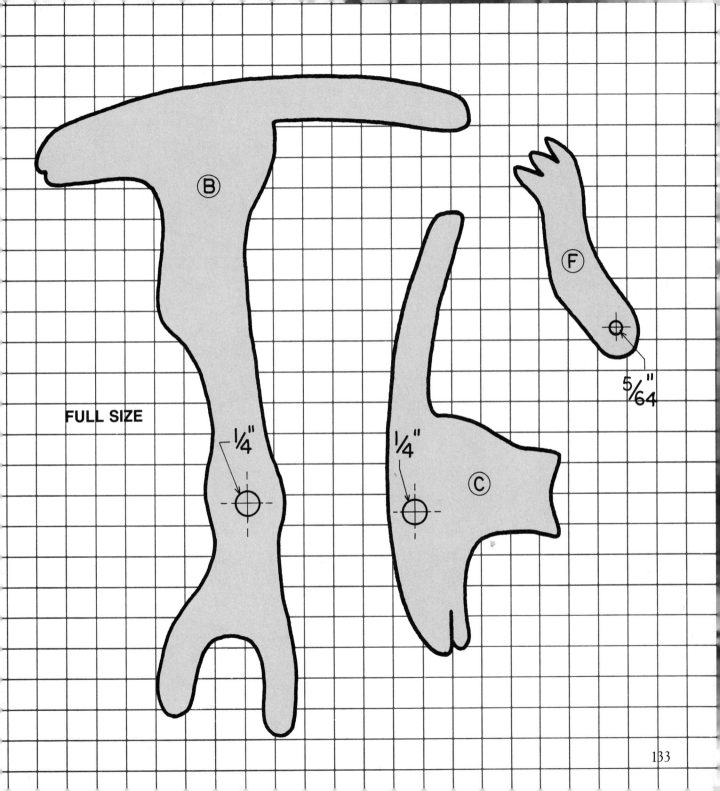

FULL SIZE

B

¼"

C

¼"

F

5/64"

133

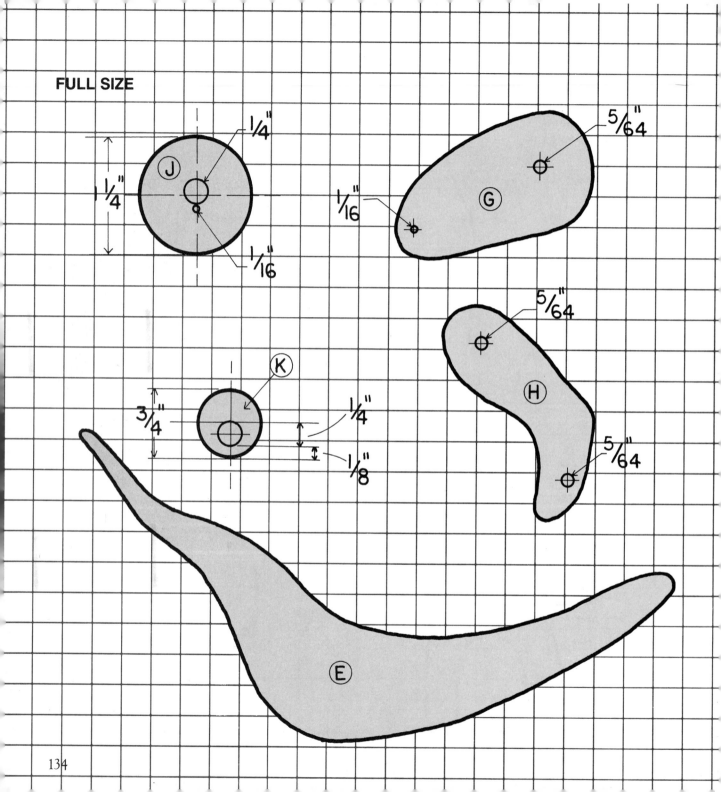

FULL SIZE

134

Figure 1. With the side missing you can see that the head piece pivots in the middle and is rocked back and forth by the cam that fits into the fork at the bottom.

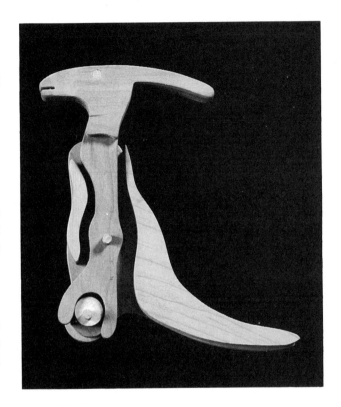

will be hidden after assembly. With the edge sander, round the ends of the spacers where they will meet the outside edges of the body sides after assembly. Do not flat-sand them because the surfaces must remain perfectly parallel.

The Arms and Legs

Lay out the arms and legs (F,G,H). Drill all the holes according to the size of the nails that you are going to use. Cut out the arms and legs. Edge-sand and flat-sand them, and break the edges by hand.

The Cam and Wheels

Lay out the cam (K), drill the ¼″ hole and carefully cut out the circle. Hand-sand any roughness so that it fits in the fork of the head pivot piece without being too tight or too sloppy. Don't hesitate to make the cam over to insure a good fit in the fork.

The wheels (J) are made by plugging the axle hole of the 1¼″ wheels and drilling them *slightly* off center. The holes for the nails are just on the other side of the old plugged center from the axle hole.

Assembly and Finishing

Lay one of the side pieces down, and without gluing, position the spacers and the pivoting head piece. See that all the clearances are correct as you pivot the head back and forth, and make any necessary adjustments.

Apply glue to both sides of the spacers and position them on one of the sides. Put the head pivot piece in place and carefully lay the second side on top. Check the movement of the pivoting head pieces and

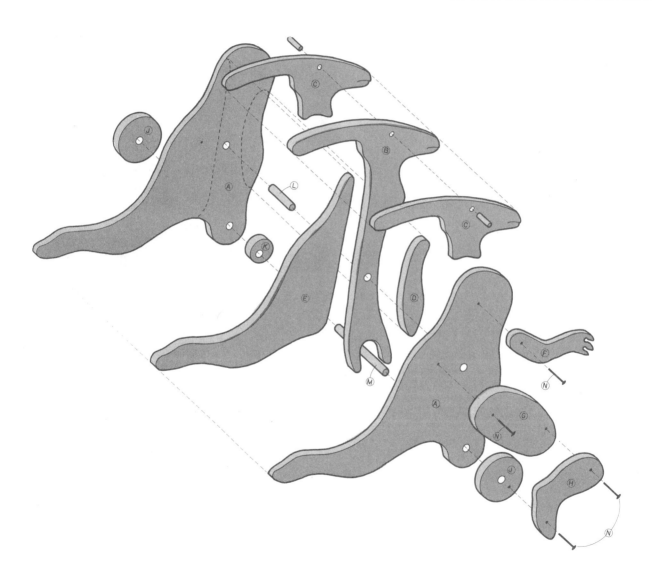

the *alignment of the wheel holes* as you apply clamps.

When the assembly has set up, edge-sand the areas where the spacers are. Rout these edges.

Lay out the top view of the tail. Cut it out and edge-sand it. With the body in a vise, tail upward, round over the edges of the tail with a four-in-hand and hand-sand it with 80# paper to get out all the cross-grain scratches. Then sand the whole body with 120#.

Glue one wheel to the axle. Slip it through the cam as you pass it through the axle holes. Glue on the second wheel with the nail holes diagonally opposed (one up and one down). When the glue is dry, sand the axle ends.

Drill a small hole through the cam and the axle and glue a toothpick in the hole. Break off the ends and smooth them.

It is a good idea to oil the body, arms and legs before assembly, since it is hard to rub them off afterwards.

When the finish has set up, nail the legs together in opposing sets, leaving adequate clearance. Nail the sets to the body and the wheels, again leaving adequate clearance. Nail the arms tightly at the body so that they can be moved, but stay in place otherwise.

One more delightful miniature dinosaur for your collection!

BILL OF MATERIALS

PART	DESCRIPTION	QTY	THICKNESS	WIDTH OR DIAMETER	LENGTH
A	Body sides	2	3/8″	4″	7 1/8″
B	Pivoting head piece	1	1/2″	4 7/8″	7″
C	Head sides	2	1/4″	2″	4 7/8″
D	Chest spacer	1	5/8″	5/8″	2 5/8″
E	Tail spacer	1	5/8″	2 5/8″	6 7/8″
F	Arms	2	3/8″	7/8″	2 1/2″
G	Upper legs	2	3/8″	1 3/8″	2 3/8″
H	Lower legs	2	3/8″	1 1/4″	2 1/2″
J	Wheels	2	3/8″	1 1/4″	
K	Cam	1	1/2″	3/4″	
L	Axle	1		1/4″	2 1/4″
M	Pivot dowel	1		1/4″	1″
N	Brass brads	8		16 gauge	7/8″

The Miniature Dimetrodon

The Dimetrodon is the oldest of all the dinosaurs. It is believed that Dimetrodons roamed the earth some 250 million years ago!!

How Does It Work?

This miniature works in a similar manner to the larger version. The only difference is that (because of space limitations) the lower jaw is attached to the sail piece, and they move up and down together as the cam on the front wheel lifts and drops them.

His low-slung legs attached to the wheels give him that lizard like gait (*See Figure 1*).

The Body Sides

Lay out the body sides (A) on ⅜″ stock and cut out the silhouettes. Line them up on top of each other and drill the axle holes, the pivot holes and the leg attachment holes at the same time (according to the size nails that you are going to use). Don't drill the eye hole until after assembly.

Flat-sand both sides of each piece. Hand-sand the inside edges, as these areas will be harder to get to after assembly (except the edges on the head and tail where the spacers will be glued or there will be a gap after glue up).

Spacers

Lay out the spacers (B,C) on ½″ stock and cut them out. Edge-sand the front of the tail spacer and the rear of the head spacer, so they will look smoother after assembly.

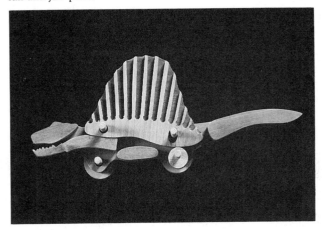

Figure 1. With one side removed you can see how the cam on the rear axle lifts the back of the sail and jaw piece.

The Sail and Lower Jaw Assembly

Flat-sand both sides of your ⅛″ stock with a belt sander. Then, lay out the central piece (E), with the grain running horizontally, to strengthen the assembly. When you cut it out, cut it exactly along the bottom line, but have ¼″ all the way around the exposed area on top. This will be cut after the sides are attached. Lay out the sides (D) (the spines) with the grain running vertically for maximum strength. Drill all the ⅛″ holes (at the base of the spines) very carefully as they will determine the width of the spines. Don't drill the pivot holes until after assembly.

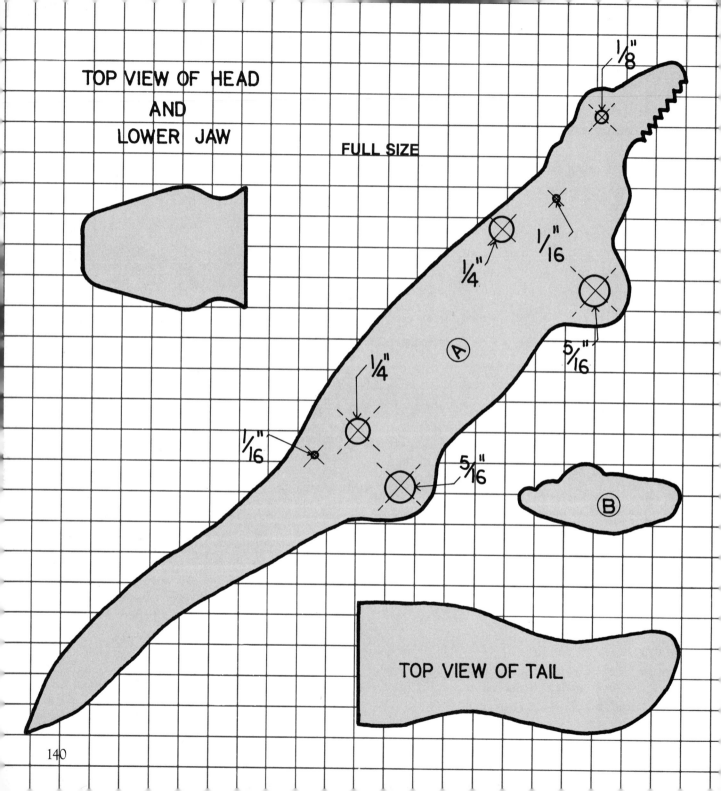

TOP VIEW OF HEAD
AND
LOWER JAW

FULL SIZE

$\frac{1}{8}$"

$\frac{1}{16}$"

$\frac{1}{4}$"

Ⓐ

$\frac{5}{16}$"

$\frac{1}{4}$"

$\frac{1}{16}$"

$\frac{5}{16}$"

Ⓑ

TOP VIEW OF TAIL

140

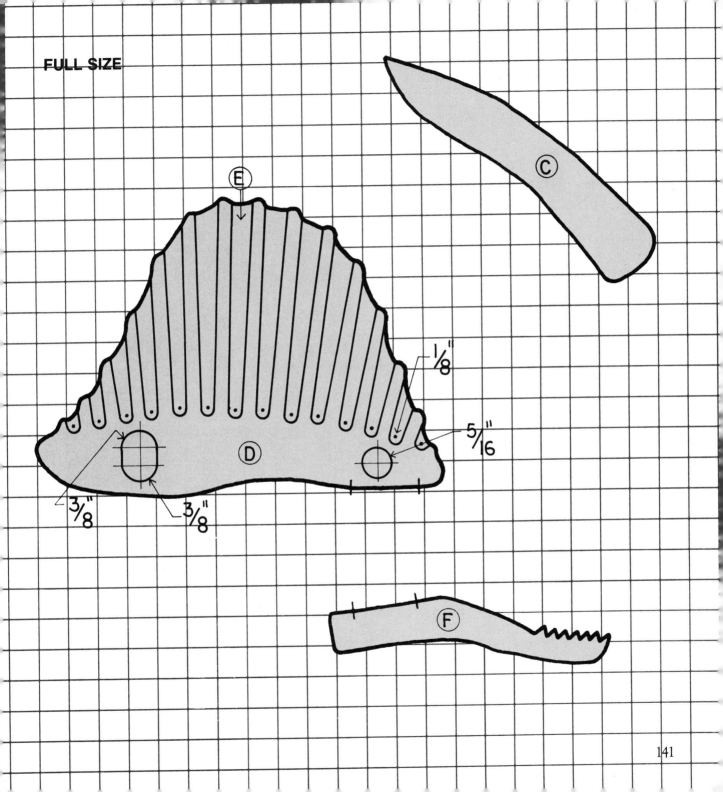

FULL SIZE

141

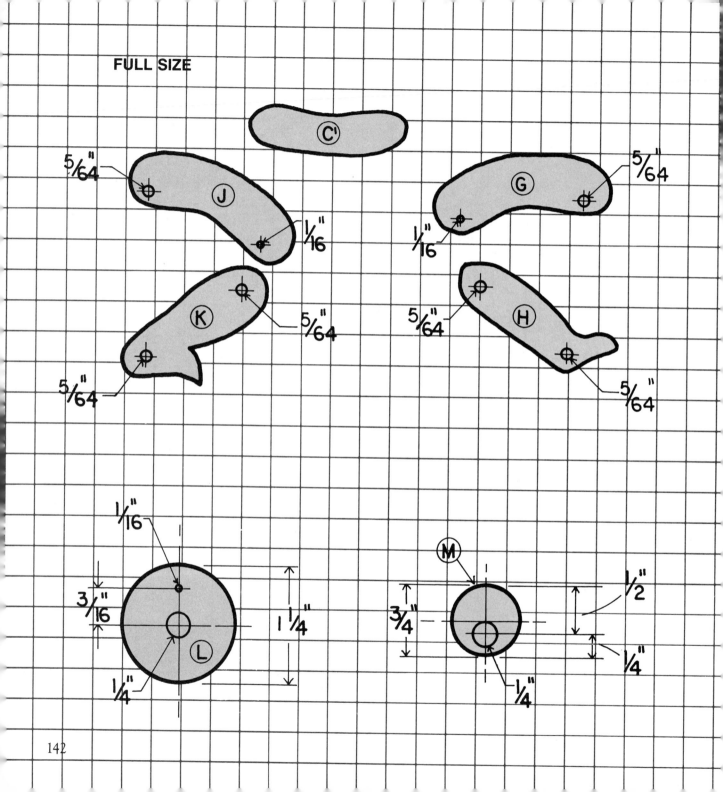

FULL SIZE

142

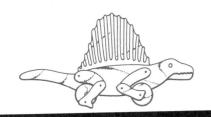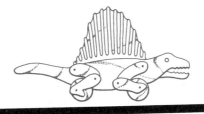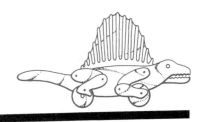

Carefully cut the spines out. Cut to the base of the spine. Turn off the saw, back it out, cut the second pass and turn the saw off to remove the scrap. Repeat the process for each spine.

If you are gentle, you can break the fuzz off the edges of the inside of the spines (by hand) so they'll look better when they're glued to the central piece. Don't sand the outside edges until after assembly.

It's important not to put too much glue on the spines, or it will squeeze out as you clamp them on either side of the central piece. Carefully line up the three pieces, by means of the bottom edge. Eyeball the tops of the spines to see that they line up perfectly. Now, put a flat board on either side of the assembly and watch for any shifting as you apply pressure with your clamps.

When the assembly is dry, drill the pivot hole in the front. Drill both pivot holes in the rear and remove the remaining material with a chisel to make a smooth channel for the pivot dowel to travel up and down in.

Now cut out the top of the assembly, making sure that each curved cut ends at the top of a spine. Edge-sand the entire assembly being sure that the bottom edge stays true to the pattern, as this determines both the proper movement of the assembly on the cam, and the proper placement of the lower jaw.

Break all the edges by hand including the spines.

Lay out the side view of the lower jaw (F) on 1¼″ stock. Cut out the silhouette and edge-sand it. With a dovetail saw, cut the diagonal line to the depth of 7/16 from either side (leaving 3/8″ in the middle—the same width as the sail assembly). Then mark a line (top and bottom) from this cut to the rear of the piece. Put the piece in a vise and again using the dovetail or back saw, saw down these lines removing the side material and leaving a strip 3/8″ wide (*See Figure 2*).

Lay out the top view of the jaw on the bottom of the jaw piece and cut away the tapered scraps (with the piece upside down on the band saw). Hand-sand the entire piece.

Transfer the intersection lines from the side view of the lower jaw and the sail. They will help you line up the two pieces as you glue them together. Make sure that sides of each piece are parallel to each other.

When the assembly is dry, drill two 1/8″ holes through the lower jaw piece into the sail piece. Glue 1/8″ dowels in these holes. Cut off any excess and sand the dowel ends.

The Legs

Lay out the legs (G,H,J,K) and drill the holes (according to the nails that you are going to use). Cut out the legs, edge-sand them and flat-sand them. Break the edges by hand with sandpaper.

Wheels and Cam

Drill the nail holes in the wheels (L). Lay out the cam (M) on 3/8″ stock. Drill the 1/4″ hole and cut the cam out with a jigsaw or coping saw. Smooth out the silhouette to form a clean circle and break the edges.

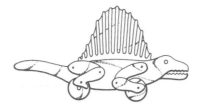
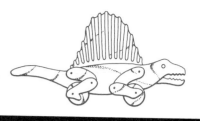

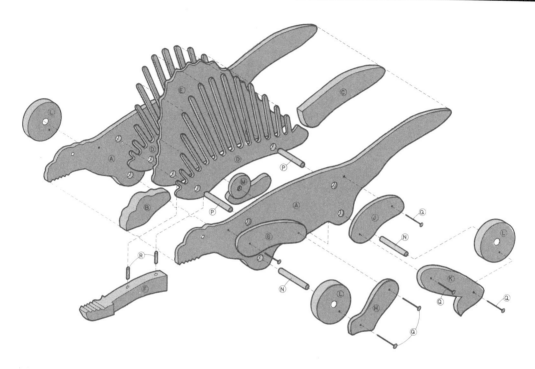

BILL OF MATERIALS

PART	DESCRIPTION	QTY	THICKNESS	WIDTH OR DIAMETER	LENGTH
A	Body sides	2	3/8″	2″	10″
B	Head spacer	1	1/2″	7/8″	1 3/4″
C	Tail spacer	1	1/2″	7/8″	3 5/8″
D	Sail sides	2	1/8″	4 1/2″	3 1/4″
E	Sail center	1	1/8″	3 1/4″	4 1/2″
F	Jaw	1	1 1/4″	3/4″	3 1/8″
G	Upper front leg	2	3/8″	3/4″	2″
H	Lower front leg	2	3/8″	5/8″	1 7/8″
J	Upper rear leg	2	3/8″	3/4″	2″
K	Lower rear leg	2	3/8″	7/8″	1 7/8″
L	Wheels	4	3/8″	1 1/4″	
M	Cam	1	3/8″	3/4″	
N	Axles	2		1/4″	2″
P	Pivot dowels	2		1/4″	1 1/4″
Q	Brass brads	12		16 ga.	7/8″
R	Dowels to fasten lower jaw to sail	2		1/4″	5/8″

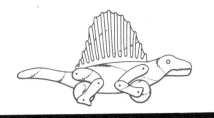 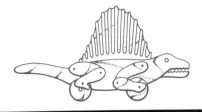 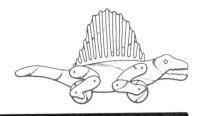

Assembly and Finishing

You'll want to try a dry run first. Lay one side on the workbench with the pivot dowels (left 1" long) temporarily in place. Position the spacers. Lay the sail in place and try pivoting it. If it does not move smoothly or hits one of the spacers, make any necessary adjustments.

Next remove the sail. Put glue on both sides of the spacers and carefully position them. With the pivot dowels still in place, slide the second side in place. The pivot dowels will help to line the sides up perfectly. You can also eyeball the alignment of the axle holes.

When the glue has dried, remove the pivot dowels, and drill the eyehole. Edge-sand the edges where the spacers are, and rout the silhouette.

Lay out the top view of the head and tail and cut them out. Edge-sand these areas. Use a four-in-hand and thoroughly round over the tail. The edges of the head should be rounded by hand with sandpaper. Hand-sand all the routed edges, etc.

Hold the sail assembly in place as you tap the pivot dowels in until they just enter the holes on the other side. Then put a little glue on the sides of the two holes and drive the dowels in until they slightly protrude. When the glue is dry, saw off the excess dowel ends and flat-sand the body sides to smooth the dowel ends.

Glue one wheel on an axle and hold the cam in position as you slide the axle through the body. Glue the second wheel on, making sure that the nail holes are diagonally opposed (one up, one down). Drill a small hole through the cam and the axle and glue a toothpick in place. Break off the excess and sand the surface of the cam again.

Repeat for the front wheels, except for the cam. Edge-sand the axle ends when the glue is dry.

It's a good idea to oil the toy at this point before the legs are attached, as it's hard to rub them off afterward.

Nail the legs together in opposing sets, leaving adequate clearance. Finally, nail the legs to the body and the wheels, again leaving adequate clearance.

One more nasty little predator on the loose!

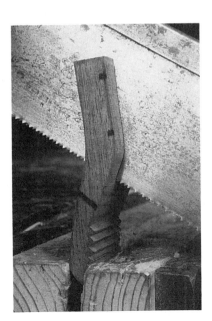

Figure 2. With the lower jaw piece in a vise use a dovetail saw to remove the sides.

145

The Miniature Pteranodon

Just recently a new theory has been advanced that many dinosaurs evolved into our present-day birds, rather than reptiles and that they were warm blooded. It will be interesting to see where the Pteranodon fits into the picture as research continues.

How Does It Work?

The head raises up by means of the hidden cam at the same time that the wings fall, being attached to the wheels by Pitman arms (*See Figure 1*). This is one of the few toys in which I resorted to metal hardware. The size dictated the need for tiny brass hinges. You can use leather if you're a purist.

This toy requires meticulous work because of the size. It is quite challenging, and it's definitely a thrill to put it all together and see those delicate wings flap up and down.

The Body Sides

Lay out the body sides (A) on ¼" stock, and cut out the silhouettes. Lay the pieces on top of each other and keep them accurately lined up as you drill the axle and pivot holes. Flat-sand both sides of each piece. Use a small drum sander or a dowel with sandpaper to smooth out the slots for the legs. The legs will be fitted into these slots after they are made.

The Spacer

Cut out the spacer (B) from ½" stock. Edge sand the area that will be hidden and the top front edge that will meet the top edge after assembly.

The Head

Lay out the head (C) on ⅜" stock. Drill the ⅛" eye hole and the ⁵⁄₁₆" pivot hole. Cut out the silhouette and edge-sand the whole silhouette. Break the edges by hand with sandpaper.

The Legs

Lay out the legs (D) and cut them out. Edge-sand them. Fit them into the slot in each leg so that they fit neatly with both legs at the same angle. Then break the edges by hand with sandpaper.

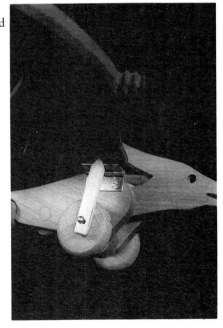

Figure 1. The Pitman arms are nailed to the wheels (off-center) and to the wings so the wings flap as the wheels turn.

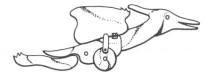

EXPLODED VIEW

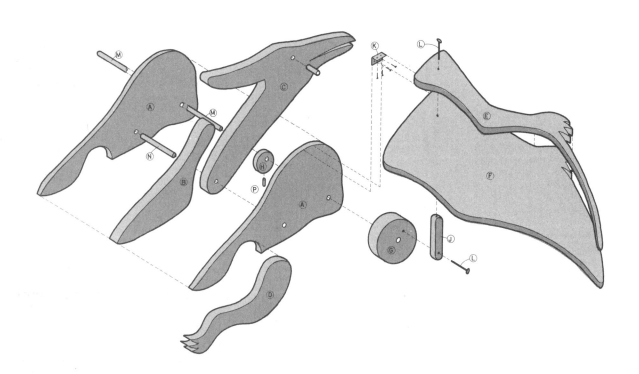

The Arms and Wings

Lay out the arms (E) on ¼″ stock and cut them out. Carefully edge-sand the silhouette of the pieces, except the claws and the forward edge of the long last claw. These will be sanded after assembly. Break all the edges (by hand) that you edge-sanded.

Lay out the wings (F) on ¼″ stock and cut them out. Edge-sand both silhouettes and hand-sand the edges, except the edge where the claw will be cut out after assembly, and the forward edge where the arm claw will be joined.

To glue the arms to the wings, put glue on the underside of the arms. Spread the glue and work it back from the edges to avoid squeeze-out. Position the arm carefully on the wing with the long claw along the forward edge of the wing and the shoulder meeting the front corner of the wing. Clamp the parts together with six or seven small C-clamps. Repeat the process for the second wing, being sure to make them exact opposites.

After the glue has set up, locate the hole through which the Pitman arm will be nailed (not the hinge holes). Drill a ¼″ hole precisely in this location and glue a ¼″ dowel in the hole to fill it. This will make a stronger socket for the Pitman arm pin. Flat-sand these dowel ends, then mark the center of this dowel and drill an ⅛″ hole (slightly larger than the head of the nail that you're going to use), leaving a ¹⁄₁₆″

BILL OF MATERIALS

PART	DESCRIPTION	QTY	THICKNESS	WIDTH OR DIAMETER	LENGTH
A	Body sides	2	¼″	1½″	4⅛″
B	Spacer	1	½″	⅞″	3⅛″
C	Head	1	⅜″	1¾″	4¼″
D	Legs	2	½″	¾″	2⅞″
E	Arms	2	⅛″	1½″	5¼″
F	Wings	2	⅛″	2⅜″	5½″
G	Wheels	2	⅜″	1″	

PART	DESCRIPTION	QTY	THICKNESS	WIDTH OR DIAMETER	LENGTH
H	Cam	1	⅜″	⅝″	
J	Pitman arms	2		¼″	1⁵⁄₁₆″
K	Brass hinges	2		¼″	¾″
L	Brass brads	4		16 gauge	⅞″
M	Axle	1		¼″	1⅞″
N	Pivot dowel	1		¼″	1″

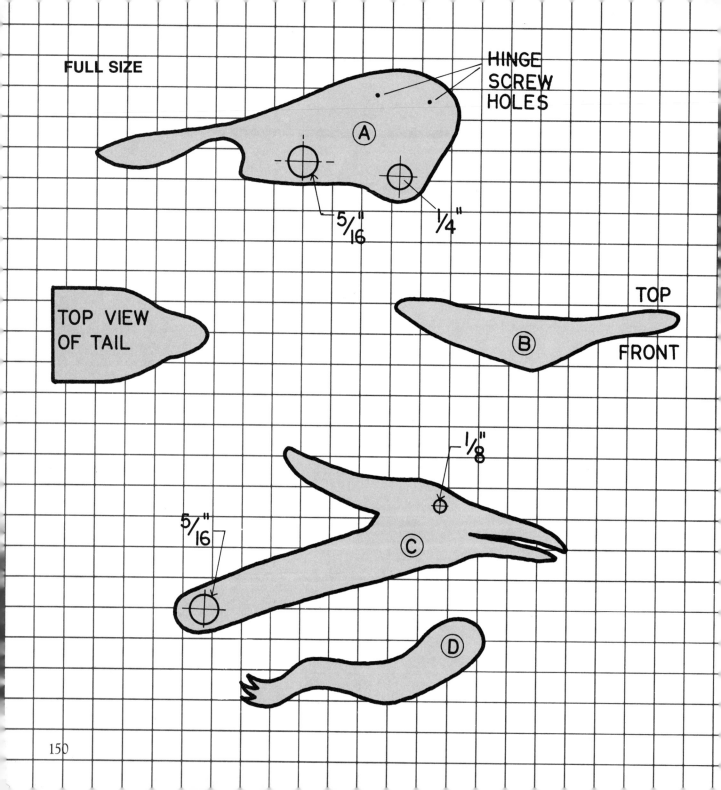

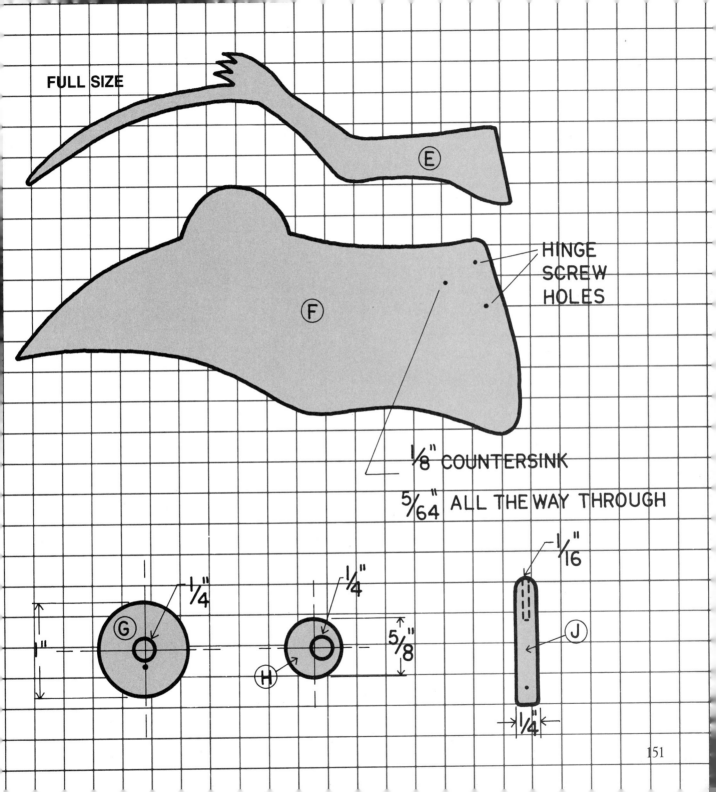

FULL SIZE

E

F

HINGE
SCREW
HOLES

⅛" COUNTERSINK

5/64" ALL THE WAY THROUGH

¼"

G

H ¼"

5/8"

1"

1/16"

J

¼"

151

thickness undrilled at the bottom of the hole. Drill the rest of the way through with a $7/64''$ bit (slightly larger than the diameter of the nail you're going to use).

Now lay out the hinge screw locations on the underside of the wings and drill the appropriate size holes to the proper depth. (You might try it on a piece of scrap first to make sure the hole won't be either sloppy or so tight that the soft brass screws break off as you tighten them.)

The Wheels and Cam

Drill the nail holes in the $1''$ wheels (G). Lay out the cam (H) on $3/8''$ stock. (You may want to make 2 or 3 to make sure you get a good one.) Drill the $1/4''$ hole. Cut out the outline carefully on a jigsaw or with a coping saw. Smooth the silhouette by hand and break the edges with sandpaper.

The Pitman Arms

Cut the $1/4''$ dowels to length. Drill the $7/64''$ hole through one end, as in the pattern. Slip the piece up onto the bit and rock it back and forth and from side to side, so the hole is $5/64''$ in the center but flares out at the ends. This will enable the Pitman arm to move freely as the pin stays stationary, with the wheel turning.

Next use a block of wood with a $1/4''$ hole drilled in it to hold the piece perfectly vertical on the drill press. Drill the $1/8''$ holes in the ends of the dowels, making sure that they are perfectly centered.

Using the sander/grinder freehand, bevel the end of the dowel so that it forms a perfect cone, the surfaces of which come right to the edges of the hole (*See Figure 2*). Don't sand off any more or you'll shorten the piece and affect the stroke of the wings. Hand-sand the other end of the dowel. Don't be afraid to make these over during final assembly to get them perfect.

Assembly and Finishing

Lay one body side on the workbench with the pivot dowel (cut $1''$ longer than finished length) temporarily in place. Position the spacer and slip the head onto the pivot dowel. Slip the cam onto a $1/4''$ dowel, and see if it can make its full revolution in the axle hole without the head piece hitting the spacer. Make any adjustments necessary by either sanding off some of the spacer or simply shifting its position.

Figure 2. The top of the Pitman arm is tapered on the sander/grinder so that the sides of the resulting cone shape end right at the edges of the nail hole.

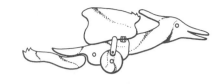

Then, remove the head piece, put glue on both sides of the spacer (except where legs will attach), and slip the second body side onto the pivot dowel to help line the sides up as you bring them together and clamp them. You can also look through the axle holes to insure proper alignment. Wipe off any glue that might have gotten on the spacer where the legs will be glued.

When the assembly is dry, take out the pivot dowel and edge-sand the silhouette of the body. Transfer the top view of the tail, cut it out and edge-sand it. Hand-sand the rough edges, and hand-sand the back to remove any cross grain scratches.

Hold the head piece in position as you pass the pivot dowel through until it just enters the hole on the other side. Then put a little glue inside the hole and drive the dowel in until it slightly protrudes. When the glue is dry saw off any excess and flat-sand both sides of the body with 120# to smooth the dowel ends. Locate and drill the hinge screw holes.

Position and glue the legs, making sure that they are lined up with each other as you clamp them in place.

Glue one wheel to the axle. Twist the axle through the cam (held between the body sides) as you pass it through the body sides. Glue the other wheel on, perfectly opposed (both holes up or down). When the glue is dry, edge-sand the axle ends.

It's easiest to oil everything at this point before final assembly. That way you can rub everything down, and the hinges won't get oil on them.

After the oil has set up, screw the hinges to the underside of the wings and then to the body sides. You may have to cut the tips off the screw to keep them from protruding through the body sides and interfering with the head piece or protruding through the top of the wing surface.

Finally, slip the brad through the wing and push the Pitman arm onto the end of the brad, leaving $1/32''$ clearance under the wing. You can tap a finishing nail into the side of your workbench and use the head to push against the head of the brad to push the Pitman arm on (*See Figure 3*).

Slip a brad through the base of the Pitman arm and tap it into the wheel (checking your clearance several times so you don't tap in too far). As I said before, if your Pitman arms are too long or too short or the $7/64''$ hole is binding, don't hesitate to make them over. They're relatively simple compared to other parts and their accuracy is imperative!

Well, there you have it. If you've made it this far, I hope your satisfaction is greater than your frustration. If it helps, just imagine the difficulties of designing this fellow!

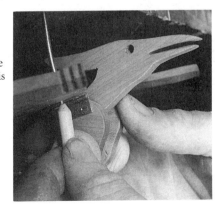

Figure 3. The head of a finishing nail (nailed into the side of the workbench) is perfect for pressing the brass nail into the Pitman arm.

Wood Burnings

These images can be used in several different ways. You can make ¾″ thick play figures out of scraps laying around the shop. You can burn the images on ¼″ stock to make ornaments (for windows and walls as well as Christmas trees) or magnets for holding notes to the refrigerator.

Kids love to color these images with colored pencils or magic markers.

Play Figures

Flat-sand both sides of the (¾″ thick) piece of wood that you're going to use. Use carbon paper to transfer the image onto one side of the block.

Next, burn the image into the wood with a wood burner. When you cut the silhouette, leave about ⅛″ around the edge of the image and cut flat across the bottom so that it will stand up on a flat surface. Edge-sand the silhouette, trying to leave an unburned border of consistent width around the image.

Then flip the piece over, carefully position the pattern and transfer the reverse image onto the back of the piece, again keeping the border consistent. Scraps of wood around the piece will help to support your hand as you burn the image into the piece.

Finally, break all the edges by hand with sand paper and oil it or apply a hard finish.

Coloring can be done after oil has set up but will have to be done before a hard finish is applied.

You may want to write the name of the dinosaur on the bottom of the block to help children learn the names.

Ornaments

The process is identical to that of the play figures with a couple of exceptions.

Use ¼″ stock instead of ¾″, and drill the hole for hanging before you cut the image out (to prevent splitting). Leave enough material around the hole to give it some strength

When it's finished, hang it by thin cord or yarn.

Magnets

To make the magnets, I use two circular ceramic magnets recessed into the back of a ¼″ thick piece, and only burn the image onto the front. You can also use plastic magnets, which can be found at craft or hobby shops. I cut the shallow flat hole for the magnet using a spade bit with its tip ground off so the point won't come through to the front of the piece (*See Figure 1*). Glue the magnets into the holes with white or yellow glue before finishing the piece. The ceramic magnets may scratch the refrigerator, but you can cover them with a little felt disk.

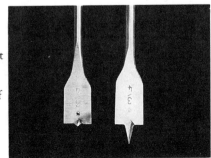

Figure 1. If you grind the tip off on a ¾″ spade bit you can drill holes to set the magnets in, without drilling through the front of the piece.

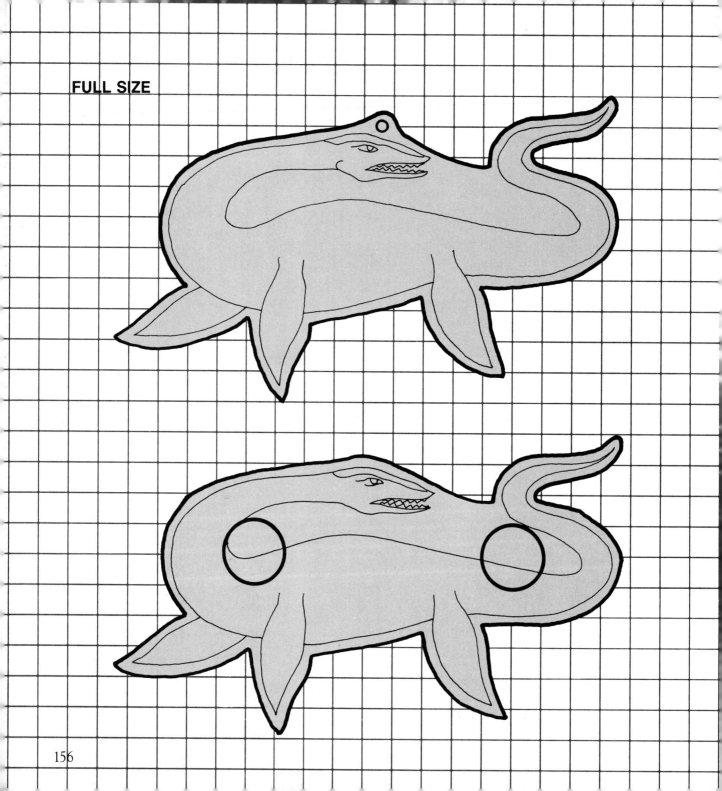

FULL SIZE

156

FULL SIZE

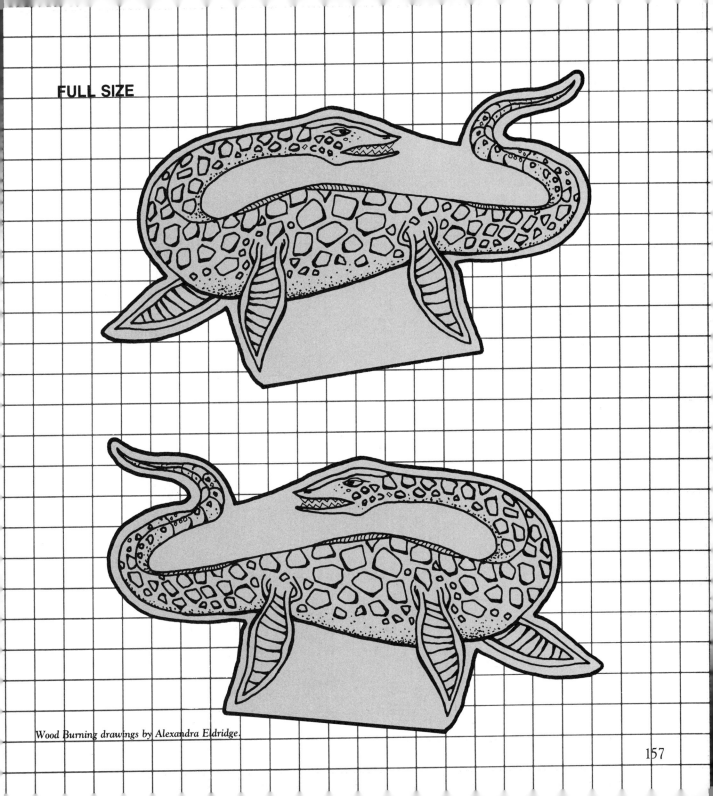

Wood Burning drawings by Alexandra Eldridge.

157

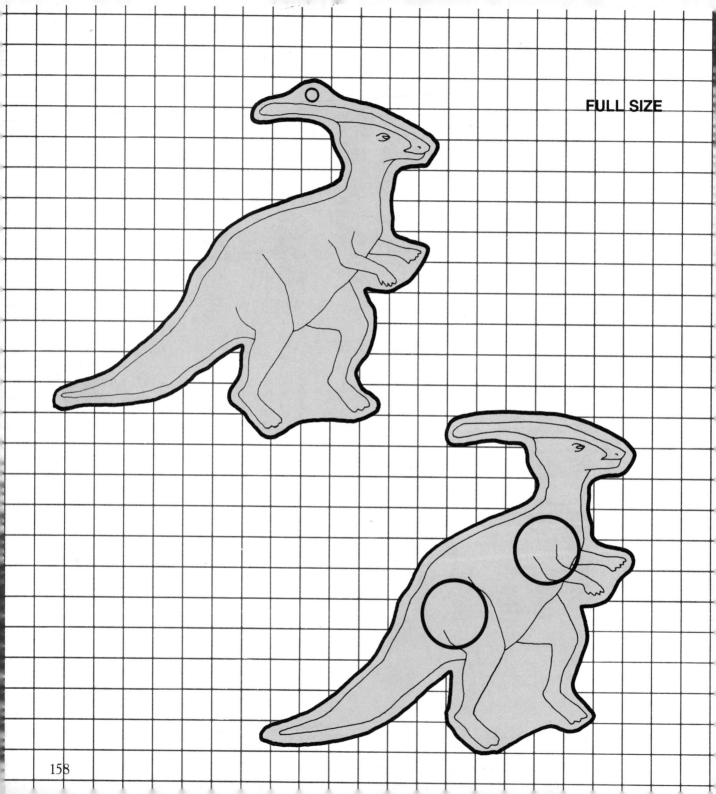

FULL SIZE

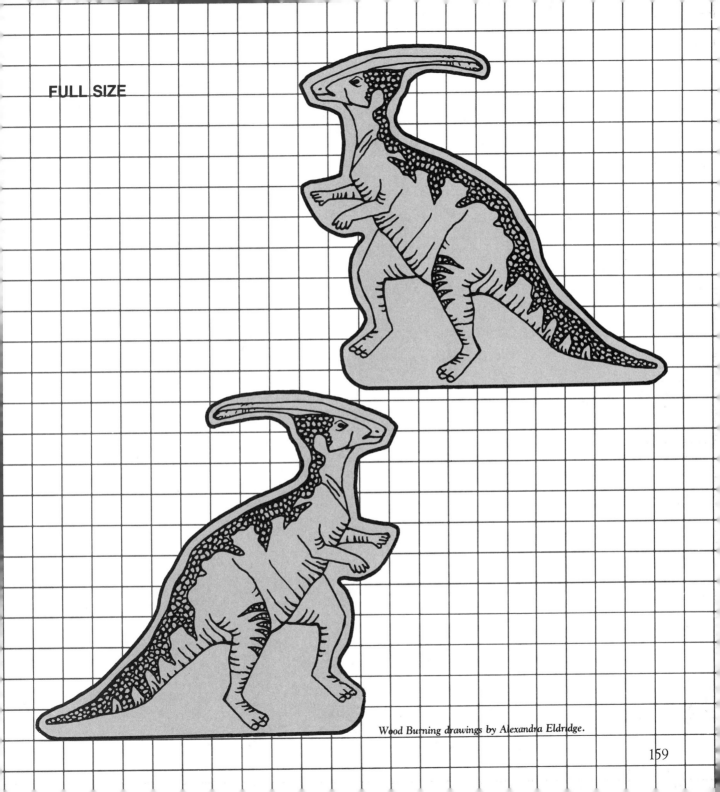

FULL SIZE

Wood Burning drawings by Alexandra Eldridge.

159

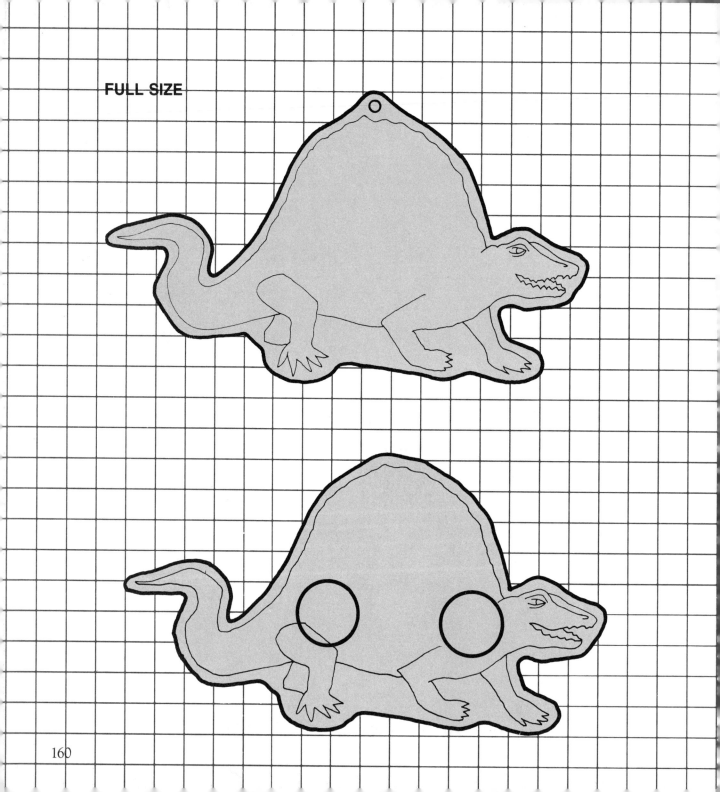

FULL SIZE

FULL SIZE

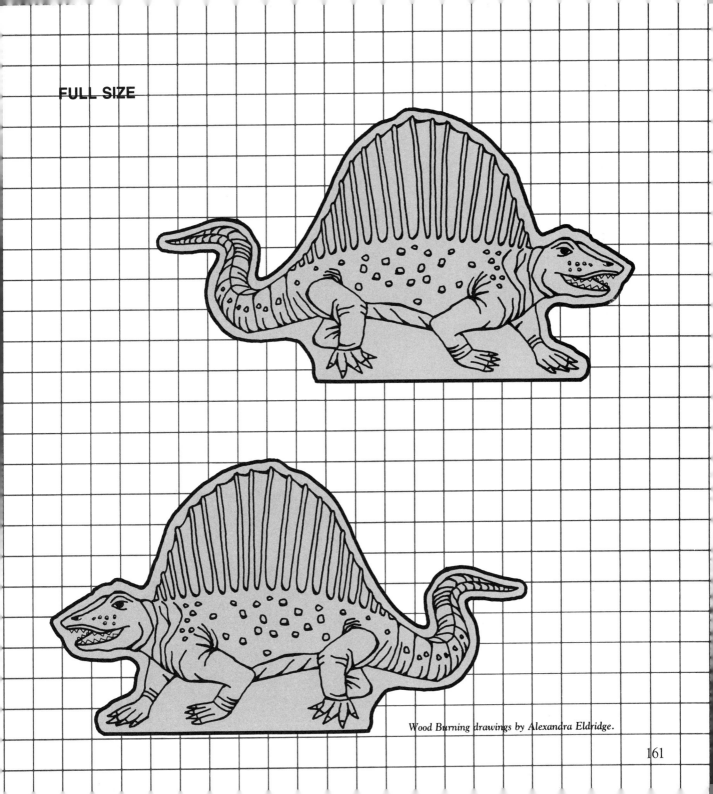

Wood Burning drawings by Alexandra Eldridge.

FULL SIZE

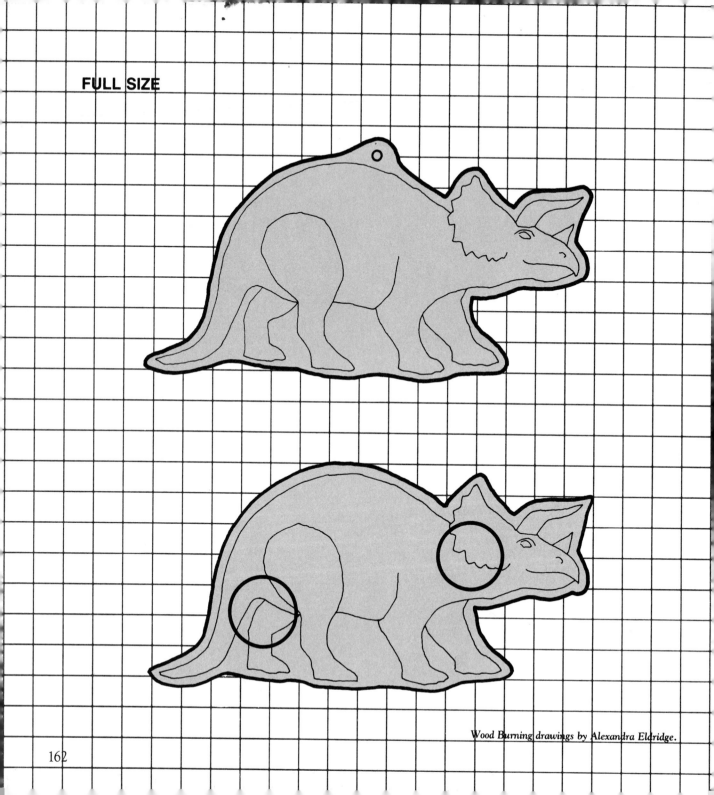

Wood Burning drawings by Alexandra Eldridge.

FULL SIZE

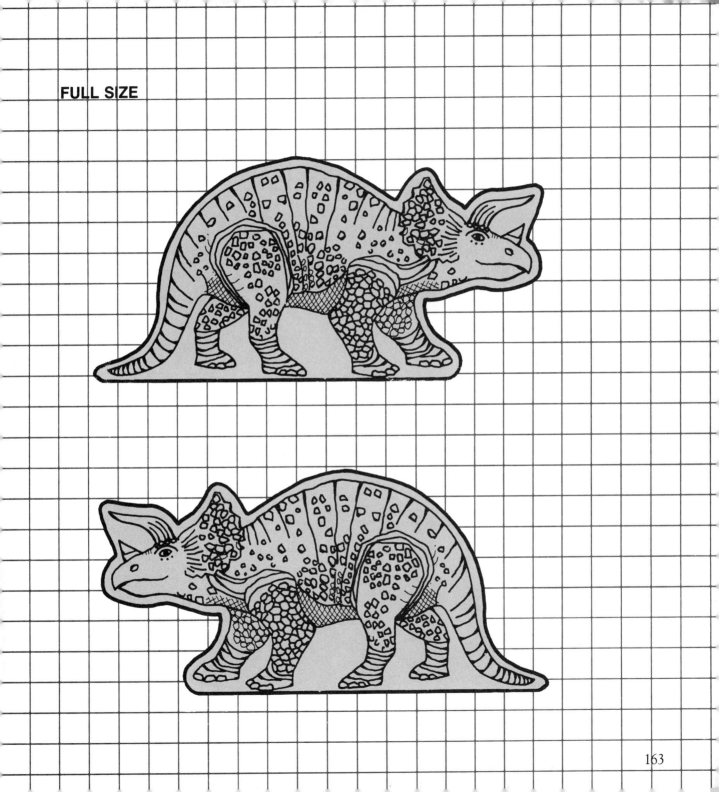

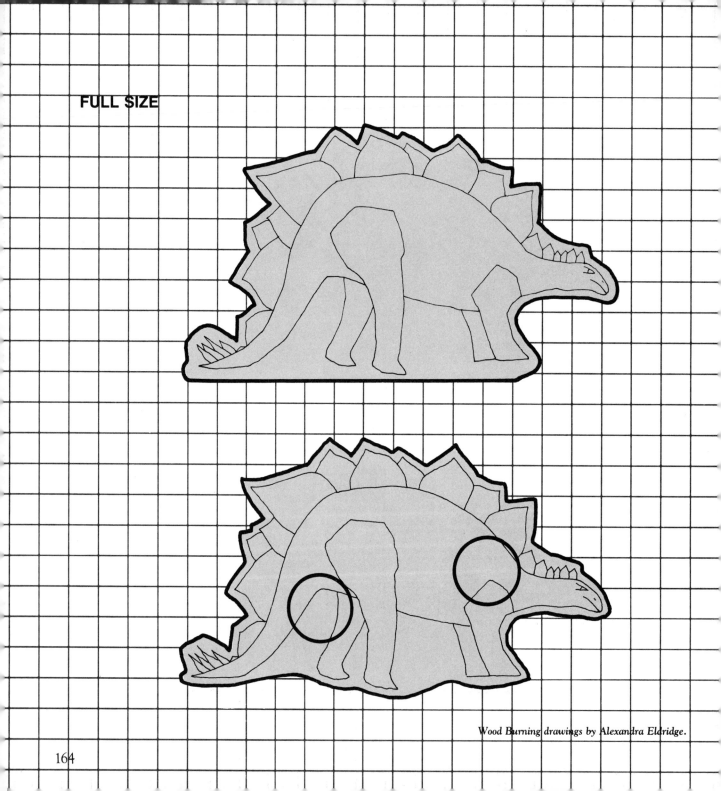

FULL SIZE

Wood Burning drawings by Alexandra Eldridge.

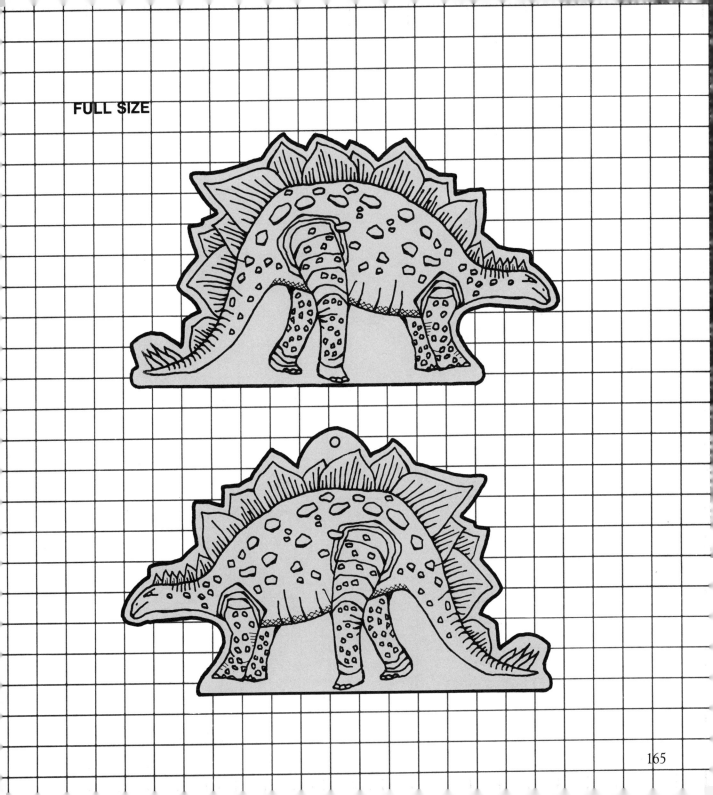

FULL SIZE

165

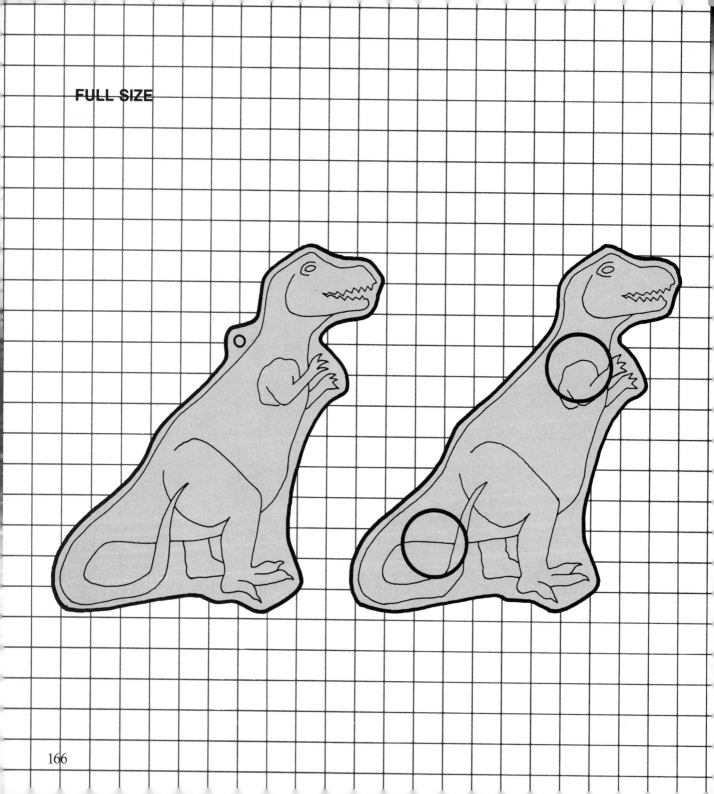

FULL SIZE

166

FULL SIZE

Wood Burning drawings by Alexandra Eldridge.

167

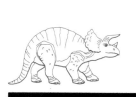

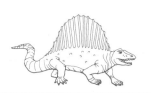

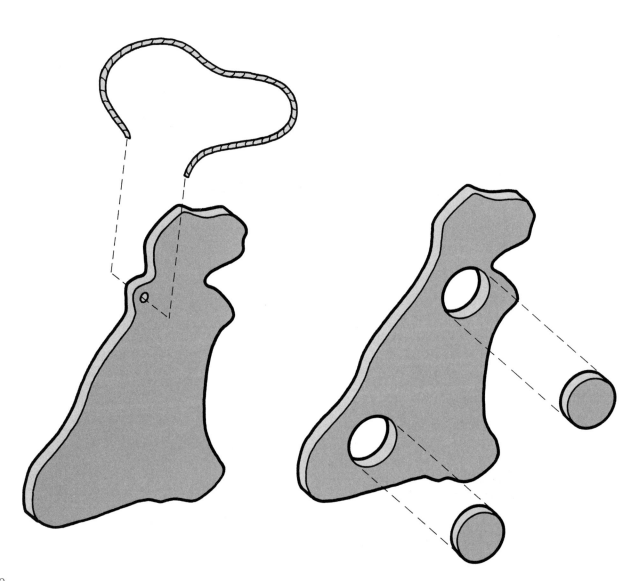

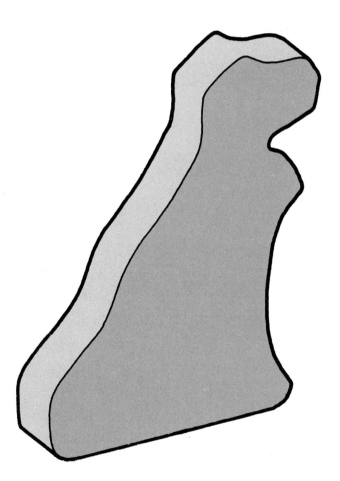

The Brontosaurus Hanger

There is no end to the possibilities for this hanger. The backboard can be made into either a tree or a plain rectangle. The rack can be made longer by simply lengthening the backboard by 3⅞″ for each additional hanger and bracket. (3⅛″ for hanger and clearance, plus ¾″ for the bracket thickness). It can also be made horizontally to fit in a different space.

The hanger can be painted, lacquered or varnished before assembly, or oiled afterwards.

The Vertical Tree Hanger

The Brontosaurus Pieces: Lay out the brontosaurus pattern (A) on ¾″ stock, making sure that the square end of the hanger is perpendicular to the edge of the board. This will facilitate accurate drilling of the vertical pivot hole.

Drill the 3⁄16″ eye holes and then (before cutting out the silhouettes) drill the 7⁄16″ pivot holes, using a square block of wood or a square to hold the hangers square to the drill press table (See Figure 1).

Next, cut the silhouettes, edge-sand them and flat-sand both sides of each piece. As you rout the silhouettes, skip the area around the pivot holes or the roller bearing or guide on the router bit will slip into the holes and tear up the corners. Round this area over by hand with a four-in-hand. Use a sharp chisel or a v-shaped gouge to cut a groove along the line where the rear leg cuts into the body. Try to duplicate the routed edge that is on the rest of the silhouette.

Now hand-sand the pieces entirely, and either paint or lacquer them or set them aside until assembly.

The Brackets: Lay out the brackets (C) with the long edge against the jointed edge of a board. This will ensure that they are perpendicular to the backboard after assembly. Drill the pivot holes. One of the brackets will have a ⅜″ hole halfway through while the remainder will have a 7⁄16″ hole all the way through. This way, when the brackets are mounted to the backboard, you can mount the hangers by easily slipping the dowel through the brackets and hangers and tapping it into the glued ⅜″ hole. This one bracket (with no dowel end exposed) can be either at the top or the bottom of the backboard, depending on the height at which you mount your hanger and which end will be more readily seen.

Figure 1. Use either a square or a block of wood with square sides to hold the hangers perfectly vertical as you drill the pivot holes.

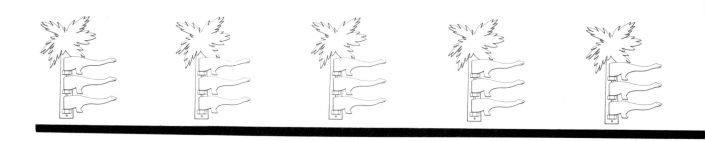

The Backboard: Glue up boards for the tree pattern to fit on and flat-sand both sides.

Lay out the pattern (B) and cut it out. I used a ½" blade on the band saw, to get a smooth line, as you can't get at a lot of the edges with a sander/grinder. You'll have to flip the piece over and transfer the pattern to the back to get at some of the cuts with a 14" band saw, but they can all be reached. Edge-sand what you can, and then hand-sand the rest. Then break all the edges by hand with sandpaper.

Drill the mounting holes (on the front) by first drilling a ½" hole (halfway through) and then drilling a ³⁄₁₆" hole the rest of the way through for ³⁄₁₆" toggle bolts. The ½" hole will serve as a countersink for the bolt head (or other fastener) and can be covered with a ½" furniture plug after the hanger is mounted.

The screw holes for mounting the brackets are drilled from behind, using the pattern to locate them.

Assembly: Fasten the brackets in place with glue and screws.

At this point, you can paint the backboard or continue assembly, if you plan to oil your hanger.

Put a little glue in the top hole (the blind one), and slide a dowel through each bracket and hanger. Tap the dowel into place.

At this point, you can either touch up the end of the dowel with a little paint, lacquer, varnish, etc., or let the glue set up and oil the hanger with a rag or a brush. And there you have it, a bunch of Brontosaurs hanging around.

The Plain Vertical Hanger

Follow all the directions for the previous hanger, except the layout of the backboard. Simply cut out a 3½" × 16" rectangle. Flat-sand both sides and sand the edges with a hand-held belt sander (with the piece in a vice). Rout the corners and the front edge silhouette. Assemble as before.

BILL OF MATERIALS

PART	DESCRIPTION	QTY	THICKNESS	WIDTH OR DIAMETER	LENGTH
A	Brontosaurus hanger	3 or more	¾"	4"	11½"
B	Tree backboard	1	¾"	14"	24½"
C	Brackets	4 or more	¾"	1⅝"	2¼"
D	Dowel	1		⅜"	12½"

PART	DESCRIPTION	QTY	THICKNESS	WIDTH OR DIAMETER	LENGTH
E	Furniture plugs	2		½"	
F	Simple backboard	1	¾"	3½"	16"
G	Horizontal backboard	1	¾"	4⅝"	12"
H	Top & bottom piece	2	¾"	1½"	12"
J	Dowels	4		⅜"	4¼"

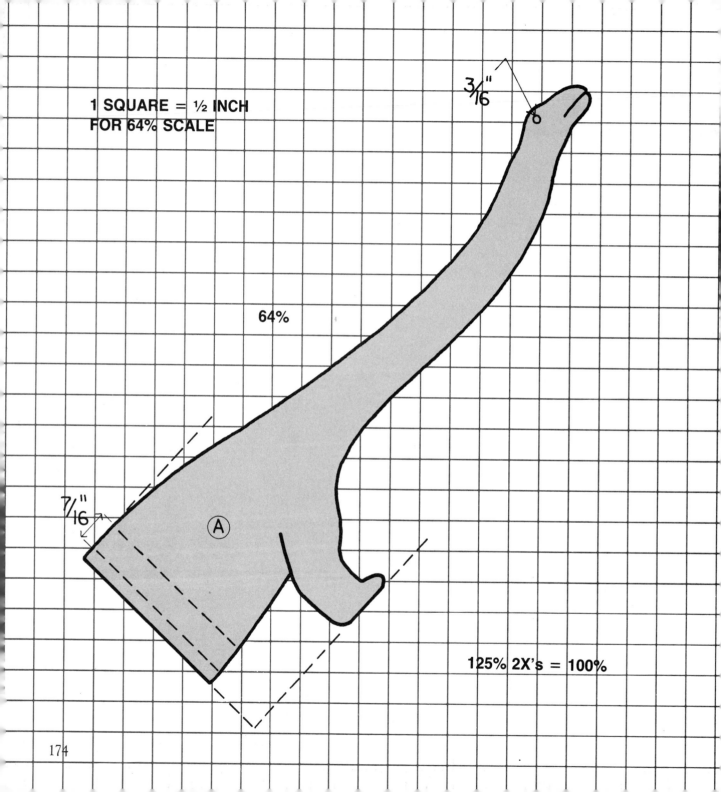

1 SQUARE = ½ INCH
FOR 64% SCALE

3/16"

64%

7/16"

(A)

125% 2X's = 100%

174

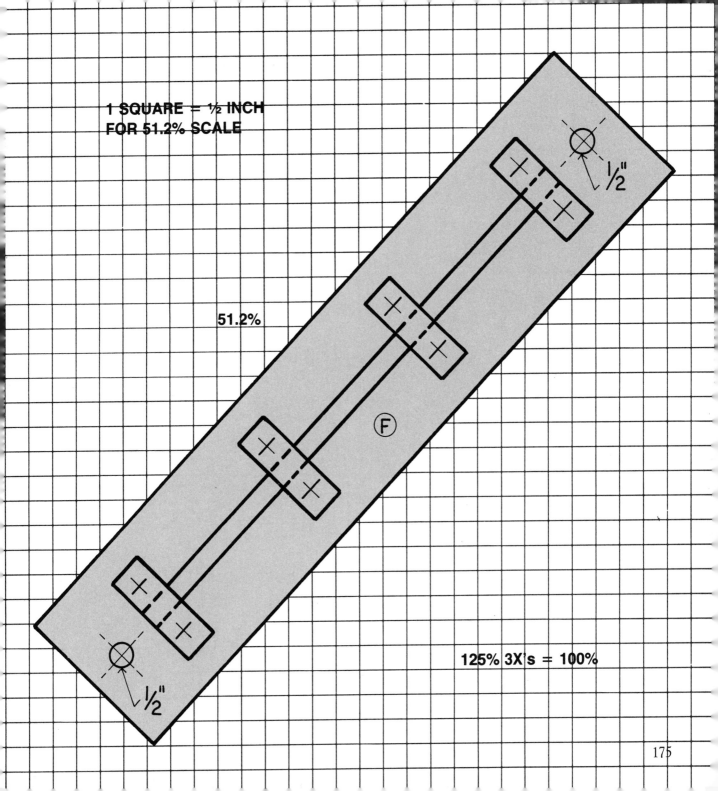

1 SQUARE = ½ INCH
FOR 51.2% SCALE

51.2%

Ⓕ

½"

½"

125% 3X's = 100%

175

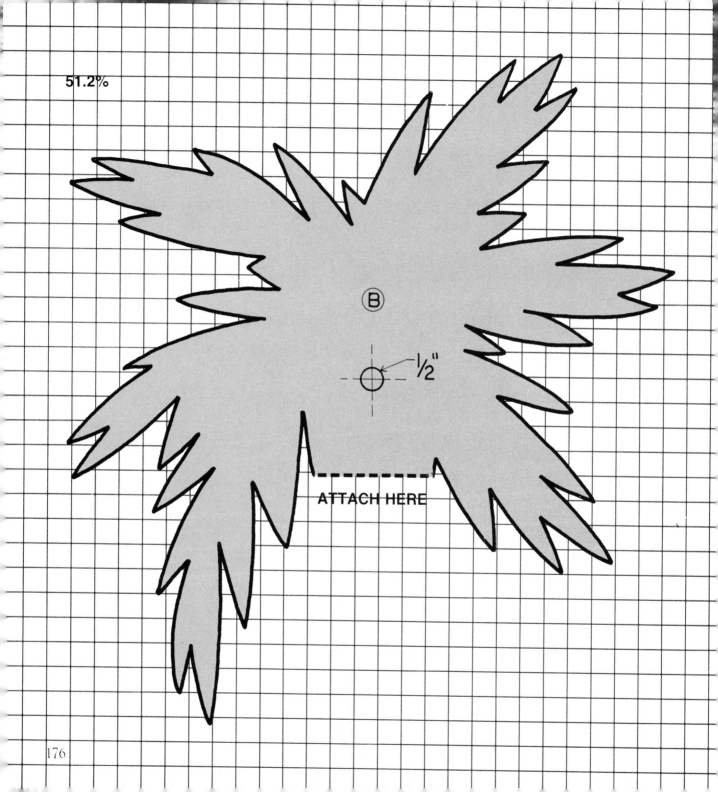

51.2%

Ⓑ

½"

ATTACH HERE

176

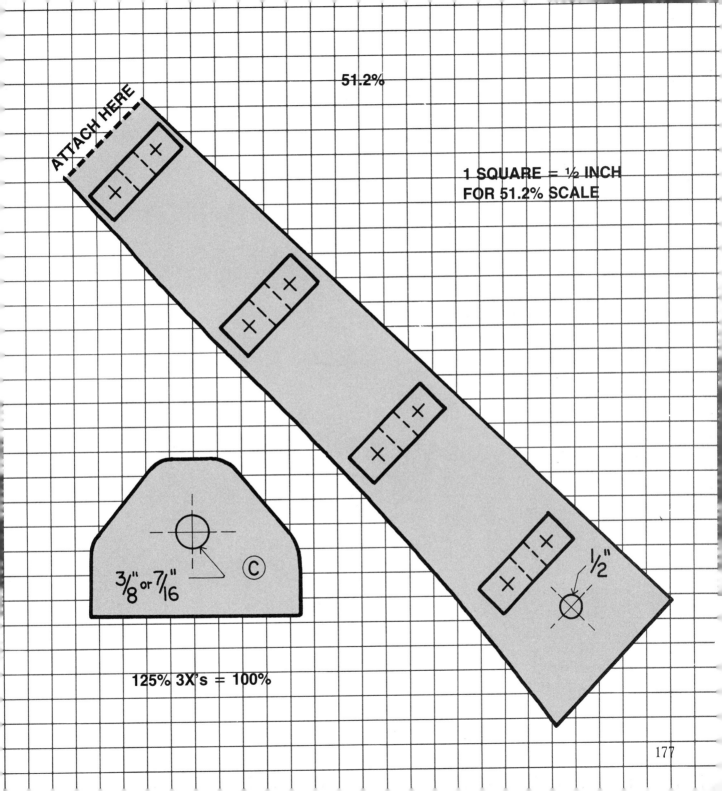

51.2%

1 SQUARE = ½ INCH
FOR 51.2% SCALE

ATTACH HERE

½"

C

3/8" or 7/16"

125% 3X's = 100%

177

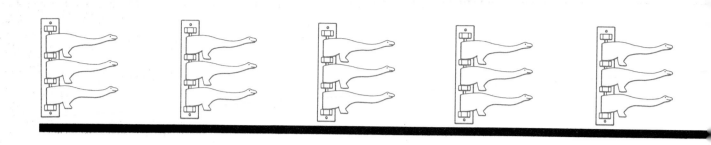

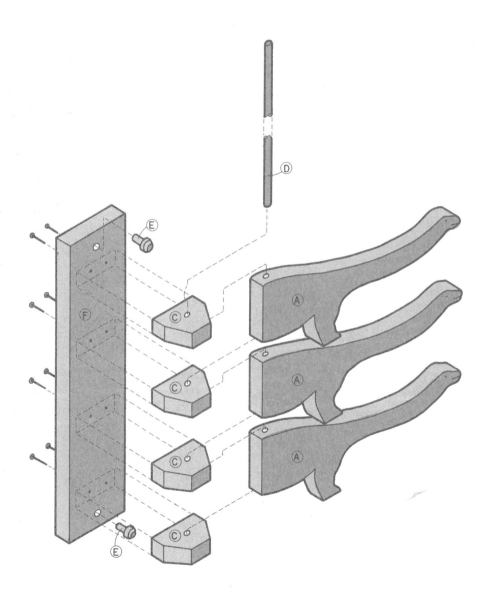

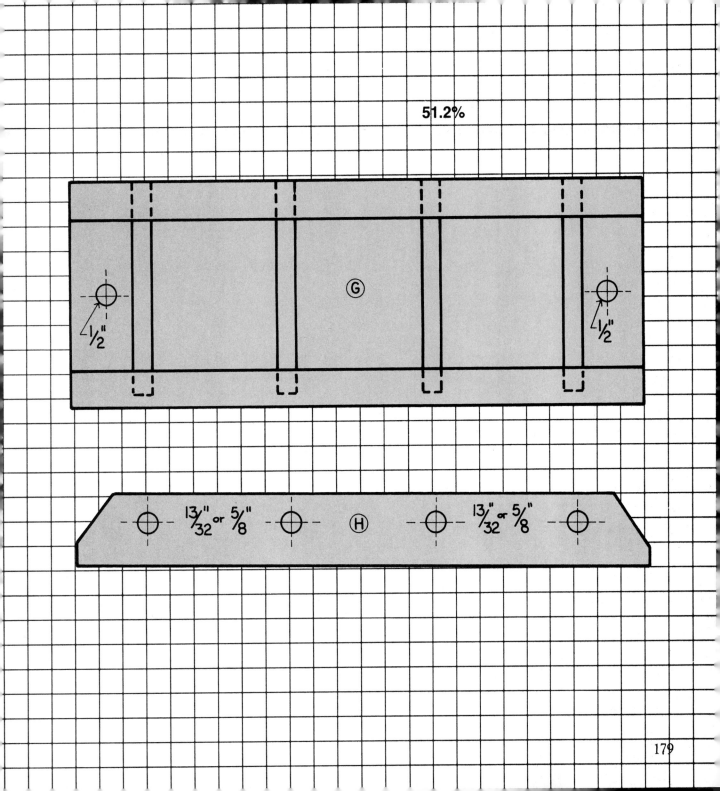

51.2%

$\frac{1}{2}"$

G

$\frac{1}{2}"$

$\frac{13}{32}"$ or $\frac{5}{8}"$

H

$\frac{13}{32}"$ or $\frac{5}{8}"$

179

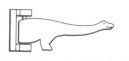

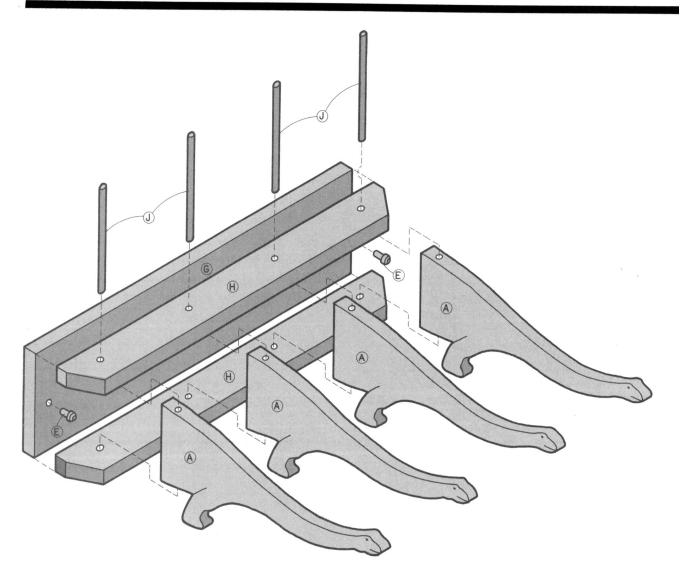

The Horizontal Hanger

Follow the instructions in the first hanger for the brontosaurus pieces, since they are the same for all three hangers.

The Horizontal Backboard: Lay out the three pieces of the horizontal backboard. The upper and lower bracket (H) are drilled slightly differently. The holes in the lower bracket are drilled slightly oversize ($13/32''$) and all the way through. The holes in the upper bracket are drilled halfway through at exactly $3/8''$. This way the dowels can be easily slipped into place and then glued snugly into the top bracket. Also, the dowels won't show on top of the hanger. You can have the unexposed dowels either above or below the hanger depending on what height you plan to mount it at and which area will show.

Flat-sand all three pieces on both sides. Use a hand-held belt sander to sand the edges of the two bracket pieces (G,H) (not the backs that will be glued). Do not rout the edge that will be glued to the back piece.

Glue the two pieces (G,H) to the back piece, working glue away from the inner edge to avoid squeeze-out. When the assembly has set up thoroughly, flat-sand all the surfaces to the bracket (top, bottom, and either end). Rout the remaining exposed edges (the front edge of the ends of the back piece).

Drill the two mounting holes in the back piece. First, drill a $1/2''$ hole halfway through and then drill a $3/16''$ hole the rest of the way through (for $3/16''$ toggle bolts).

Assembly

If you're going to paint the hanger, this is the time to do so, before assembly. When all the painting is done and dry, put a little glue in the $3/8''$ holes (with the rack upside down). Now position the hangers, (one at a time and upside down) and slip the pre-cut and sanded dowel through $13/32''$ hole in the bracket, and the hanger, and into the glued $3/8''$ hole. Repeat for each hanger. When the glue is dry, you can oil the hanger if you didn't apply paint or lacquer already. You can touch up the dowel ends with paint at this point and you're done. Mount it on the wall and put those dinosaurs to work.

The Dimetrodon Clothes Rack

This piece can serve as a coat, tie or hat rack. Whether you paint this fellow or use some type of clear finish, you'll want to use hardwood for the main body to give it some strength. The back of the sail can be made of masonite, however, if you're going to paint it.

The Body

Glue up boards to make a piece big enough to encompass the enlarged pattern (A). When the glue has set up, belt-sand both sides. Lay out the pattern. Drill all the 7/16" holes at the base of the spines with a Forstner bit or a brad point bit. Position the holes carefully since they will determine the width of the spines. (Note the two 3/8" holes for the last spine, front and rear.)

Drill the 3/8" hole for the eye, the holes for the shaker pegs and the mounting holes. The mounting holes have a 1/2" hole drilled halfway through from the front (for plugs). Then drill a 3/16" hole the rest of the way through the center of the hole for 3/16" toggle bolts, or the appropriate holes for whatever fastener you decide to use.

With the piece in a vise, use a coping saw to cut out the rest of the eye, including the line that extends slightly beyond the eye hole to give definition to the eyelid.

Now, cut out the body silhouette. You'll have to flip the piece over and lay out the pattern on the reverse side to make some of the cuts. Cut out the mouth minus the teeth. They'll be added later. It's a good idea to edge-sand the silhouette before you cut

out the spines since they'll be quite fragile and prone to breaking after they're cut out.

The spines should be cut out very carefully, since it's next to impossible to sand their sides after they're cut out without breaking them off. Cut carefully but quickly to keep the lines straight.

Make sure that each cut ends right on the tangent of the 1/2" hole at the base of the spine. Make a pass down one spine to the hole, turn off the saw,

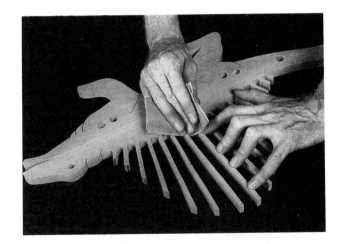

Figure 1. You can round the edges of the spines, before assembly, if you hold down the entire spine with spread fingers, as you sand.

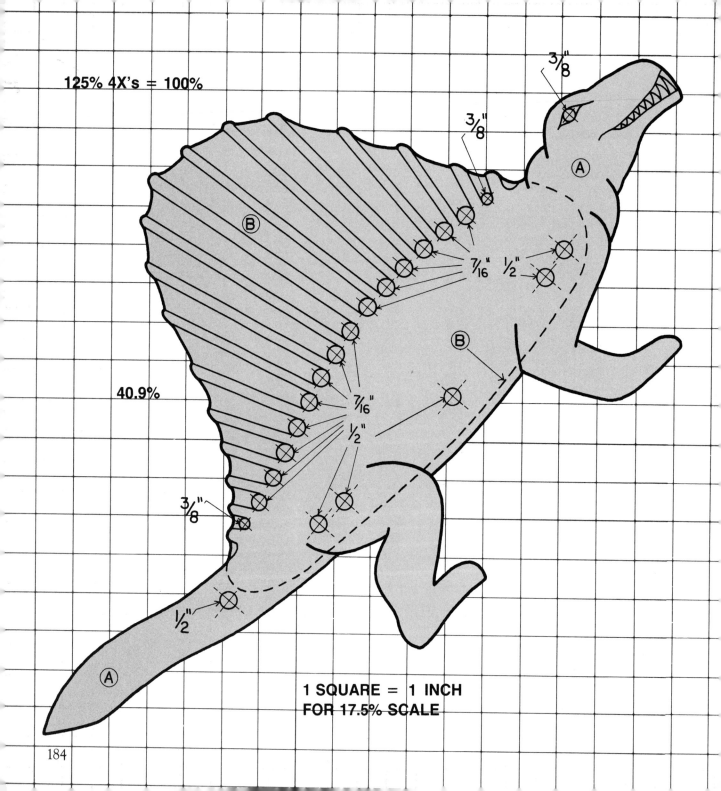

125% 4X's = 100%

3/8"

3/8"

A

3/8"

B

7/16" 1/2"

B

7/16"

40.9%

1/2"

3/8"

1/2"

A

1 SQUARE = 1 INCH
FOR 17.5% SCALE

FULL SIZE

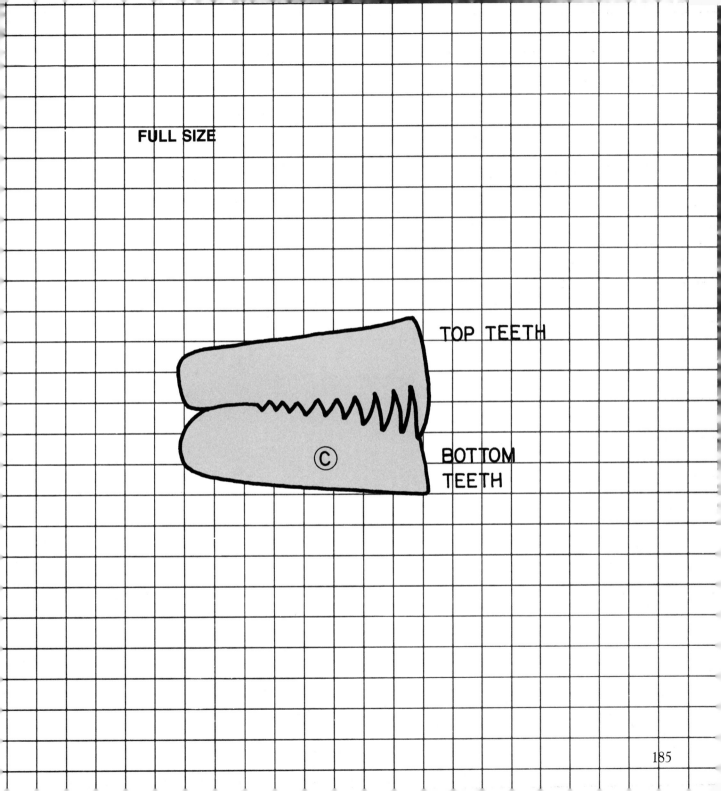

TOP TEETH

BOTTOM
TEETH

185

BILL OF MATERIALS

PART	DESCRIPTION	QTY	THICKNESS	WIDTH OR DIAMETER	LENGTH	PART	DESCRIPTION	QTY	THICKNESS	WIDTH OR DIAMETER	LENGTH
A	Body	1	½"–¾"	13½"	24"	D	Shaker pegs	4		½"	3½" (total)
B	Sail	1	⅛"–¼"	10½"	13"	E	Plugs	2		½"	
C	Teeth	2	½"–¾"	1½"	2"	F	Eye	1		⅜"	½"–¾"

  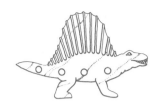

back out of the cut, turn the saw on, make the second cut, and turn the saw off to remove the scrap.

Again, you'll have to flip the piece over to cut some of the spines.

Break all the edges by hand with sandpaper. To break the edges of the spines, spread your fingers out and hold the whole length of the spine as you gingerly sand the edge (*See Figure 1*).

This is the time to paint the body, if that's your intention. As you paint the cracks entering the body from the legs, blow into the cracks—this will spread the paint into the cracks without actually filling them.

Paint the ½″ plugs and the shaker pegs at this point.

If you're going to oil the toy you can glue the ⅜″ dowel (F) in place for the eye (with the end flat-sanded and rounded over slightly). Otherwise, paint it the same color as the sail and glue it in place, when all the paint has dried.

The Sail

If you're making the sail out of hardwood, glue up several ¼″ boards with the grain running vertically and flat-sand both sides after the glue has set up.

Lay out the sail (B) on the hardwood or masonite. Cut out the silhouette, edge sand it, and break the edges with sandpaper.

If you're painting the sail, it will look best if you fan your strokes out radially to match the angles of the spines.

The Teeth

The teeth (C) are tricky to make but they look great when you're done. Lay out both sets of teeth on two pieces of hardwood (use maple or some light colored wood if you're not going to paint them). The grain must run vertically for strength.

Cut them out, leaving a big scrap to hold onto. Edge-sand them carefully, until the two sets of teeth fit tightly together.

Now is the time to paint them, if that's your plan. When the paint has dried, spread glue carefully over the surfaces of the teeth that will meet. Be careful not to use too much glue or the squeeze-out will detract from the clean sharp look of the teeth. Clamp the two sets of teeth together.

When the assembly is dry, mark the mouth outline onto the top of the assembly and cut it out carefully, leaving some extra material to edge-sand down to fit them perfectly into the mouth.

When you've fitted them as best you can, glue them into the mouth opening, again watching for squeeze-out.

Glue the shaker pegs into their holes.

If you're putting a clear finish on, that's the last step, after all the glue has set up.

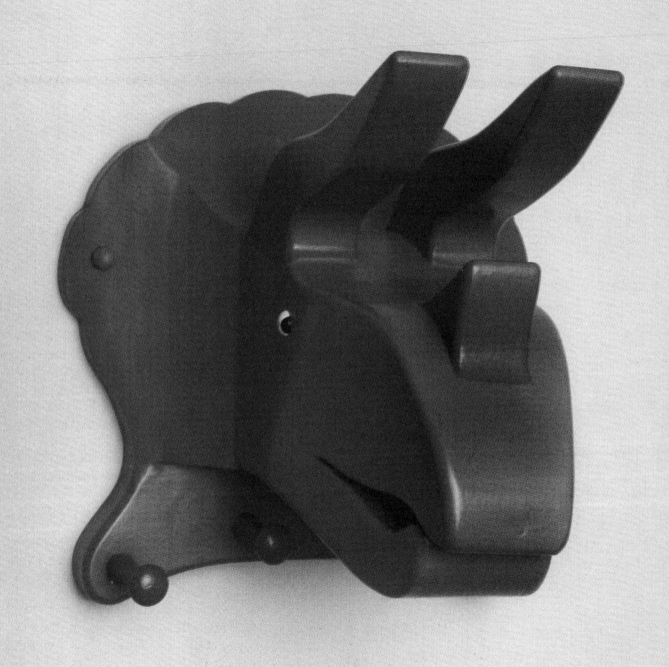

The Triceratops Coat Rack

This massive trophy-like coat rack is relatively easy to make, but it does require some serious wood removal. You'll want to use a light, fairly soft wood because of the mass and the sculpting. I used poplar, but pine or basswood would work fine, as all the pieces are so thick that strength is not a real consideration.

First, enlarge the patterns. Make two copies of the head piece pattern (one for the sides with the brow horn, and one for the center with only the nose horn).

When you cut these pieces out (of 1¾″ stock) be extremely faithful to the pattern. This will avoid a lot of sanding afterward. Also, the mouth area is unsandable, so saw this very carefully. (Turn the band saw off after the first pass, to back it out. Turn it off again after the second pass to remove the scrap.)

When the pieces are cut out, edge-sand the areas that will be inaccessible after assembly. On the central piece (B), this will be the single horn and the area on top of the head which will be between brow horns on either side. On the two side pieces it will be the area on either side of the nose horn. Edge-sand the brow horns and rout their inside edges. Rout either side of the brow horn.

Apply an even layer of glue to both sides of the center piece (except the horn). Work the glue away from the edges to avoid squeeze-out. Be sure to use scraps or pads to protect the work from the clamps, especially with such soft wood.

Be very particular about the way the three pieces line up as you apply pressure to the clamps.

When the assembly has set up thoroughly, edge-sand all the edges that you can reach.

With a hand-held belt sander, sand both sides of the assembly flat (with the grain) and rout the entire silhouette on both sides. Sand the back of the head assembly with the hand-held belt sander, being careful to keep the surface perfectly flat. Drill the ½″ eye holes.

Now remove the material of either side on the nose and mouth. Transfer the diagonal dotted line from the pattern to both sides of the head. Make a pencil mark on the front surface of his nose, 1¼″ in from either side surface.

Use the edge of a piece of stiff paper (something that will follow the curve of the nose and still make a straight line) and lay it from the top of the side view dotted line to the mark on the tip of the nose and scribe a line. Repeat this on the other side. These lines mark the material that is to be removed.

There are several ways to remove this material. I believe the easiest way is to use a hand-held power planer and take it off starting at the nose and working your way back, keeping the same angle as the scribed line and ending at the dotted line that you transferred to the side of the head (See Figure 1). Clean it up with a hand-held belt sander, and smooth out the transition from the side to the tapered nose.

You can saw the pieces off with a hand saw, with the piece (chin upward) in a vise. Follow the taper line and come out at the dotted line (watching out for the brow horns).

The last method may take longer than the handsaw method but might give you more predictable results. Use a hand-held belt sander and a 40# belt and sand away the excess material. Switch to a finer belt to finish it up.

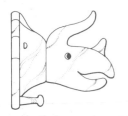
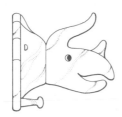
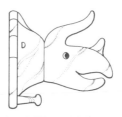
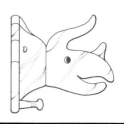

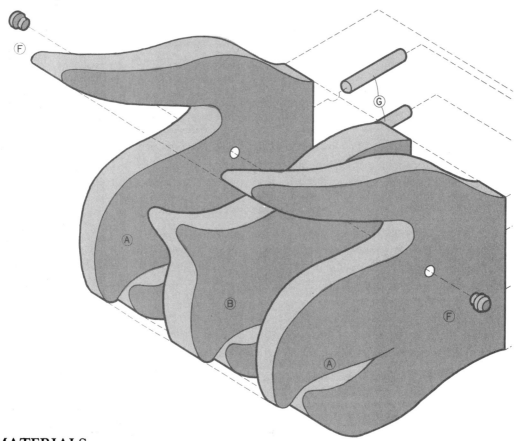

BILL OF MATERIALS

PART	DESCRIPTION	QTY	THICKNESS	WIDTH OR DIAMETER	LENGTH
A	Head sides	2	1¾″	11½″	12″
B	Head center	1	1¾″	8½″	12″
C	Transition piece	1	1½″	7½″	8¼″
D	Shield	1	1½″	13″	13″

PART	DESCRIPTION	QTY	WIDTH OR DIAMETER	LENGTH
E	Shaker pegs	4	½″	3½″ (total)
F	Furniture Plugs	4	½″	
G	Dowels to attach head to transition piece	4	½″	2″

190

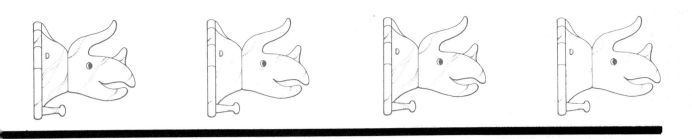

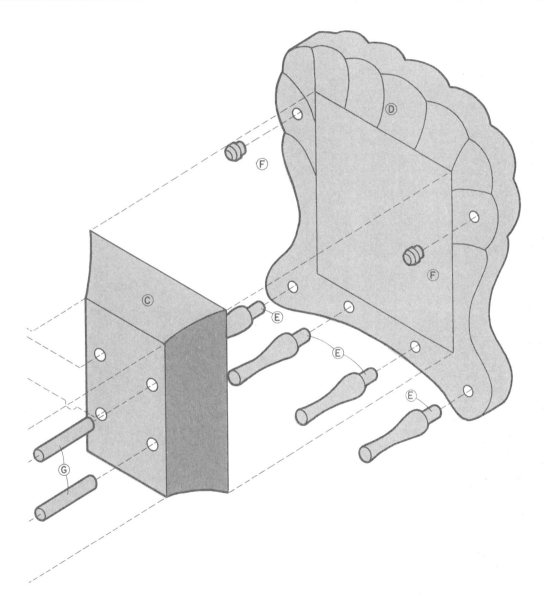

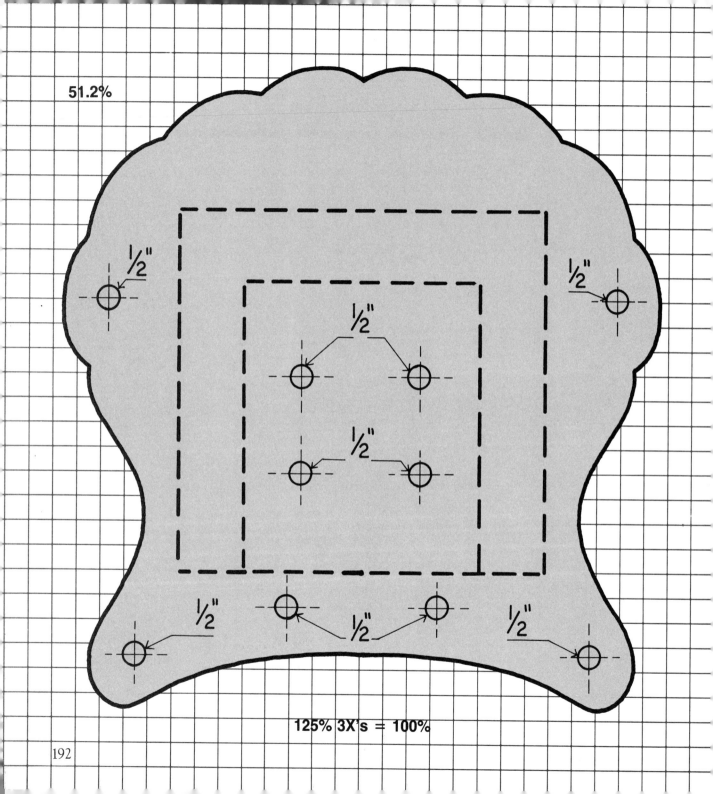

51.2%

½" ½" ½" ½" ½" ½" ½" ½" ½"

125% 3X's = 100%

192

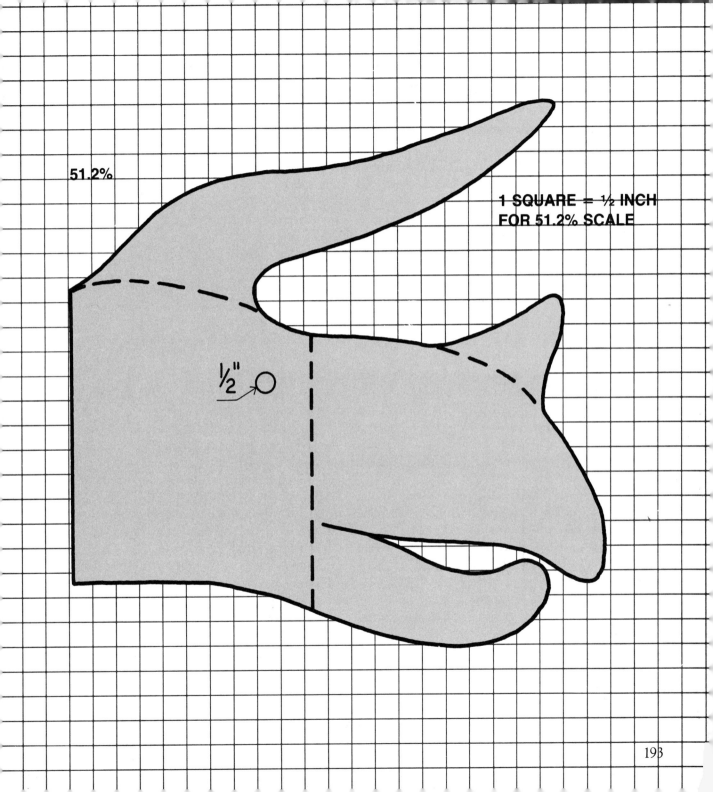

51.2%

1 SQUARE = ½ INCH
FOR 51.2% SCALE

½"

193

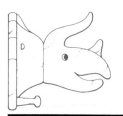 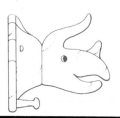 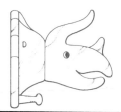 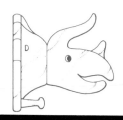

Whichever way you do it, when it's finished round over all the edges with a four-in-hand and sandpaper. You'll want to use a chisel to round the areas of the mouth that you can't reach with the rasp and file.

With the head in a vise, drill the four ½" holes in the back of the head to attach it to the shield.

The Shield

The shield assembly is made of two pieces. The transition piece (C) is made by starting with a block 8" wide × 7½" tall × 1½" thick. On the top and two sides, make a cut with the table saw set at 45° to put a bevel on these edges as shown in the exploded view.

Lay the shield (D) out on 1½" stock. Drill the ½" holes for the shaker pegs. Cut out the silhouette, and edge-sand it. Flat sand both sides of the piece. Rout the edge below the pegs, where the transition piece will not be.

Now lay the transition piece on the shield, center it and scribe its outline onto the shield. The shield should be tapered away from this line. This is done by one of the methods described for removing the sides of the tapered nose. These surfaces are left tapered and flat until after assembly, at which point they are scooped out to make more of a flare.

Glue and clamp the transition piece to the shield. When it has set up thoroughly, you can scoop out more of the angled sides with the front roller of the hand-held belt sander. Keep the belt sander moving all the time to avoid gouges, and try to keep the curve uniform. The edges where the curves meet are a good indicator of how even the flair is. You may

want to try it with a scrap first to get the hang of it. Hand-sand as much as necessary.

Using dowel points, transfer the ½" hole locations from the head to the shield assembly, and drill the ½" holes.

Use a Forstner bit to drill the ½" holes in the shield for countersinking the mounting bolts. Then drill the holes all the way through, for whichever fastening device you decide on (³⁄₁₆" for ³⁄₁₆ toggle bolts).

Glue the dowels in place (with the ends rounded) and glue the head to the shield, avoiding squeeze-out by working glue back from the edges. You can use a board across the top of the head (from nose to brow horn) for a clamping surface.

I used a little water putty to smooth the transition from head to shield and to fill any roughness that couldn't be sanded easily.

When the putty is totally dry, sand the whole head finally and paint him up. You'll probably need three coats with light sanding in between coats. Don't let my conservative paint job inhibit you. And remember to paint the shaker pegs and the ½" furniture plugs for the eyes and the fastener holes. Glue the shaker pegs in place after the painting is done, and touch it up if necessary. Glue the eyes in place. The plugs (F) will probably stay in place without glue if you anticipate moving it at some point, otherwise glue them in place after you've mounted this monster on the wall.

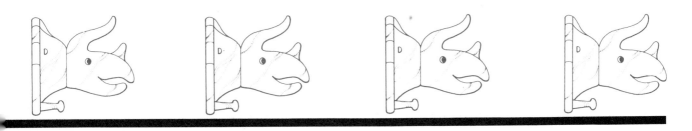

Figure 1. A small power planer will make short work of removing the sides of the nose and mouth area.

The Brontosaurus Rocker

A new twist on the old rocking horse, this rocking Brontosaurus, though a somewhat lengthy project, is not a difficult one. You can let yourself go in painting it, choosing whatever colors you like.

The Body

Enlarge all the pattern pieces for the body. Lay the pattern for the body side (D) out onto ¾" AC plywood and cut it out on the band saw. Leave about ¼" extra all the way around for final cutout after glue-up. Cut all the edges that you can on the band saw and then mark the pattern on the reverse side to cut the last few lines.

Lay out and cut the second body side (D). Again, leave ¼" extra all around and make sure that it is a reverse of the first side so that you'll end up with two "A" surfaces facing outward after assembly.

The central pieces of the body sandwich (A,B,C) are made of 2" × 12". These are cut so that the belly piece goes horizontally and the head and tail pieces go vertically. This increases the strengthening effect of the 2" × 12".

Glue the 2" × 12"'s to one body side first. Put the good side of the plywood outward with plenty of clamps and pads to protect your work. When it's dry, roughly cut away the excess 2" × 12". Then glue the second side on, being careful to line it up with the first side. Again, use plenty of clamps.

When you make your final cut with the band saw, cut smoothly, as any roughness will have to be rasped, filed and sanded. As you rasp the rough spots, you'll probably tear some edges out—don't worry,

they'll be filled later. When the silhouette is as smooth as you want it, rout the entire silhouette (except the mouth) with a ½" quarter-round bit. This will also tear out some edges.

Drill the ½" eye holes for the furniture plugs and the 1" hole in the neck for the handles. Now the sides can be screwed to the core with 1¼" #8 wood screws or drywall screws. Put a screw every 3" to 6" around the silhouette. Countersink your holes first with a ⅜" or ½" bit. Glue and plug the holes with dowels after you've put in all the screws. Belt-sand both sides to get the dowels flush to the plywood.

Now, mix up some "water putty" (powdered filler) and work it into all the core cavities in the plywood that were exposed. Fill any splintered areas and work some into the routed edges all the way around, to fill the roughness.

When the filler is thoroughly dry, sand it smooth by hand. You'll want to use the screen type of sandpaper (used for drywall finishing) as it won't clog up with all the fine dust you'll be making.

When you've got the whole body as smooth as you like, put it aside until assembly.

The Legs

The legs should be made out of hardwood for several reasons. They need to support the rocker and the rider. The rockers get screwed to the legs and the wood mustn't strip out. Lastly, the legs are fairly thin at the top where they're countersunk and screwed to the body and this area must be strong.

Lay out the legs (E,F) and cut them out, with the band saw table perfectly square (at 0°). Flat-sand both

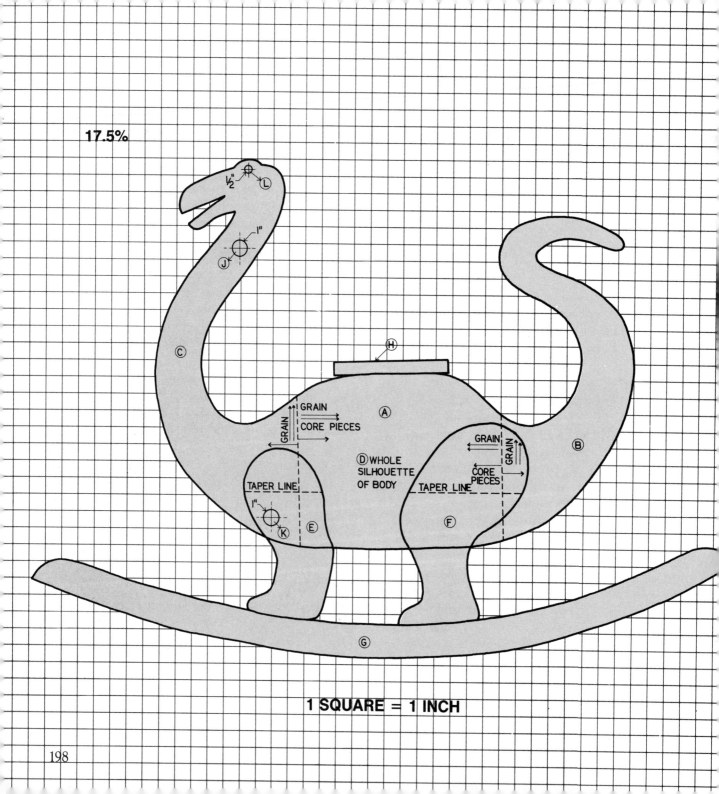

17.5%

1 SQUARE = 1 INCH

198

sides and edge-sand the entire silhouette of all four legs. Rout all the edges (except the bottoms of the feet). Hand-sand the routed edges.

Now divide the legs into sets, left side and right side. Tilt the band saw table 20° to the right. With the leg to the right and the good side upward cut along the bottom of the foot. This way the foot will rest flat on the rocker which is also cut at 20°. Be sure you end up with matching sets, (front and back, left side and right side).

This angled cut on the bottom of the feet will be belt-sanded to fit the top of the rockers later.

The Rockers

Lay out the pattern for the rockers (G) on a clear piece of 2″ × 8″ hardwood. With the band saw table still at 20° cut out one rocker. The two surfaces should end up parallel.

Flip the pattern over for the second rocker, so that they form a matched (opposite) pair. I found it easier to use a hand-held belt sander on the edges than the sander/grinder. Keep the belt sander moving and use just the front roller on the upper concave surface of the rockers. Flat-sand both sides.

Now lay out the rockers and legs in two sets (right and left sides). Use the pattern to position them, and then sand either the bottom of the feet or the top of the rockers until you have a good fit.

The Seat

Lay out the seat with the grain running across the seat (H) to strengthen the overhanging sides. Cut it out, edge-sand it and flat-sand both sides. Rout the top

edge with a ½″ quarter round bit (to make it comfortable) and the bottom edge with a ¼″ quarter round bit. Hand-sand any roughness and set it aside until the end of the assembly procedures.

Assembly

The legs and rockers are assembled into two identical sets before they are tapered and attached to the body.

Lay down some wax paper and one rocker.

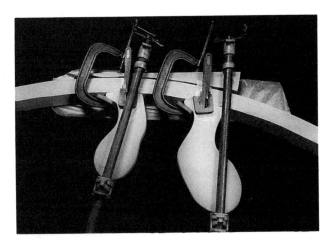

Figure 1. Clamping the rockers down to the workbench will keep them from slipping as you glue and clamp the legs to the rockers.

Clamp the rocker to the edge of the workbench. This will prevent them from slipping upward as they're glued and clamped (*See Figure 1*).

Lay the cut away scraps (from the bottom of the rocker) against the bottom edge again. This will serve as a flat clamping surface.

Carefully position the legs (from the pattern) as you glue and clamp them in place with a pole clamp (on the leg) and C-clamp (on the toe) on each leg (*See Figure 1*).

When each set is dry, drill a countersink and a pilot hole for two screws straight up through the rocker into the feet. I used 3″ #8 drywall screws but wood screws will work fine. Then glue and plug the holes and sand the dowel ends back to the rocker surface.

Now that both sets of legs and rockers are assembled, you can round off all the edges of the rockers with a four-in-hand and then hand-sand both assemblies.

The taper must be cut on the inside of the legs now before they are attached to the body. With a pencil, make a mark 3″ from the *inside* top of each leg. Lay a straight edge along both marks and draw a line across both legs. This will be the top of your cut on the band saw (*See Figure 2*).

With the band saw table at 20° and the rip fence ½″ to the right of the blade, run the entire assembly by the blade with the outside top of the leg against the fence and the rocker up in the air. This cut should follow the line you drew, and remove the taper from both legs on exactly the same plane, so that the assembly can be glued flat to the side of the body (*See Figure 3*).

BILL OF MATERIALS

PART	DESCRIPTION	QTY	THICKNESS	WIDTH OR DIAMETER	LENGTH
A	Body core (center)	1	1½″	10½″	12½″
B	Body core (tail)	1	1½″	8½″	20″
C	Body core (head)	1	1½″	9½″	23″
D	Body sides	2	½″	24″	30″
E	Front legs	2	1¾″	6″	10¼″
F	Rear legs	2	1¾″	7″	13¾″
G	Rockers	2	1¾″	6″	44½″

PART	DESCRIPTION	QTY	THICKNESS	WIDTH OR DIAMETER	LENGTH
H	Seat	1	¾″	7″	7″
J	Handlebar	1		1″	
K	Foot pegs	2		1″	
L	Plugs	2		½″ plug	
M	Screws (body)	60 approx.		#8	1¼″
N	Screws (legs & rockers)	30 approx.		#12	3″

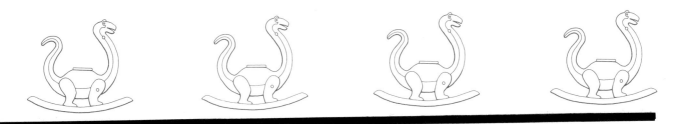

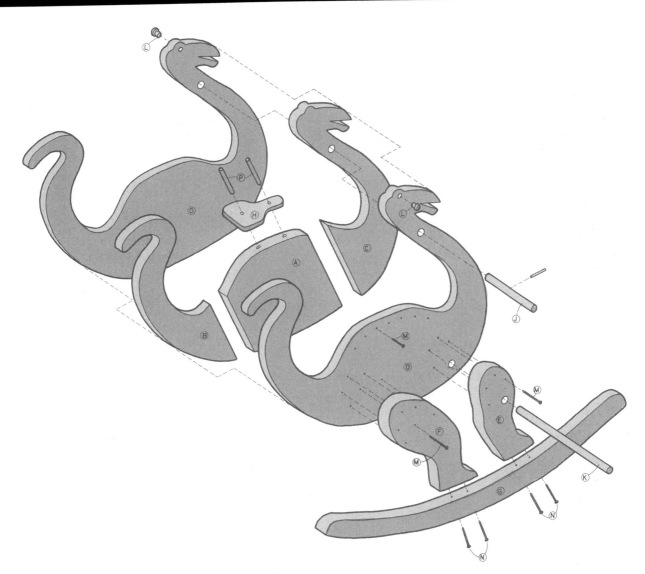

Save the tapered scraps to help glue the assembly to the body. You can use the hand-held belt sander to smooth off these sawn surfaces. Make sure that you keep the surface perfectly flat or the assembly won't fasten securely to the body.

Next, glue one (legs and rocker) assembly to the body, using the tapered scraps to make the shoulders parallel to the body so the clamps won't slip. If you wet the smooth surface of the tapered scraps, it will keep it from slipping as you apply pressure to the clamps (*See Figure 4*).

When the glue has set up thoroughly, countersink and drill three holes in the top (glued) area of each leg. Screw them in with 3″ #8 wood screws or drywall screws. Glue and plug the holes, saw off excess dowel material and sand flat.

Now that one side is securely in place, you can locate and drill the 1″ foot peg hole on the drill press. Drill halfway through the body. This dowel will serve as a foot peg and also strengthen the rocker (later).

Now you're ready to attach the second leg and rocker assembly. This one is tricky and it must be perfectly aligned with the first one, to work smoothly.

Use a scrap under the body of the rocker to hold it perfectly vertical with the one rocker resting on the ground. Position the second rocker and leg assembly. Glue and clamp it carefully in place, again using the tapered scraps to provide a square clamping surface. Check the positioning several times as you clamp the assembly. The right and left tips of the rockers should be the same distance off the ground (front right and left the same, rear right and left the same) (*See Figure 5*).

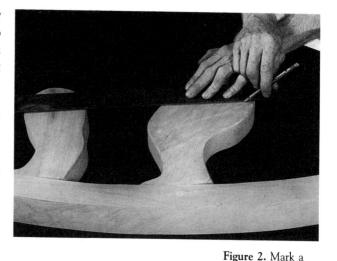

Figure 3. With the table tilted at 20° set the rip fence and cut along the line that you've marked inside both legs.

Figure 2. Mark a line across both legs for the taper cuts.

When the glue has set up, fasten the second assembly in the same way as the first. The foot peg will have to be drilled by hand. You might have someone help you eyeball the angle of your drill so it comes out identical to the other foot peg.

The foot pegs and handlebar can be glued in place now. Cut them to length, edge-sand the ends of the dowels and rout both ends of the handlebar and one end of each foot peg. Hold the dowel *firmly* in a vertical position as you pass it counter-clockwise around the ¼″ quarter round bit. You'll probably have to hand-sand the surface of the dowels to get them to slip into the 1″ holes.

The handlebar can be slipped into place and centered (without glue). Then drill and peg it with a ¼″ dowel glued through the neck. Cut off excess and sand smooth.

To attach the foot pegs, put glue into the body hole (not the leg hole) and twist them into place (watching that the final exposed pieces are the same length). Drill a ⅜″ hole up through the chest and each foot peg. Glue a ⅜″ dowel in the hole. Cut off the excess and sand it flat.

The seat can be glued and clamped in place with the ½″ quarter round edge facing upward. When it's dry, drill the two ½″ holes through the seat into the body. Glue the ½″ dowels in place. Cut off any excess and sand smooth.

Finishing

Once you've gotten the whole rocker as smooth as you can, the finish is next. Sanding sealer can be applied to the plywood to get a smoother finish.

You can use latex or oil, but I think a gloss enamel finish will look best and will stand up well to heavy use. I recommend using a primer first.

You'll want to apply at least two coats for good protection, leaving the bottom of the rockers unpainted to avoid paint rubbing onto a floor or carpet. Pay special attention to end grain as it will soak up more paint and may require a third coat. Paint the eyes before you glue them into the eye holes.

There aren't many children who have the opportunity to ride on a Brontosaurus!

Figure 4. Support the center of the body as you attach the second leg and rocker assembly, making sure that they are positioned identically and the body is perfectly vertical.

The Plesiosaurus Scooter

This one-of-a-kind dino-scooter has pivoting steering that makes him easy to drive, and a low-slung sleek look. The flippers in front serve as steering pedals which turn the front head, neck and wheels as he coasts along.

The Body Piece and the Head and Neck Piece

Lay out the enlarged body pattern on a piece of 1½" clear hardwood (A) and two pieces of ½" A-C plywood (B). Keep in mind that the good side of the plywood should end up outward on each side.

Cut the pieces out about ¼" to ½" oversize, so that you can cut the assembly out cleanly after it's glued. (*Don't* cut the slotted pivot area out yet.)

Glue and clamp the three pieces together (with plenty of clamps). When the glue has set up, countersink and drill screw holes all over the body sides, keeping clear of the edges (to allow cut out and routing) and the pivot area (to allow cut out, rounding and drilling pivot hole). Screw sides securely with 1¼" #8 wood screws, or drywall screws. Now cut out the silhouette accurately, leaving the pivot fingers slightly oversize to fit them with the head piece later.

Drill the axle hole, the holes where flippers are doweled to the body, and the eye holes for the ½" furniture plugs.

Edge-sand and rout the silhouette, again skipping the pivot area till later.

Repeat the previous section exactly for the head and neck piece (C,D) (Drill the eye holes and handlebar holes as well.)

Now to fit the pivot fingers together. Remove a little material at a time, (with the band saw, rasp and/or edge sander) until the two pieces slip together with enough space to slide in and out freely (keeping in mind that you're going to increase the thickness slightly by painting). The rounding of the front edges will enable them to actually pivot.

Transfer the top view of the finger joint onto the top finger of the head piece. Then, stand the two assemblies up on the drill press. Fit the pivot fingers together with about ³⁄₁₆" clearance at the ends of the fingers. Make sure that the sides are truly parallel and the head piece is vertical and not tilted forward. *Carefully* drill the ¼" hole, stopping ⅜" short of the bottom.

Now, to round over the fingers of the joint so they can pivot. Scribe the top view of the joint onto the top of the body piece and on the bottom of the bottom finger of each piece. The semicircle should touch the front edge and the two side edges of each finger.

Clamp each piece (one at a time) in the vise, with the pivot upward. Round over the fingers with a four-in-hand (or a belt sander if you're really good with one). Leave the steel pin long and put it in the hole to try the pivoting action. Keep filing and sanding until the pivot works smoothly.

Use water putty to fill all the countersunk holes and any exposed voids in the plywood. Sand both pieces with a belt sander and by hand when the putty has thoroughly set up.

The Flippers

Lay the flippers (E) out on square pieces of stock with

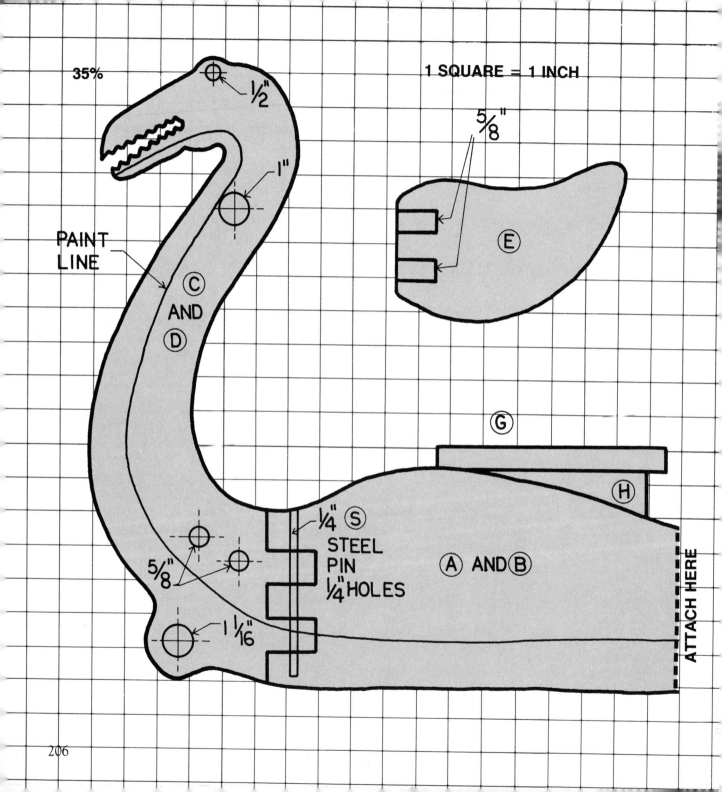

35%

1 SQUARE = 1 INCH

½"

5/8"

1"

PAINT
LINE

C
AND
D

E

G

H

5/8"

¼" S
STEEL
PIN
¼" HOLES

A AND B

ATTACH HERE

1 1/16"

206

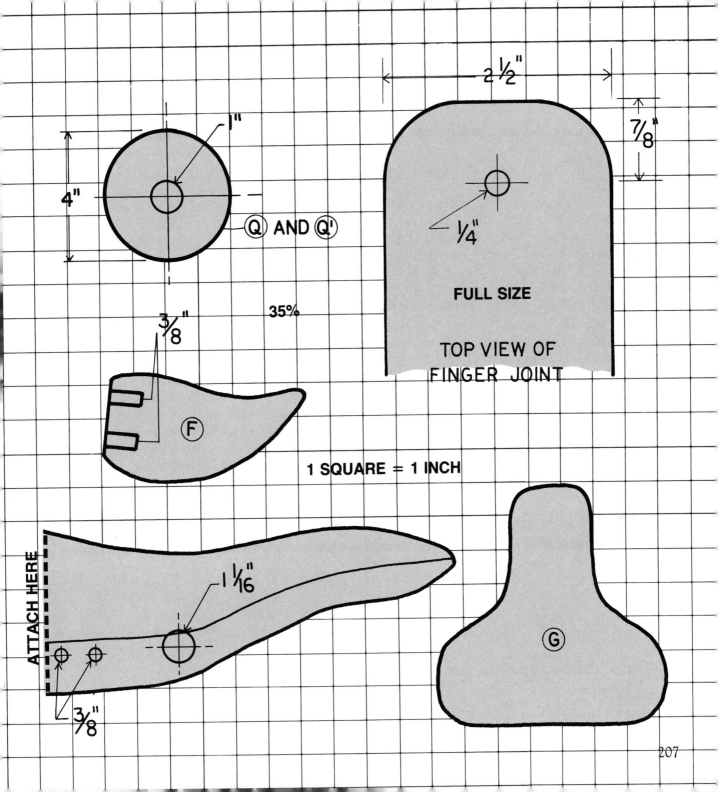

1"

4"

Q AND Q'

35%

2 ½"

7/8"

¼"

FULL SIZE

TOP VIEW OF
FINGER JOINT

3/8"

F

1 SQUARE = 1 INCH

ATTACH HERE

1 1/16"

3/8"

G

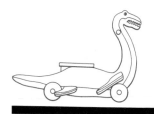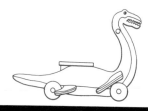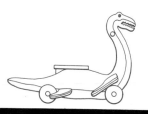

the flat edge of the flipper flush to the end grain edge of your stock.

Mark the hole locations, using dowel pins in the body sides, or simply by positioning the flippers next to their respective holes on the body and carefully marking the hole positions on the flipper blanks.

Stand the flipper blanks on end, on the drill press, and drill the dowel holes.

Cut out the silhouettes. Flat-sand them on both sides, and edge-sand them. When you rout the silhouettes, skip the inside edges where the holes are, or the router's roller bearing will slip into the holes and mess up the edge. With the flippers in the vise, one at a time, round over these areas with a four-in-hand. Then hand-sand these edges and all the routed edges as well.

The Seat and the Seat Wedge

Cut the seat out (G) with the grain running sideways

for greater strength. Flat-sand both sides and edge-sand the silhouette. Rout the top edge with a ½" quarter round bit (for greater comfort) and the bottom edge with a ¼" quarter round bit.

For the seat wedge (H), cut out a block of hardwood 1¾" thick by 2" wide by 6" long. Use either the pattern or the actual edge of your body piece, to mark the bottom edge of the wedge shaped piece. Cut this line and edge-sand it, until it fits on the top of the body. Break the edges by hand.

The Wheels

The wheels (Q) are made in the same fashion as the body. The plywood on either side of the wood core eliminates the wood grain's tendency to crack. This way the wheels are almost indestructible. The rear wheels are fat (2½") for plenty of strength and stability, while the front wheels are thinner (1¾) for easy steering. Cut square blanks (4½" × 4½") for the

BILL OF MATERIALS

PART	DESCRIPTION	QTY	THICKNESS	WIDTH OR DIAMETER	LENGTH
A	Body core	1	1½"	6⅝"	25½"
B	Body sides	2	½"	6⅝"	25½"
C	Head & neck core	1	1½"	7½"	18½"
D	Head & neck sides	2	½"	7½"	18½"
E	Front flippers	2	1"	4½"	7⅛"
F	Rear flippers	2	¾"	3⅛"	6"
G	Seat	1	¾"	7"	7"
H	Seat wedge	1	1¾"	2½"	5¾"
J	Seat dowels	2		½"	2"

PART	DESCRIPTION	QTY	THICKNESS	WIDTH OR DIAMETER	LENGTH
K	Front flipper dowels	4		⅝"	2"
L	Rear flipper dowels	4		⅜"	1¾"
M	Handlebar	1		1"	
N	Axles	2		1"	4¾"
P	Eyes (furniture plugs)	2		½"	
Q	Wheels	4	1"	4"	
R	Axle wedges	4	¼"	1"	1"
S	Pivot pin (steel)	1		¼"	4¾"

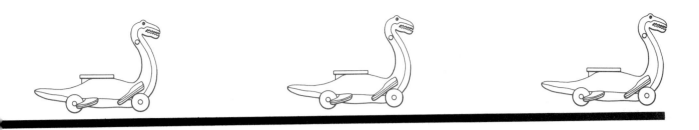

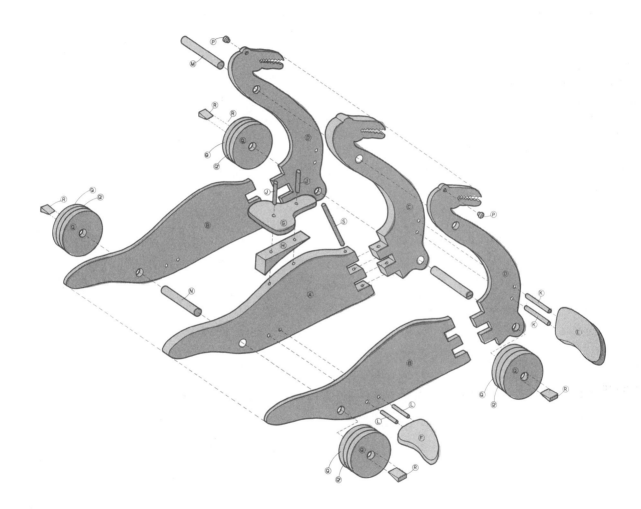

wheel parts. The front wheels are made of a ¾″ hardwood core and two ½″ plywood sides. The rear wheels are made of a 1½″ hardwood core and two ½″ plywood sides.

Glue and clamp all four wheel sandwiches. Lay out the patterns for the wheels when the glue has set up. Countersink and drill holes for wood screws or drywall screws, staying clear of the axle hole and the edges that will be sawn out and routed. Screw the sandwiches together. Drill the axle holes and cut out the silhouettes.

Edge-sand all four wheels and rout all the edges. Fill all screw holes, rough areas and exposed plywood voids with water putty. Sand everything smooth.

The Axles and Handlebar

Cut the axles (N) to length with about ⅛″ clearance on each side of the body. Cut a slot in the ends to drive the wedges in (R) after assembly. Sand the ends of the dowel flat on the sander/grinder and round the edges slightly by hand.

Cut the handlebar (M) to length, and sand the ends on the sander/grinder. Rout the ends by holding the dowel firmly in a vertical position and passing it clockwise around the router bit. Hand-sand the entire dowel.

Painting

All the parts should be primed first. Then lay out the paint lines. Masking tape will help where the colors meet. Be sure not to get any paint in the ¼″ holes in the finger joint, the handlebar holes in the neck and the axle holes. Also, don't paint surfaces that will be glued together (the middle of the underside of the seat, the top and bottom of the seat wedge, and the top of the body where the seat will be fastened).

Some polyurethane in the axle holes and on the axles (except the ends where the wheels will be glued) will help prevent deterioration, if the scooter happens to get wet.

Don't paint the handlebar until it is in place.

Final Assembly and Touch-Up

Cut the ¼″ steel rod (available at most hardware stores) to length so that it will end ½″ below the top surface of the finger joint.

With both body parts positioned together, tap the rod into place. Use a nail punch to drive it all the way in (½″ below the surface). Glue a ¼″ dowel in on top of it. Cut off any excess and sand smooth.

Glue one wheel onto each axle, glue and tap the wedges into place, cut off any excess and sand smooth. Slip the axles through the body and attach the other two wheels in the same fashion.

Tap the handlebar into place (perfectly centered) and drill and dowel it in place through the front of the neck.

Cut the dowels (L) to attach the flippers to length. Round the ends off by hand, and glue them into place in the body. Put glue inside the holes in the flippers (just on the sides of the holes and *not too much!*). Make sure that the protruding dowels aren't longer than the holes are deep. Tap the flippers onto their respective dowels.

Glue the eyes (furniture plugs or "buttons") in place, after they're painted.

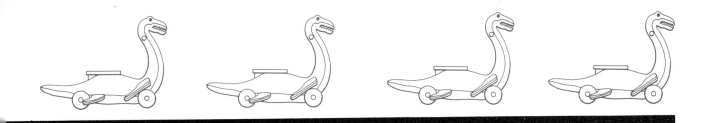

Glue and clamp the seat wedge in place. When the glue has set up, glue and clamp the seat in place and let it set up. Drill the ½" holes through the seat and the wedge and into the body.

Cut the ½" dowels slightly shorter than the hole depth. Sand one end flat on the sander/grinder and round over the other end of each dowel. Put glue on the sides of the holes and drive the dowels in until the flat end is flush with the top of the seat.

Now touch up all the unpainted areas (dowel ends and handlebar). Remember the end grain will need two or three coats.

Now he's ready for a spin, so find your favorite little driver, and give a push.

The Tyrannosaurus Swing

A swing may not be a new idea, but a Tyrannosaurus swing is certainly a new twist. Kids seem to love this one, and will swing for hours. This project can be made out of hardwood with a clear finish, or out of plywood and softwood, and painted.

The ropes are spaced at 16″ across the front and approximately 24″ front to back, so you can mount the eye hooks in the ceiling joists or rafters whether they're on 16″ or 24″ centers.

If you don't have a porch roof to hang your swing from, you can build an outdoor rack to hang it from. (See "*Variable Swing Rack*.")

You can also hang it from a tree but it isn't easy to get the ropes at the proper distances and same heights. You may have to fasten a board as a cross piece to provide mounting in the appropriate position.

If your swing is going to stay outside, you'll have to be sure that you apply a good thick finish over the entire piece, paying special attention to the end grain, which will absorb more finish and will also absorb moisture easily if not totally covered with finish.

You can also make this fellow adult-size simply by enlarging the patterns to the appropriate size. Get yourself comfortably in a chair, with your arms outstretched as if you are riding a swing, and have someone measure the distances from the seat forward to the hand and foot hold, and the distance from hand hold to foot hold.

The Body Assembly

Cut the two side pieces (A) out of ¾″ A/C plywood or hardwood, leaving ¼″ extra all the way around the pattern. This will facilitate one smooth finish cut after glue-up. Don't cut out the teeth yet. If you use plywood, be sure that the A side faces outward on each side.

Cut the central head piece (B) out of 1¾″ material (again ¼″ oversize), without cutting out the teeth. The only area that should not be cut oversize is the bottom line or hidden area. This line should be cut exactly, edge-sanded, and carefully positioned during assembly. Don't drill the 1″ holes till after assembly.

Take each side, one at a time, good side up, on the drill press, and drill ⅜″ holes about ¼″ deep every 3″ to 6″ around the silhouette. These are the countersinks for the drywall screws or wood screws that will hold the sides securely to the core piece. Since the silhouette will be routed, be sure to keep the holes far enough away from the edge.

If you're using ¼″ drywall screws, simply glue one side to the core and screw it in place. The drywall screws will pull the side in tight. Repeat for the second side. If you're using 1¼″ wood screws, position the side and drill all the tapered pilot holes, then glue and clamp the side in place and screw in the wood screws. Repeat for the second side.

When the assembly is dry, cut out the final shape, making sure that the interior hidden line is in the proper relationship with the final cut.

Edge-sand and rout the silhouette, except the teeth. Carefully locate and drill the 1″ holes, using a 1¾″ scrap between the two sides to prevent tear-out behind the first surface, on the lower hole. Drill until the point breaks through the underside, flip the piece

over, and drill from behind using the little hole to center the spade bit. This is the best way to prevent tear-out. Drill the ¾″ holes for the eye plugs.

If you're using hardwood, plug the ⅜″ holes with dowels. When the glue is dry, saw them off flush and flat-sand.

If you're using plywood, you can fill the holes (and any roughness on the surface) with water putty. When it's set up, sand both sides flat. Mark the positions where the legs and arms will be glued to the body. The painting is done now since it's hard to paint a clean belly line with the arms and legs in the way. Paint the entire body assembly except these areas where glue will be applied. You can overlap these areas slightly to avoid unpainted areas later. The eyes can then be painted and glued in place (after the paint dries) so that the rounded surface protrudes. Make the eyes by rounding the end of a ¾″ dowel

(into a hemisphere) on the sander/grinder, the belt sander, or by hand and with a file and sandpaper.

The Tail Assembly

Cut out the two side pieces (C) slightly oversize as with the body. In this assembly, though, the sides are shorter than the central piece, so the front edge of the two side pieces should be cut exactly, edge-sanded, and routed since you won't be able to get at it after assembly.

Cut out the central piece (D) oversize (out of 1½″ material) and drill the 1¹⁄₁₆″ hole. Carefully glue and screw the pieces together (just like the body assembly).

Next make your final cut on the band saw. Edge-sand the silhouette and route the edges. Drill the ⅜″ hole in the tail for the rope. Plug the ⅜″ holes with dowels and saw off the excess when the glue has

BILL OF MATERIALS

PART	DESCRIPTION	QTY	THICKNESS	WIDTH OR DIAMETER	LENGTH
A	Body sides	2	¾″	10½″	23½″
B	Body core	1	1¾″	8¾″	20″
C	Tail sides	2	¾″	7″	28″
D	Tail core	1	1½″	9″	33″
E	Legs	2	1¾″	10″	18¼″
F	Arms	2	1½″	2½″	6″
G	Seat	1	¾″	7″	7″

PART	DESCRIPTION	QTY	WIDTH OR DIAMETER	LENGTH
H	Handle & foot bars	2	1″	18″
J	Pivot dowel	1	1″	3″
K	Eye dowels	2	¾″	¾″
L	Seat dowels	2	½″	1½″
M	Screws	60 approx.	#8	1¼″
N	Screws	30 approx.	#10	2¼″
P	Hanging rope		⅜″	20′ approx.

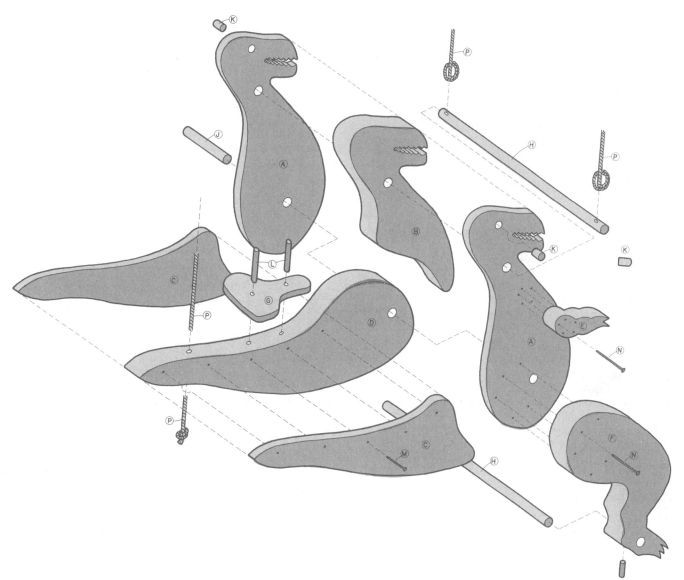

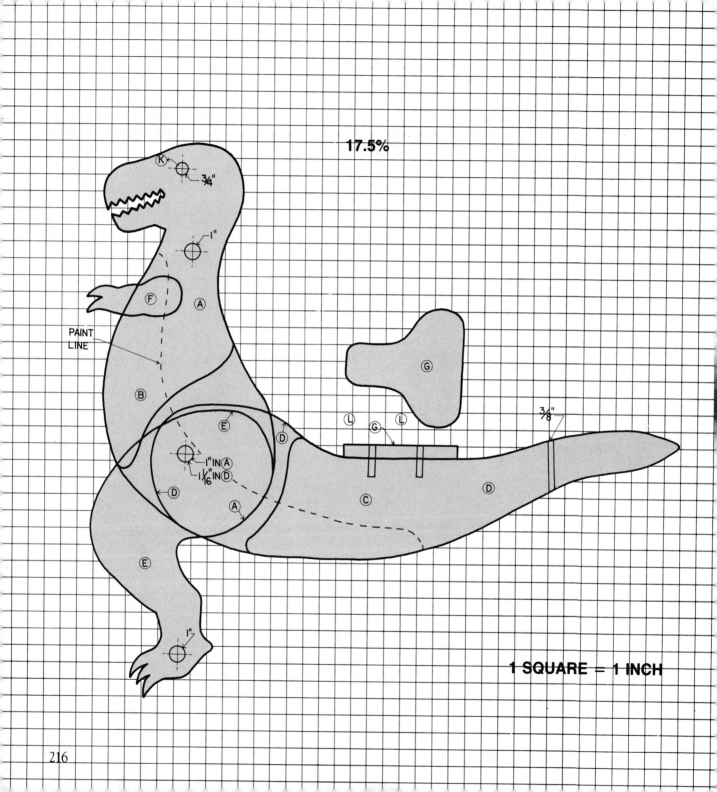

17.5%

Ⓚ 3/4"

1"

Ⓕ Ⓐ

PAINT
LINE

Ⓑ

Ⓔ

Ⓓ

Ⓓ 1" IN Ⓐ
1 1/16" IN Ⓓ

Ⓐ

Ⓔ

Ⓖ

Ⓛ Ⓖ Ⓛ

3/8"

Ⓒ

Ⓓ

1"

1 SQUARE = 1 INCH

216

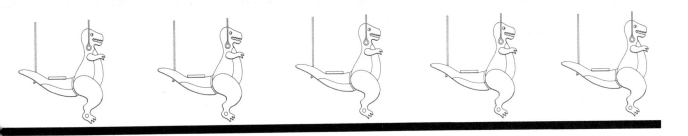

dried, or fill with water putty. Flat-sand both sides. Fill any roughness and voids in the plywood with water putty. When the putty has set up, hand-sand the entire piece. Any areas of the front edge of the central piece that could not be routed can be rounded over with a four-in-hand and sandpaper.

Now you can paint the tail piece, leaving the area unpainted where the seat will be glued.

The Arms, Legs and Seat

The arms, legs and seat are made out of hardwood or solid softwood such as pine. Drill the holes in the legs (E) before cutting them out. Cut out the arms (F) and the legs and the seat (G). Edge-sand the silhouettes, flat-sand the sides, and rout the entire silhouette on both sides of all four pieces (except between the claws on the arms and legs). Hand-sand the routed edges, and they're ready for paint. When you paint the arms, legs and seat remember to leave unpainted the surfaces that will be glued.

Handlebar and Foot Bar

Cut the 1″ dowels to length for the handlebar (J) and foot bar (H). Hold them vertically (and firmly) over the router table and rout the ends, one at a time. Drill a ⅜″ hole 1″ from either end of the handlebar. A piece of wood with a V-shaped notch is handy to keep the dowel positioned as you drill the holes (*See Tools, Techniques & Production Procedures, Figure 4*). Make

sure that both holes are drilled parallel (both vertical).

Final Assembly

The first step is to join the body and tail assemblies. Position the two pieces. Cut the 1″ dowel to length and tap it into place. It doesn't need to be glued because the legs get glued and screwed over the ends of the dowel and there's nowhere for it to go.

The legs are next. Slip the 1″ foot bar through the hole in both legs. Center the dowel as you glue the legs in place. Make sure that the legs are positioned perfectly. The dowel will help you keep them opposed. Use several clamps and plenty of pads to protect your paint job.

When the glue has set up, countersink and screw the legs to the body with either 3″ wood screws or 3″ drywall screws. Plug the holes with either dowels or wood putty. Saw off dowel ends and sand smooth.

Repeat this whole process for the arms and the seat.

Slip the dowel through the upper body and center it with the holes facing up and down. Drill a ¼″ hole through the chest and the 1″ dowel. Glue and peg it with a ¼″ dowel. Cut off the excess and sand it smooth. Repeat this process from under the feet to hold that dowel in place.

Touch up your paint job and you're ready to swing. See "The Variable Swing Rack" chapter for hanging instructions.

The Brontosaurus Double Swing

The idea of a double swing may seem a little outrageous at first, but really, it's quite practical. It will prevent siblings from fighting over their single swing. Also, most children have a good friend that they could ride with. I've made quite a few double swings in my time as a toymaker. I had one in front of my toy store, and I can testify to the heavy use it was put to.

The Handlebars and Foot Pegs

The handlebars (L) have a ⅜″ hole drilled 1″ from both ends (for the rope). A V-shaped support will help to keep the dowel from shifting as you drill the holes (*See Tools, Techniques, and Production Procedures*).

The ends of all your dowels are routed holding the dowel firmly in a vertical position and passing it clockwise around the bit.

The 1″ dowels (N,P) that go through the body and the uprights are held in place by wedges in the rear and by the legs in the front. So, both dowels should be cut to length and the rear dowel will need a slot cut ¾″ deep in both ends of it for wedges to be tapped into it, after assembly. Sand both ends of this dowel flat, as it will be exposed after assembly.

The wedges can be cut on the band saw from 1″ stock with the grain running the long way for strength.

The Body

The body assembly is formidable in appearance but not too difficult to make. It is a large and heavy piece to pass through the band saw though, and you may want some help supporting it when you make the final cut. Or you may use a reciprocating saw to cut it out. If you want to reduce the weight, you can cut away portions of the core, at this point. Be sure to stay away from the pivot holes and rope hole. You'll want to mark this piece onto the sides to avoid placing screws where there's no core.

Glue up a couple of 1½″ softwood boards for the core of the assembly (E). Cut out both side pieces (B) (good side out) leaving ¼ to ½″ extra all the way around the silhouette except the areas in the front that do not reach the edge of the core to be cut off after. These edges should be edge-sanded, routed and hand-sanded now, as you won't be able to get at them after assembly. Don't drill any holes until after assembly.

Drill countersink holes and screw holes all over the outer surfaces of both sides, staying away from the edges and the hole locations. Apply glue to the inner surface of one side and carefully position it as you press it onto the core. Screw the side to the core with 1¼″ drywall screws. Repeat this process for the other side. Eyeball the assembly before screwing it together to make sure the two side pieces are lined up on either side of the core.

Cut the whole body piece out. Try for a smooth cut, rather than extreme accuracy. A ½″ blade on the band saw will make it easier to get a smooth line.

Use a hand-held belt sander and a four-in-hand to smooth out the edges and then rout the entire silhouette. Drill the two 1¹⁄₁₆″ pivot holes. Drill the hole in the tail for the hanging rope.

Fill any voids in the plywood with water putty as you fill the ⅜″ countersink holes and any rough areas.

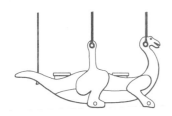 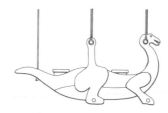 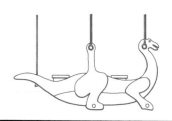

When the water putty has thoroughly dried, sand the whole assembly smooth.

Paint the assembly with primer or sanding sealer. Do not paint the top of the body where the seats will be attached. When the primer is dry, lay out the painting pattern and paint the assembly. You'll want two or three good coats to really protect your swing. Pay special attention to end grain as it will soak up more paint. Polyurethane in the pivot holes and rope hole will help prevent deterioration.

The Head Assembly

The head assembly is made in the same way that the body was except that the *bottom* edge of the central piece is the area that is not cut oversize and is edge-sanded before assembly. When the three pieces (C,D) are fastened, make your final cut, and edge-sand and rout the silhouette. Then drill the two 1" holes. A scrap of 1¾" wood (the same thickness as center piece of the assembly) between the two sides will help you drill the lower hole without tearing it out between the sides. For both of the other holes, drill until the tip of the bit sticks through. Flip the piece over, and drill the rest of the way through from behind, using the small bit hole to center your spade bit.

Fill all the core cavities, the countersink holes and any roughness with water putty. Sand it all smooth when the filler has set up.

Mark the location of the front legs (E) onto both

MATERIALS

PART	DESCRIPTION	QTY	THICKNESS	WIDTH OR DIAMETER	LENGTH
A	Body core	1	1½"	14"	62"
B	Body sides	2	½"	14"	59"
C	Head sides	2	¾"	9"	20¼"
D	Head core	1	1¾"	8½"	16½"
E	Front legs	2	¾"	13"	14"
F	Rear pivot legs	2	¾"	15"	27¾"
G	Pivot leg spacer	1	1¾"	3"	7¼"
H	Seats	2	¾"	7"	7"
J	Front seat wedge	1	1¾"	1½"	6½"
K	Rear seat wedge	1	1¾"	2"	6½"
L	Handlebars & foot bar	3		1"	18"
M	Rear foot pegs	2		1"	7½"

PART	DESCRIPTION	QTY	THICKNESS	WIDTH OR DIAMETER	LENGTH
N	Front pivot dowel	1		1"	3"
P	Rear pivot dowel	1		1"	4½"
Q	Rear foot peg support	2	¾"	2¼"	
R	Pivot dowel wedges	2	¼"	1"	1"
S	Dowels to fasten seats	4		⅜"	3½"
T	Eyes (furniture plugs)	2		½"	
V	Screws	50 approx.		#8	1¼"
V	Hanging rope			⅜"	40' approx

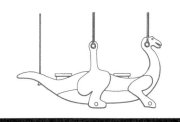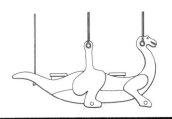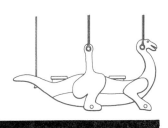

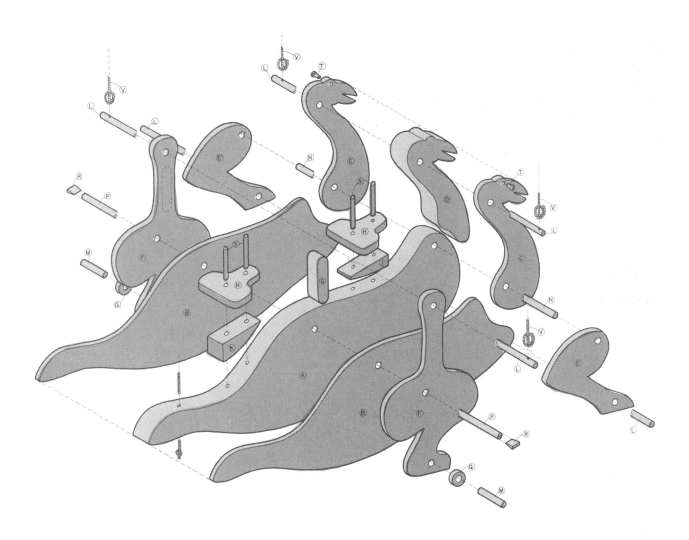

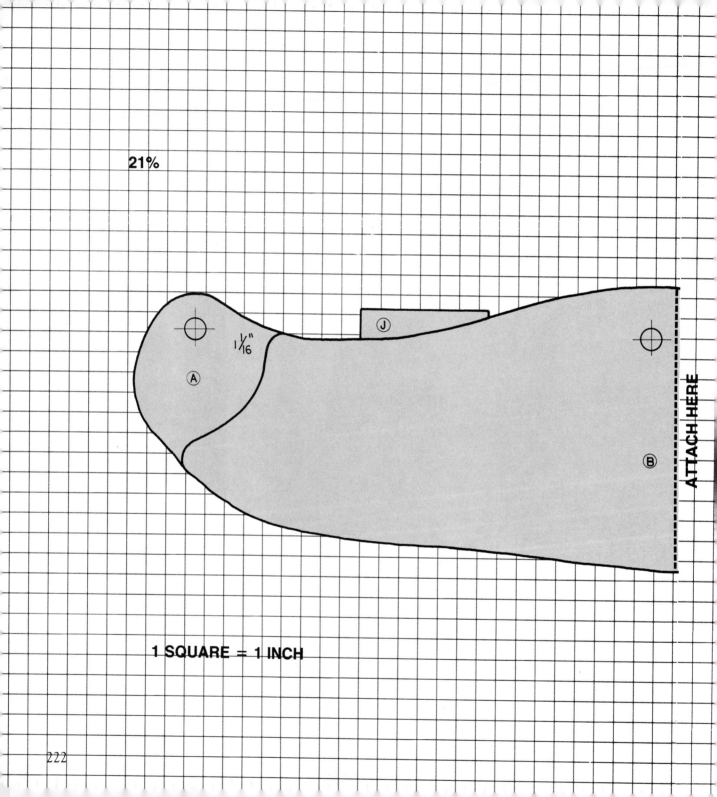

21%

1¹⁄₁₆"

Ⓐ

Ⓙ

ATTACH HERE

Ⓑ

1 SQUARE = 1 INCH

222

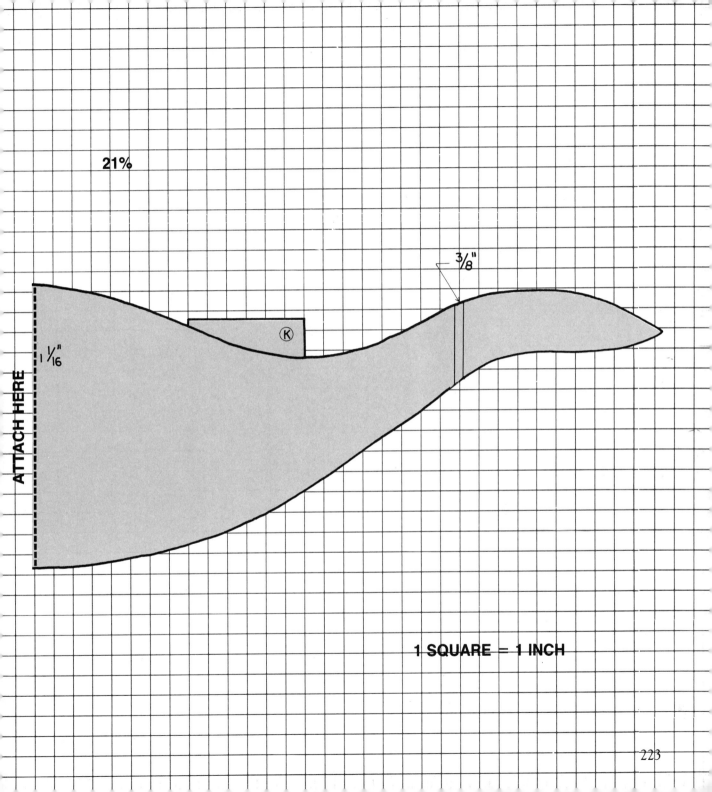

21%

³⁄₈"

ⓀK

ATTACH HERE

1 ¹⁄₁₆"

1 SQUARE = 1 INCH

223

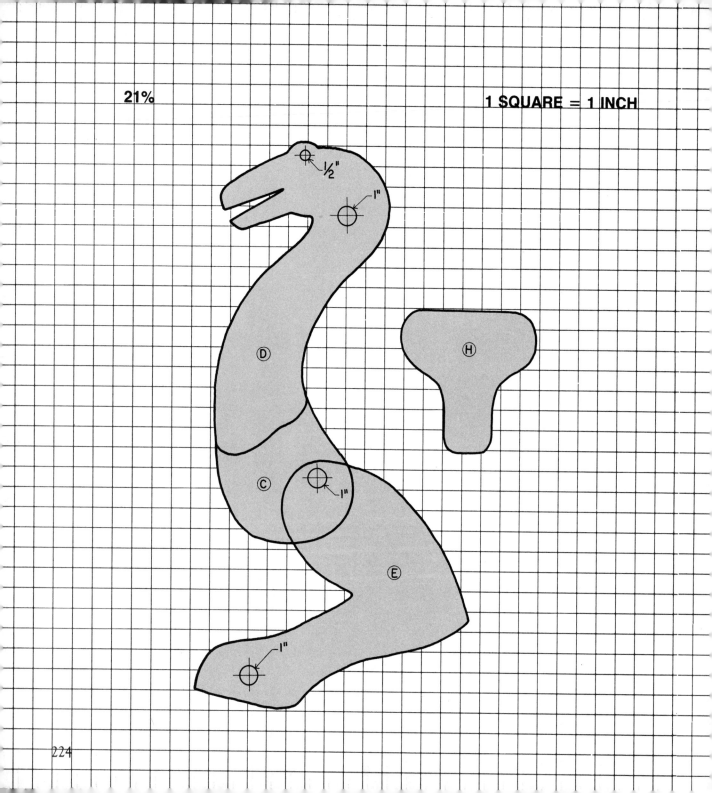

21%

1 SQUARE = 1 INCH

½"

1"

D

H

C

1"

E

1"

224

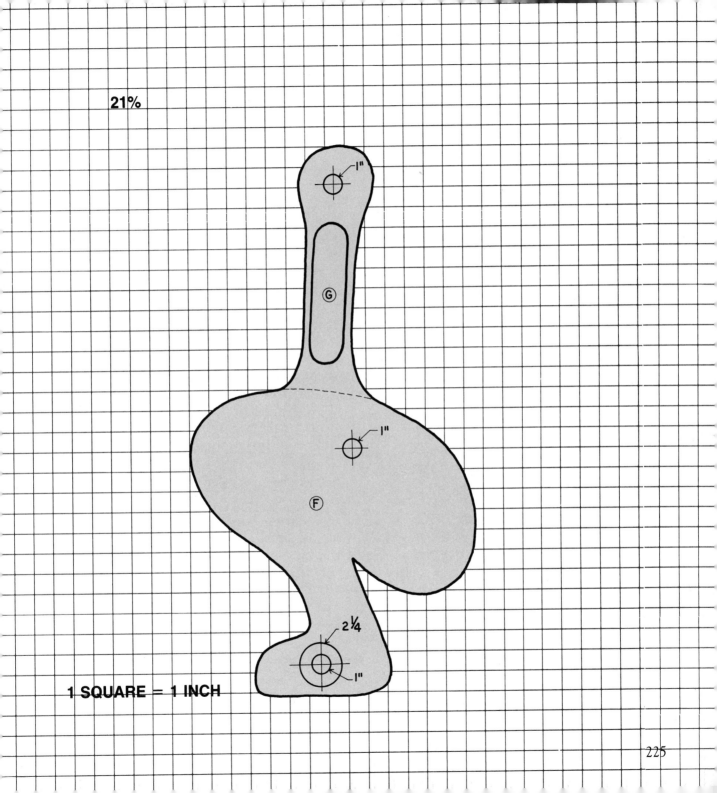

21%

1"

G

1"

F

2¼

1"

1 SQUARE = 1 INCH

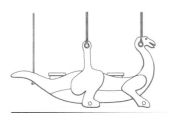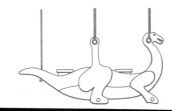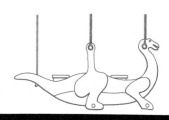

sides of the head assembly. This area should not be painted, otherwise the glue won't be able to grab. So prime the head assembly except this area and inside the 1″ holes where the dowels will go. You can go slightly over the line to avoid having unpainted areas later. Masking tape will help make a clean line where different colors meet. You'll want several coats of paint.

Front Legs

Cut the front legs out of ¾″ A-C plywood with the A side outward on both pieces. Drill the 1″ holes. Edge-sand and rout the silhouettes. Fill any core cavities and roughness with water putty and sand it smooth when it has set up. Mark the inside surface where each leg will be attached to the head assembly, and prime and paint both legs leaving this area unpainted, again overlapping the line slightly to avoid having unpainted areas later.

Rear Leg Assembly

Cut out both pieces (F) with the good side outward. Drill the 1″ holes in both pieces together to keep positions identical. Lay one on top of the other and drill till the tip sticks through. This will locate the hole on the second piece and give you a hole in the back of the first piece to locate the bit and drill from behind. Repeat for all three holes and then flip the piece over and drill from behind. Now finish the holes in the second piece in the same fashion. Edge-sand and rout both pieces. Fill any core cavities and roughness with water putty, and sand the pieces when it has set up.

Cut out the spacer (G) that joins the two rear legs, and edge-sand it. With dowels through the top and bottom holes of both leg pieces to position them, glue and clamp this block in place. When the glue has dried, remove the dowels, countersink about six holes on each side, and screw the assembly together. Plug the holes with water putty, and sand it smooth when it's dry. Glue and screw the footpeg supports (Q) onto the outside of the feet. Position the handlebar (with ⅜″ vertical holes 1″ from each routed end) and the foot bars. Drill ⅛″ holes through the edge of the legs into the dowels, far enough to keep the 1″ dowels from moving. Glue and plug the holes with ⅛″ dowels. Cut off the excess and sand smooth.

Prime and paint the entire assembly. Watch not to get any paint in the 1″ hole in the center, which will be doweled during assembly.

Seats (and Wedges)

Cut out the seats (H), and edge-sand and rout the silhouettes on both sides. Running a ½″ quarter round bit along the top edge will make the seat more comfortable. Prime and paint both seats after hand-sanding. Again, don't paint the center of the underside of the seats where they will be glued to the wedges.

To cut the wedges that support the seats (J,K), use the body for a pattern to get a good fit. Lay the body down with a piece of paper under the seat area. Run a pencil along the body silhouette and then mark a straight line where the seat will be. Draw lines vertically in the front and the rear of the wedge. Repeat this for the other seat. Cut the wedges out of

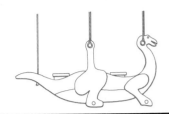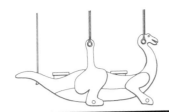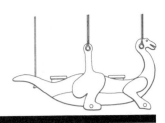

2″ stock. These pieces can be edge-sanded now, checking the fit on the body as you go. When they fit fairly well, you can prime and paint the sides (not the top and bottom surfaces). Set them aside till assembly.

Assembly

The first part of the assembly is joining the body and the head piece. With both pieces flat on the workbench, position the head piece over the front of the body, so that the holes line up.

The front pivot dowel is simply tapped into place. Now slip the 18″ long 1″ dowel through both front leg pieces. Center the dowel with legs spread slightly farther apart than the width of the head assembly. With glue on the sides of the head piece, bring the legs up on either side, position them carefully and clamp the legs to the head piece, twisting the dowel to let the legs pull together where they want to be without any tension against the dowel. Drill and peg the legs through the dowel to hold it in place. When the glue has set up countersink and screw the legs to the head piece making sure that the screws don't protrude on the insides, where the head piece overlaps the body. Fill the holes with water putty and sand smooth. You might as well leave your touch-up painting until the swing is totally assembled.

The rear leg pivot assembly can now be attached. Position it over the body as you tap the 1″ dowel (with the slots) in place. Squeeze a little glue into the wedge slots and drive the wedges in. Saw off any excess and sand the dowel ends.

Now, glue and clamp the seat wedges onto the top of the body. When the glue has set up, glue and clamp the seats in place. Drill the ⅜″ holes through the seats and wedges into the top of the body. Put glue on the insides of the holes and drive the dowels (cut to length and sanded on the upper end) into place until the smooth end is flush with the seat.

Finally, touch up your paint job (with several coats on the dowel ends). There are instructions on hanging your swings in the chapter "The Variable Swing Rack."

Of course, now they'll fight over who gets to sit in front! Oh well.

The Stenosaurus Swing

I want to start with a note of *caution*. A child who's reckless could get hurt if he put his hand in the mouth of this guy while he's riding. Most children, however, will have enough sense to hold onto the handlebars instead.

This works on the same principle as most swings, with one exception. As the swing goes forward, a rope attaching the upper jaw to the pivot arm lifts the mouth open in an awesome display of flashing teeth!

The Body

Glue up a couple of 2″ × 8″s to make a piece large enough to lay out the enlarged body core pattern (A). Lay out the pattern and cut it out, leaving ¼ to ½″ extra around the entire silhouette, except the head where the sides will not be attached. This area should be cut out exactly. The extra will be cut away after the body sides have been attached. You'll want to have some help, as the piece will be heavy and awkward.

If you want to make the swing lighter you can remove some of this piece, staying well away from the edges and the pivot hole. If you do this, you'll want to mark your final piece onto the body sides so you'll know where you can screw the lamination together without missing the core.

Drill the eye hole.

Lay out the body side pattern (B) on two pieces of A-C plywood so that the good sides will face outward during assembly. Cut these pieces out, again leaving ¼ to ½″ extra around the silhouette, except where the front of the piece will not reach the edges of the body core.

Edge-sand this line (the front edge of the body side) and rout the outside edge, as it will be inaccessible after assembly.

Now glue one of the sides to the body core (being careful to position the front edge as in the pattern). Countersink and drill holes every 3″ to 6″ around the silhouette and scatter holes over the entire side (keeping far enough away from the edge that you can make your final cut and rout the edge later). Screw the side on with 1¼″ wood screws or drywall screws, being sure that they end up below the surface.

Flip the assembly over and repeat the process.

Cut out the silhouette (with some help). Sand the edges with a belt sander where possible and file and hand-sand the remaining edges. Rout the silhouette on both sides (except the teeth). The teeth can be filed to break the edges cleanly.

Fill all the screw holes, and any exposed plywood voids, with water putty. Belt-sand the sides and hand-sand all the routed edges etc.

Drill the 1⅛″ pivot hole with a spade bit. Set the depth on the drill press so the tip of the bit just pops through the other side. Then flip the piece over and use that hole to center the bit as you drill the rest of the way through.

Drill the hole for the ⅜″ cord.

The Head

Lay out the head sides (C) on ½″ hardwood stock and cut out the two silhouettes. Lay them on top of each other to drill the eye holes identically. Flat-sand both sides of each piece. Edge-sand the teeth and the rear of the head (where the spacer does not reach the edge of the assembly). Break the edges of the teeth with a

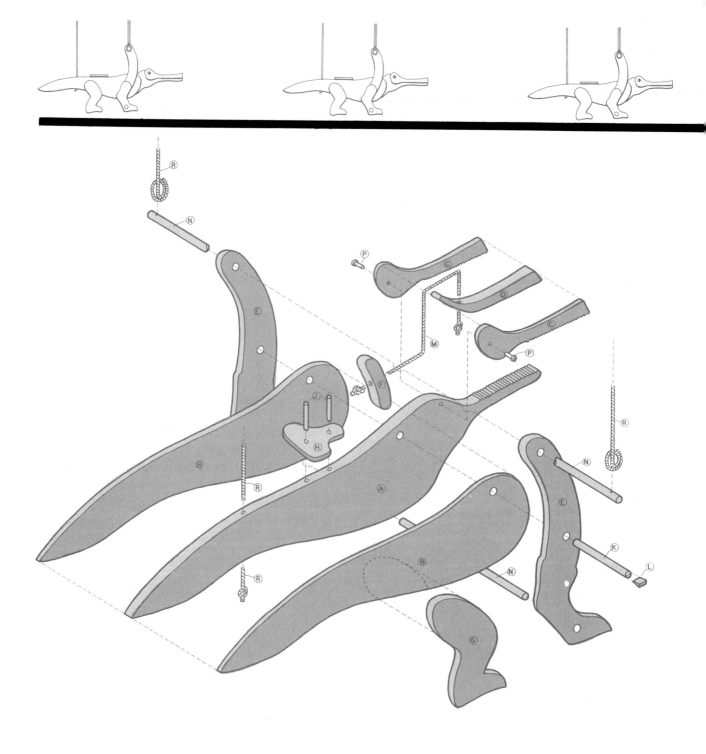

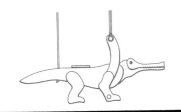 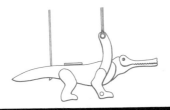 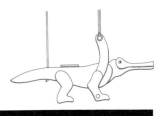

file, as it will be hard to get at them after assembly (especially the inside edges).

Lay out the spacer (D) on 1¾" stock. Cut it out and edge-sand the silhouette, except the top edge which will be sanded after assembly. Do not flat-sand the sides of the spacer or you will risk making the head sides unparallel after assembly. Drill the holes for the ¼" cord, a ½" hole from underneath (to hide the knot) and then the rest of the way through at ¼".

Put glue on either side of the spacer and glue the assembly together, making sure that the eye holes are perfectly opposed. Use plenty of clamps.

When the glue has set up, edge-sand the front and top edge of the snout. Rout the entire silhouette, except the teeth. Hand-sand the routed edges, and the inside edges of the sides.

The Pivot Legs

Lay out the pivot legs (E) on ¾" A-C plywood, with the good side outward. Cut them out and edge-sand

MATERIALS

PART	DESCRIPTION	QTY	THICKNESS	WIDTH OR DIAMETER	LENGTH
A	Body core	1	1½"	10½"	61"
B	Body sides	2	½"	10½"	45¾"
C	Head sides	2	½"	4¼"	14½"
D	Snout spacer	1	1¾"	3"	13¼"
E	Pivot legs	2	¾"	8¾"	26"
F	Pivot leg spacer	1	1¾"	2¾"	6¾"
G	Rear legs	2	¾"	7¾"	13"
H	Seat	1	¾"	7"	7"

PART	DESCRIPTION	QTY	THICKNESS	WIDTH OR DIAMETER	LENGTH
J	Seat dowels	2		⅜"	1½"
K	Pivot dowel	1		1"	4¼"
L	Pivot dowel wedges	2	¼"	1"	1"
M	Snout cord	1		¼"	12" approx.
N	Handle & foot bars	2		1"	18"
P	Eye pegs	2	½" head	5/16"	1 9/16" shaft
Q	Screws	30 approx.		#8	1¼"
R	Hanging rope	1		⅜"	20 ft. approx.

231

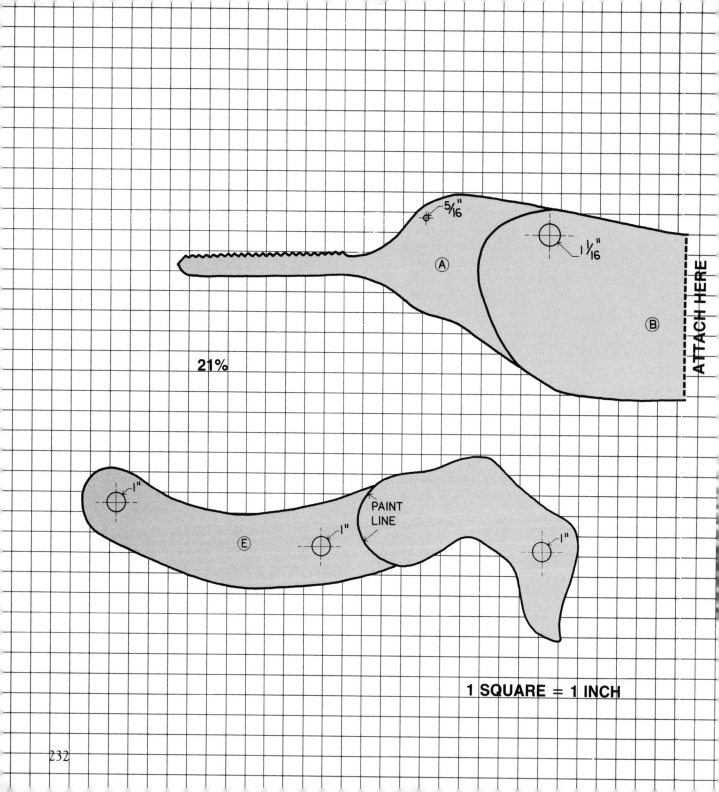

21%

Ⓐ

⌀ 5/16"

1 1/16"

Ⓑ

ATTACH HERE

PAINT
LINE

1"

Ⓔ

1"

1"

1 SQUARE = 1 INCH

232

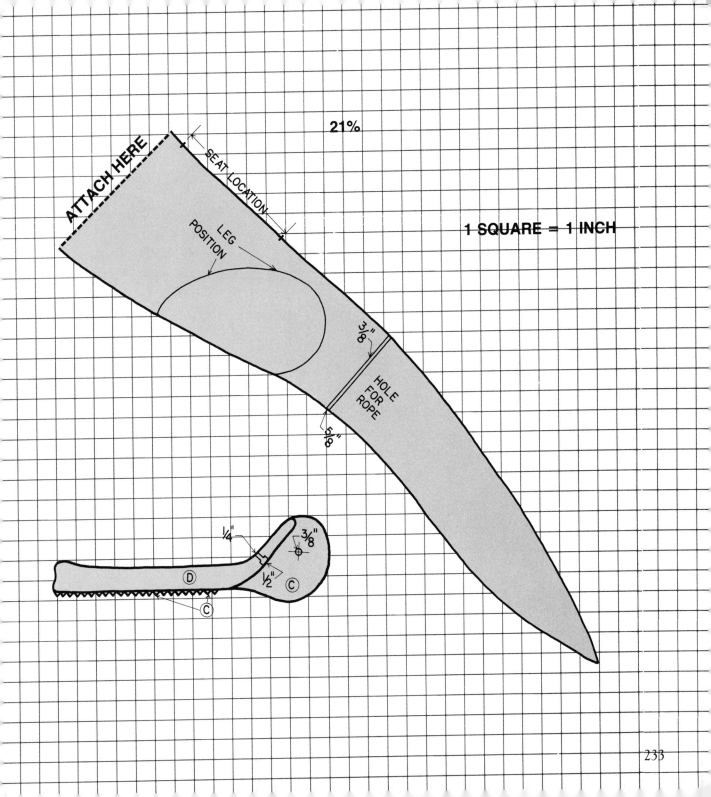

21%

1 SQUARE = 1 INCH

ATTACH HERE

SEAT LOCATION

LEG
POSITION

3/8 "

HOLE
FOR
ROPE

5/8 "

1/4"

3/8"

Ⓓ

1/2"

Ⓒ

Ⓒ

233

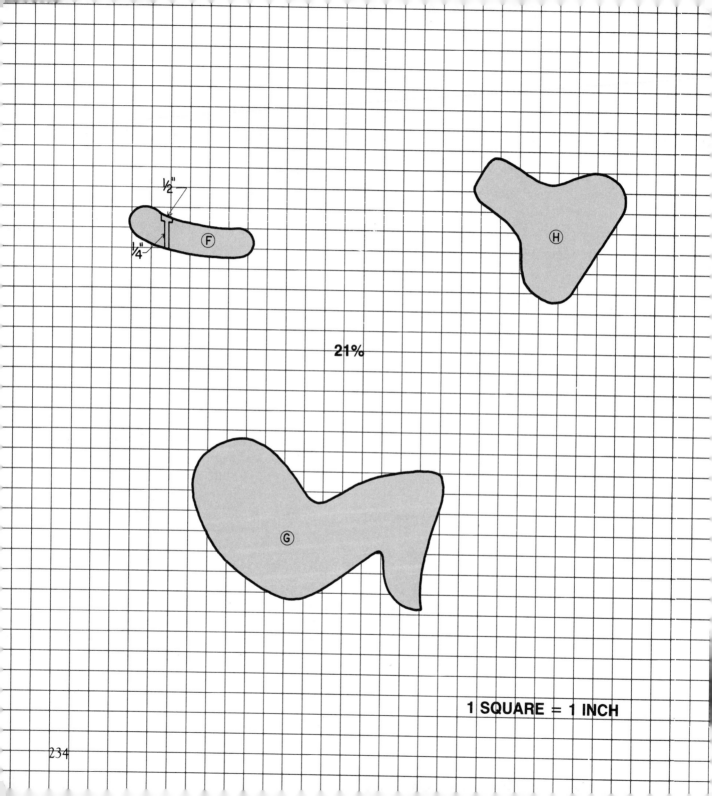

½"

¼"

Ⓕ

Ⓗ

21%

Ⓖ

1 SQUARE = 1 INCH

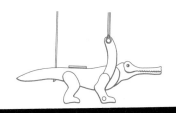
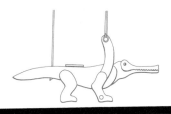
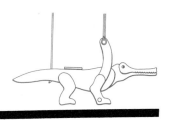

them. Rout the entire silhouette on both sides. Fill any exposed voids with water putty. Hand-sand all the routed edges and filled areas.

Lay the pieces on top of one another to drill the pivot holes identically. Set the drill press so the tip of the spade bit just enters the piece underneath. This will locate the hole on the second piece and give you a hole to center the bit as you flip the top piece over and finish the hole from the other side. Switch the pieces and repeat for the second piece.

Lay the spacer (F) out on the edge of a board (1¾″ × 2¾″ × 6¾″). Cut it out and edge-sand it. Drill the hole for the cord, a ½″ hole to hide the knot and then a ¼″ hole the rest of the way through.

Put glue on both sides of the spacer and use two 1″ dowels through the hand and foot holes in the leg pivot pieces to keep them positioned as you bring them together. Position the spacer and clamp the sides in place. When the glue has set up, countersink and drill six screw holes through the leg pivot pieces into the spacer on one side and then the other. Screw them together with 1¼″ × 8 wood screws or drywall screws. Remove the positioning dowels and fill the holes with water putty. Sand them smooth when the putty has set up.

Cut the two 1″ × 18″ dowels (N) to length. Drill the ⅜″ holes through the handlebar dowel for the hanging ropes (*See Tools, Techniques and Production Procedures, Figure 4*). Rout both ends of both dowels. Hold them firmly in a vertical position as you pass counter-clockwise around the bit.

Twist the two dowels into position (perfectly centered with the holes in the handlebars vertically positioned). You may have to ream the 1″ holes in the leg pivot pieces to get the dowels in place.

Drill ⅛″ holes through the front of the plywood sides and into the dowels, on either side, top and bottom. Glue the ⅛″ dowels in place, cut off any excess and sand the ends smooth.

The Rear Legs

Lay out both rear legs (G) on ¾″ A-C plywood with the good side outward. Cut them out, edge-sand them and rout the entire silhouette. Fill any exposed voids in the plywood with water putty and hand-sand both pieces when the putty has set up.

The Seat

Cut the seat (H) out of ¾″ hardwood with the grain running across the seat for strength. Flat-sand both sides and edge-sand the silhouette. Rout the top edge with a ½″ quarter-round bit (for comfort) and the bottom edge with a ¼″ quarter-round bit, and hand-sand all routed edges.

Painting

The Body: Lay out the painting lines, including the position of the rear legs and the seat. These two areas should not be painted or the glue won't hold during assembly. You can, however, paint slightly over these lines to avoid having unpainted areas later on.

Masking tape will help you to get a clean line where the belly meets the upper body. Avoid getting paint in the pivot and eye holes. You can put some polyurethane in the pivot hole to keep this inner area

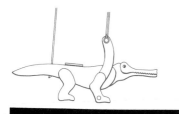 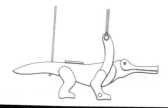 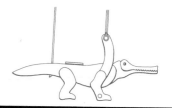

from deteriorating. This goes for the rope hole in the tail as well. Drip some polyurethane into the tail hole. Feed a piece of ¼" cord through the hole and pull it up and down to work the finish into the sides of the hole and prevent big drops from blocking the hole. Do this several times since the end grain will soak up a lot of finish.

You'll need several coats of paint to thoroughly protect the piece.

The Head: Again, several coats of paint are necessary and masking tape will help you get a clean line along the teeth. Also, polyurethane in the pivot holes and rope hole will help to keep the water out.

The Pivot Legs: Mark the paint line where the leg meets the pivot arm and use masking tape for a clean line. Don't get any paint in the pivot hole, since the 1" dowel will be glued here during final assembly. Polyurethane in the rope holes will keep the water out.

The Rear Legs: The inside surfaces don't get painted (where they are glued to the body sides).

The Seat: Don't put any paint on the underside (where it gets glued to the body).

The Eye Pegs: Paint the head of the peg and apply polyurethane to the shaft except the end of the shaft that will be glued into the body.

Final Assembly: Cut the 1" pivot dowel (K) to length and cut a slot in both ends to insert the wedges. Give it several coats of polyurethane in the middle where it will pass through the body. Cut two (1" wide) wedges with the grain running the long way to drive into the ends of the 1" dowel.

Slip the pivot leg assembly over the body into position. Tap the 1" dowel through the entire assembly until it enters the hole in the second side of the pivot leg assembly. Put some glue on the sides of this hole and drive the dowel home. Squeeze a little glue into the slots and drive the wedges into place. Cut off any excess wedge material and sand smooth.

Glue the seat in place and clamp it. When the glue has get up, drill two ½" holes through the seat and into the body. Cut the ½" dowels and sand one end on the sander/grinder so that when you drive them in, they end up flush to the seat surface and smooth.

Glue and clamp the rear legs in place (identically

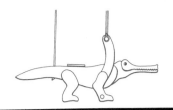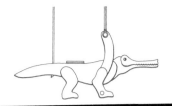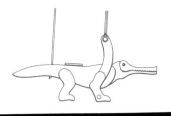

positioned) countersink and drill six or eight screw holes on either side. Screw in place with 1¼″ × #8 wood screws or drywall screws. Fill the holes with water putty and sand smooth when it has set up.

Put glue in the eye holes and peg the head in place, being careful to center it with about an ⅛″ clearance on each side.

With a knot on one end of the ¼″ polypropylene cord pull it through the snout spacer so that the knot sets into the ½″ hole. Then feed the other end through the pivot leg spacer. Tie this knot so that when the pivot legs are forward, the mouth is open (with the knot set into the ½″ countersink). It will be slack when the legs are perpendicular.

Finally touch up the pivot dowel end, seat plugs, filler on the legs, etc. and he's ready go, chomping his way into infamy (See *The Variable Swing Rack for hanging instructions*).

The Dinosaur Egg Swing

This swing has a seat compartment that will hold a small child securely as you push the swing back and forth. The bulk of this swing does make it heavy, and so it should always be used by an adult with a small child, rather than by two children.

This swing does take a lot of sanding, and so a good belt sander is recommended if you're going to build it.

Cutting Out the Pieces

Lay out the enlarged patterns on ¾" plywood. There's only one "A" piece, but two of each of the others. You'll want to lay them out so that you can cut off manageable pieces with the circular saw.

Next cut out all the pieces on the band saw. I think that the weight is nice for momentum, so you don't have to push the swing as often. But you can reduce the weight by cutting out sections of the pieces. Just make sure that you leave plenty of material for screwing the parts together. Keep in mind, also, that you'll be sanding quite a taper on the edges which will reduce the outer circumference of them. Make your entrance cuts in different places (on each piece) so that you won't lose strength.

Assembly

You'll have to screw together parts B_1-G_1 and pieces B_2-G_2 on either side first.

Start with B_1 on the workbench. Lay C_1 on top of it, so that the inner compartment edges meet up perfectly. Screw it in place with #6 or #8 drywall screws (keeping well away from the outer edge of the egg which will be rounded over) (*See Figure 1*).

Repeat the process with D_1, E_1, F_1 and G_1 until you have one side of the seat compartment totally assembled. Then cut the inner edge again on the band saw carefully to even off all these edges and make a comfortable surface for the seat (*See Figure 2*). Repeat this process for the other side.

Next position first one and then the other of these assemblies on either side of A_1 and adjust the seat line on the band saw to conform to the two side assemblies.

Repeat this entire process for B_2-G_2 on either side, except the last step of adjusting A_1.

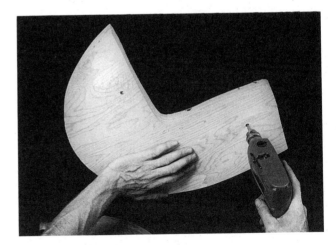

Figure 1. Start by screwing C_1 to B_1 with the inner compartment edges lined up.

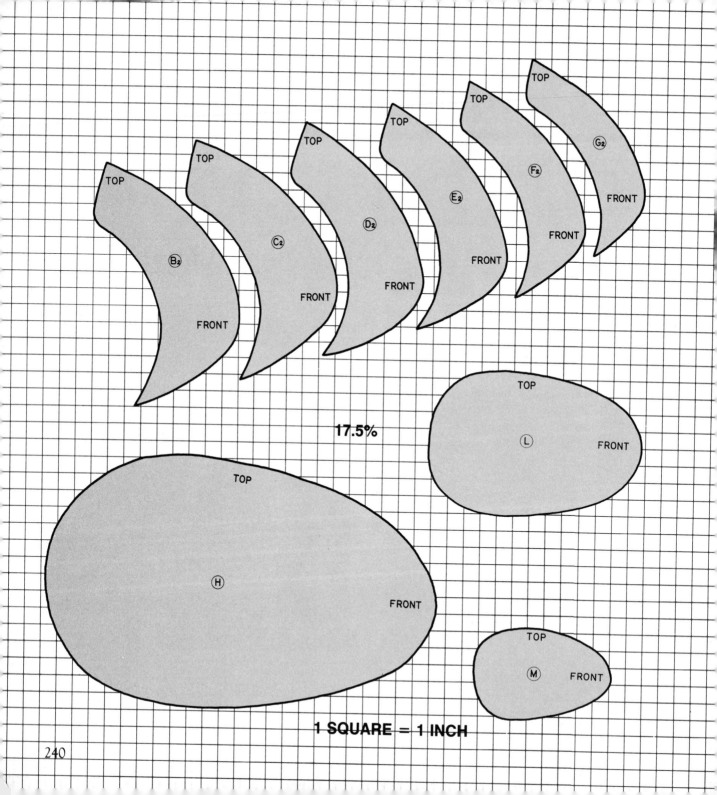

TOP

B_2

FRONT

TOP

C_2

FRONT

TOP

D_2

FRONT

TOP

E_2

FRONT

TOP

F_2

FRONT

TOP

G_2

FRONT

17.5%

TOP

L

FRONT

TOP

FRONT

H

TOP

M

FRONT

1 SQUARE = 1 INCH

240

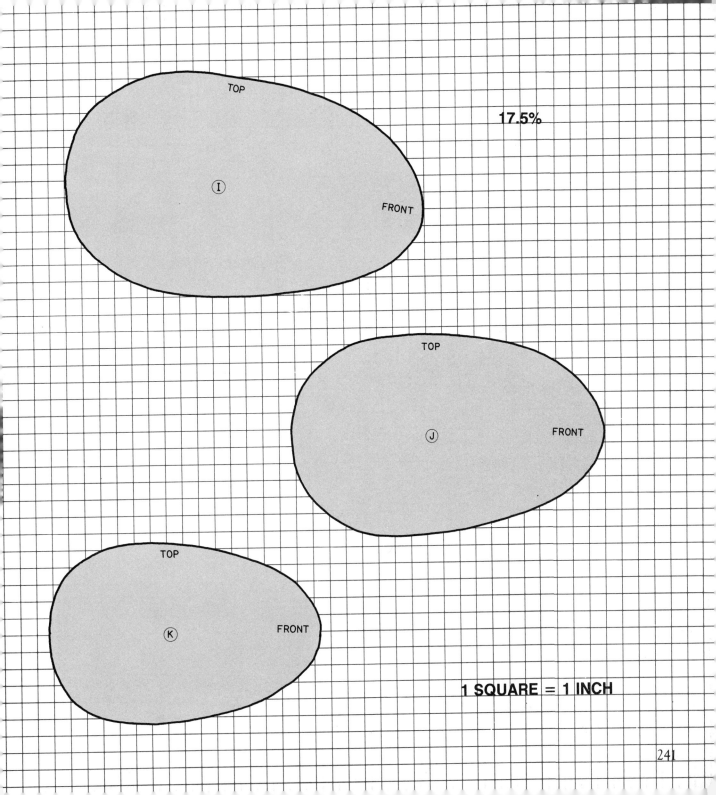

17.5%

TOP

FRONT

I

TOP

FRONT

J

TOP

FRONT

K

1 SQUARE = 1 INCH

241

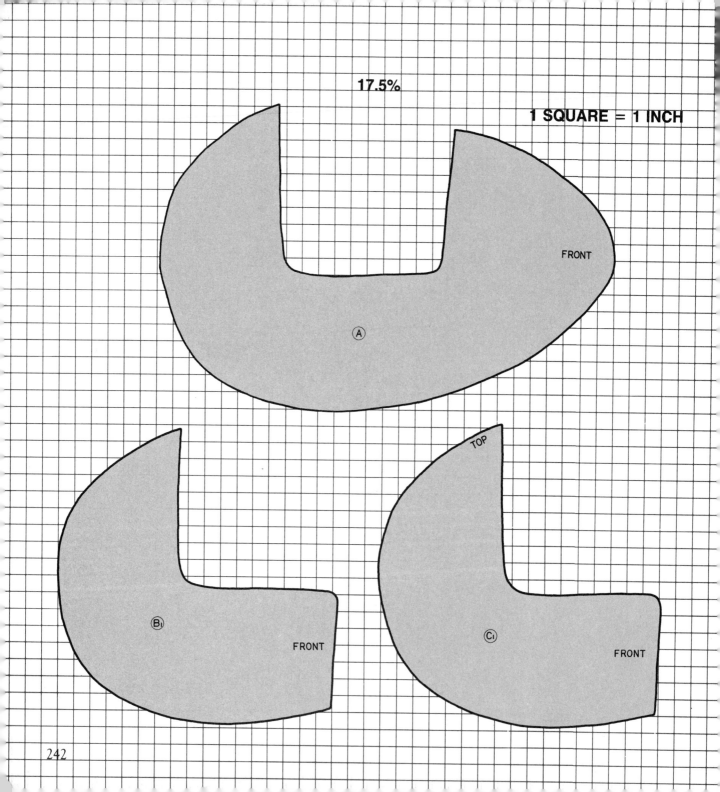

17.5%

1 SQUARE = 1 INCH

FRONT

Ⓐ

Ⓑ

FRONT

TOP

Ⓒ

FRONT

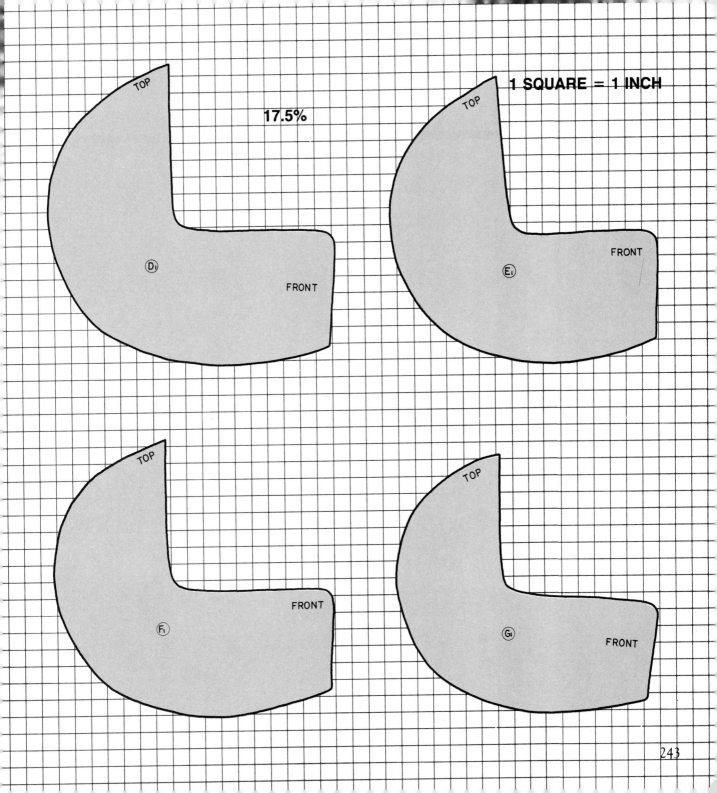

17.5%

1 SQUARE = 1 INCH

TOP

TOP

FRONT

FRONT

D₁

E₁

TOP

TOP

FRONT

FRONT

F₁

G₁

243

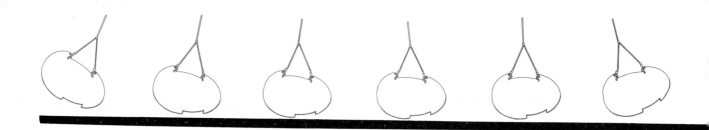

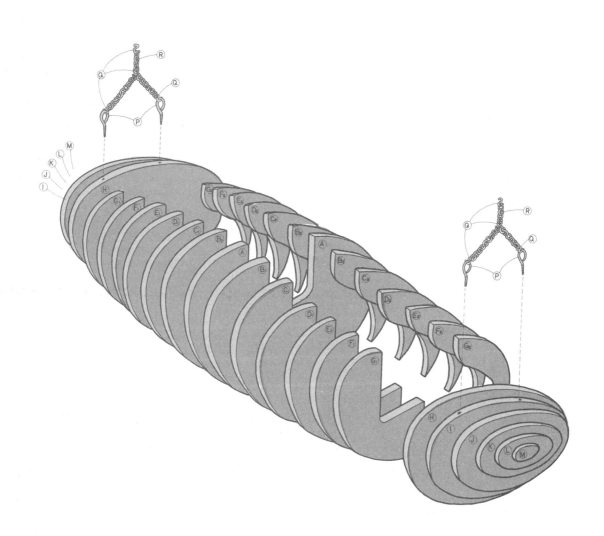

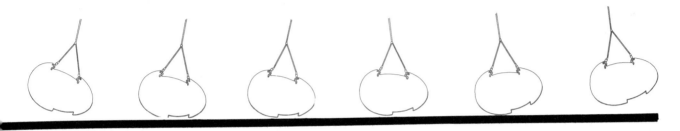

Now unscrew all four assemblies. Spread glue on the inner surface of B_1 and screw it to A_1, then B_1 to A_1 on the other side, and continue until B_1 through G_1 are glued and screwed to either side of A_1. Repeat this process for B_2-G_2 on both sides.

Scrape off any glue squeeze-out from the inner surfaces.

Before gluing and screwing the remaining pieces in place, stack them up on one side (H-L). And position them so that there is a consistent curve with the fattest area (the rear, center of the last piece) ending up at the center of seat compartment (*See Figure 3*).

When you are satisfied with the rough shape, scribe around each piece to mark its location on the piece below it.

Now remove all the pieces (H-L) and glue and screw them in place one at a time. Keep in mind that the taper in the front will be flatter, so the screws will have to be farther back from the front edge to remain unexposed (and unsanded).

As you repeat the process for the other side, try to match the two sides as closely as possible.

Now for the sanding!

You'll want to make some sort of nest to cradle your egg in as you sand it, just something to keep it

BILL OF MATERIALS

PART	DESCRIPTION	QTY	THICKNESS	APPROX. WIDTH OR DIAMETER	APPROX. LENGTH	PART	DESCRIPTION	QTY	THICKNESS	APPROX. WIDTH OR DIAMETER	APPROX. LENGTH
A	Center of egg	1	¾"	18½"	29"	G_2	7th Front piece	2	¾"	15"	24"
B_1	2nd Rear piece	2	¾"	18½"	18"	H	8th Piece	2	¾"	15"	24"
B_2	2nd Front piece	2	¾"	8"	14½"	I	9th Piece	2	¾"	14"	22"
C_1	3rd Rear piece	2	¾"	18½"	18"	J	10th Piece	2	¾"	12"	20"
C_2	3rd Front piece	2	¾"	7½"	14½"	K	11th Piece	2	¾"	10½"	16½"
D_1	4th Rear piece	2	¾"	18"	17½"	L	12th Piece	2	¾"	8½"	13"
D_2	4th Front piece	2	¾"	7"	14¼"	M	13th Piece	2	¾"	5½"	9"
E_1	5th Rear piece	2	¾"	17¼"	17½"	N	Drywall screws	200		#8	1¼"
E_2	5th Front piece	2	¾"	5¾"	13½"	P	Eye screws	4		⅜"	4"
F_1	6th Rear piece	2	¾"	16½"	17"	Q	"S" Hooks	4		⅜"	3"
F_2	6th Front piece	2	¾"	5"	13"	R	Nylon			⅜"	20' approx.
G_1	7th Rear piece	2	¾"	16"	16½"						

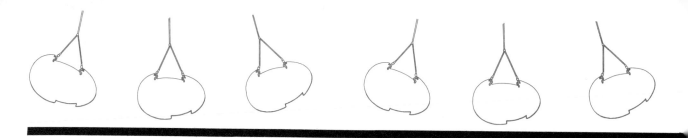

from rolling. An easy way to make one is to screw together some of the cut out scraps from all the pieces you screwed together. Or just stack up some boards around the egg.

The belt sander will cut faster if you sand perpendicularly across the edges of the pieces. Sweep the sander from side to side as you sand to get a smooth curve. This process will take a while, so don't lose heart. Keep in mind that the belt will heat up, so it's a good idea to take breaks (for your arms as well) to let the belt cool down or the glue will give out and the belt will come apart long before the material is worn out.

When the whole outside surface of the egg is sanded to your satisfaction, round off the edges of the seat compartment with a four-in-hand and sandpaper. Drill the four holes for the eye screws.

Painting

Fill all the voids in the plywood with water putty. Hand-sand the entire surface. Prime all of the surfaces and apply several coats of paint. Let the paint dry thoroughly and sand lightly between coats.

Figure 2. When parts B_1- G_1 are screwed together, go over the inside edge of the seat on the band saw to smooth the seat surface.

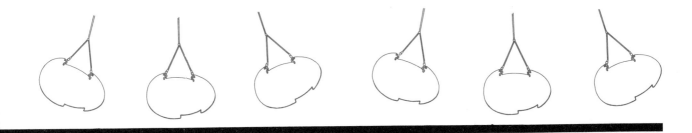

Hanging the Egg

Screw in the eye screws. Cut two lengths of ⅜″ nylon to 2½′. Tie one piece of rope to the front and back eye screw on one side with three half-hitches, and then tape the ends. Repeat this for the other side. Now fasten the hanging rope to each side by means of a bowline knot (*See Figure 4*). Make sure that the knots are located identically on each side so that the swing will hang straight.

Tie an "S" hook to the upper end of each rope, again making sure that both sides are the same length. Tape the rope ends to the hanging rope to prevent the knots from slipping. You may want a friend to help you actually hang the swing since it is very heavy.

Now you're ready to swing. Put your favorite hatchling in the cockpit and give a push.

Figure 4. A bowline knot is best for fastening the rope.

Figure 3. Position the remaining pieces so that there is a smooth egglike curve and the widest part of the egg is right over the middle of the seat compartment.

247

The Variable Swing Rack

efore I explain how to make the Variable Swing Rack, I'd like to go over hanging the swings, since you may not need to build a swing rack.

There are several ways to hang these swings other than from a rack.

On The Porch or Indoors

If you have a porch, that's an ideal place to hang these swings. It keeps the swing out of the weather so it lasts longer. It also means that children can ride on it in foul weather (when they may not be able to think of other things to do). A basement or den will do equally well.

In standard house framing the joists are set at either 12", 16" or 24" centers. The handlebar holes are 16" apart and the front to back holes are 24" apart, so, one way or the other, you should be able to fasten your eye bolts into the joists. (Using "S" hooks on the upper end of your ropes will keep the ropes from wearing out and also enable you to take the swing down.)

From a Tree

It's hard to find a tree with branches positioned just right for this. Keep in mind that the ropes need to be perfectly vertical for the swing to work properly (See Figure 1). Sometimes a board between two branches will give you the hanging points that you need.

"S" hooks on the upper end of the ropes (through the eye bolts) will enable you to take the swing down for the winter and prevent unnecessary weathering.

General Hanging Instructions

Use ⅜" nylon or polypropylene cord to hang your swing or glider. They should be hung from ½" eye screws with ⅜" "S" hooks to reduce the wear on the ropes.

The ropes on the handlebars should go through the hole from the top, circle 1½ times around the handlebar and tie back to the vertical rope with three half-hitches (See Figure 1). These wraps will keep the handlebars from splitting. Taping the ends of the rope will ensure that the knots don't come untied.

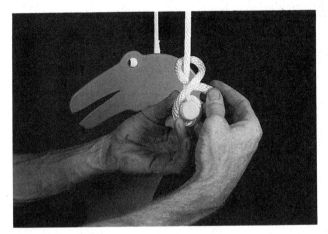

Figure 1. Use three half-hitches to attach the ropes.

The ropes in the tails of the animals should come up from underneath with a double knot, (large enough that it won't slip through the hole).

The ends of the ropes should be melted to prevent fraying or unraveling.

The ropes should be as close to vertical as possible (*See Figure 1*).

Figure 2. When you're looking at the glider or swing (simplified drawing) from the front, the ropes should hang parallel. If they spread out a little, the swing will be more stable; but don't let them come together. When you're looking at the swing or glider (simplified drawing) from the side, all the ropes must hang parallel. Don't let them come together or spread apart.

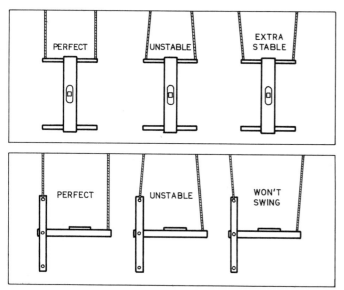

The Rack

This rack can be made to hang one, two, three or four swings depending on the length of the top pieces "F" (front and back).

It's a good idea to make this rack entirely out of treated lumber since it will be exposed to the weather. When you're buying your treated boards, pick out straight ones without any flaws, if possible.

Cut the four legs to length (A). These receive a 20° angle and a 20° bevel on the top. To make these cuts, scribe a line at the top and bottom of the legs at a 20° angle. Then set your circular saw blade at a 20° bevel, and cut along the lines.

Next cut the notches out of the top of each leg for the long top boards (F) to set into. A hand saw is easiest for this cut. Notice that the bottom of the notch is cut at 20°, parallel to the top edge (*See Figure 4*).

Lay out the two middle cross supports (B) and the two top supports (C), cutting the ends at a 20° angle (with no bevel). With all cuts completed, lay the two "A" frame assemblies on the floor, with scraps under the joints. Note that the top cross support (C) is lined up with the edge of the notch rather than the edge of the board. When all is lined up, drill three holes through each joint, drilling through into the scraps underneath (*See Figure 5*). Bolt the assemblies together with flat washers and lock washers.

Determine the length of the long beams (F) from which the swings will hang according to how many

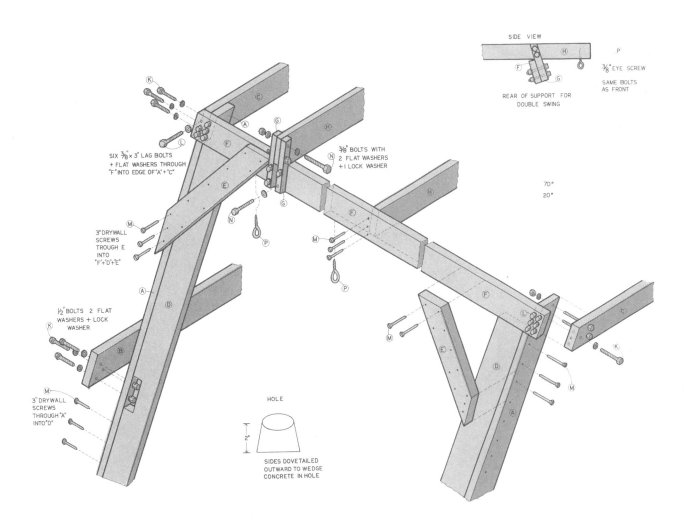

SIDE VIEW

P

Ⓗ

Ⓕ Ⓖ

3/8" EYE SCREW

SAME BOLTS
AS FRONT

REAR OF SUPPORT FOR
DOUBLE SWING

Ⓚ

Ⓒ

Ⓐ Ⓖ Ⓗ

Ⓕ

SIX 3/8" x 3" LAG BOLTS
+ FLAT WASHERS THROUGH
"F" INTO EDGE OF "A"+"C"

Ⓛ

3/8" BOLTS WITH
2 FLAT WASHERS
+ 1 LOCK WASHER

Ⓝ

Ⓔ

70°

20°

Ⓜ

Ⓝ

Ⓖ

Ⓕ

Ⓗ

3" DRYWALL
SCREWS
TROUGH E
INTO
"F"+"D"+"E"

Ⓟ

Ⓜ

Ⓐ

Ⓓ

Ⓟ

Ⓕ

1/2" BOLTS 2 FLAT
WASHERS + LOCK
WASHER

Ⓚ

Ⓛ

Ⓑ

Ⓜ

Ⓔ

Ⓓ

Ⓜ

Ⓜ

3" DRYWALL
SCREWS
THROUGH "A"
INTO "D"

HOLE

2"

Ⓐ

Ⓚ

SIDES DOVETAILED
OUTWARD TO WEDGE
CONCRETE IN HOLE

EXPLODED VIEW

251

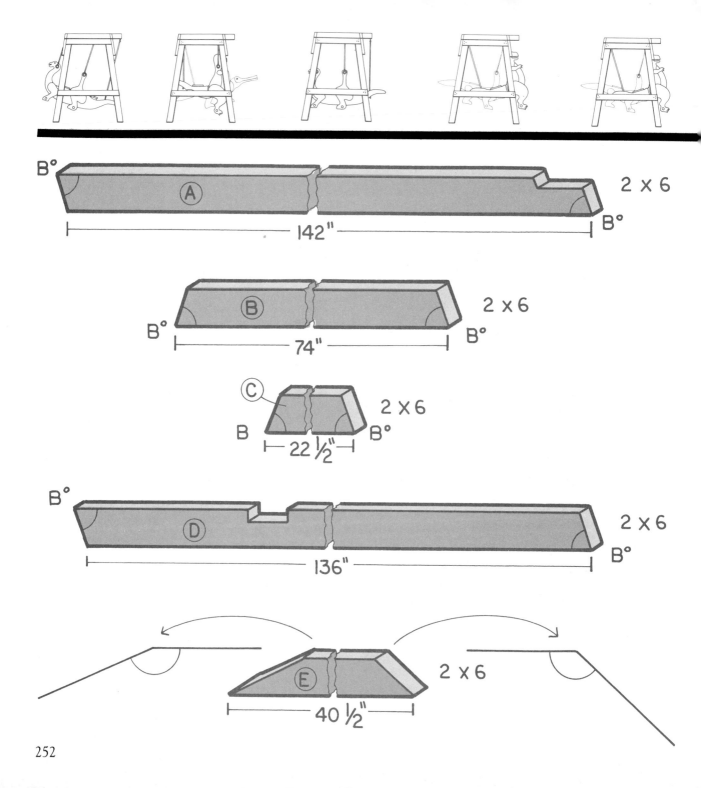

B° · ⓐ · 142" · B° · 2 x 6

B° · ⓑ · 74" · B° · 2 x 6

ⓒ · B · 22 ½" · B° · 2 X 6

B° · ⓓ · 136" · B° · 2 x 6

ⓔ · 40 ½" · 2 x 6

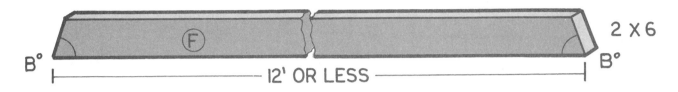

F 2 X 6

B° 12' OR LESS B°

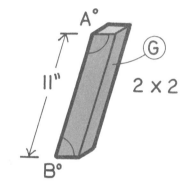

A°

11"

G 2 x 2

B°

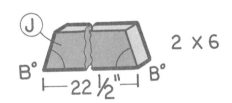

J 2 X 6

B° 22 ½" B°

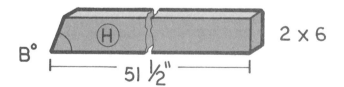

B° H 2 x 6

51 ½"

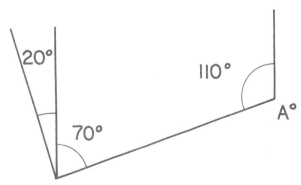

20°

110°

70° A°

swings you're going to have. (One swing: 48″, Two swings: 80″, Three swings: 112″, Four swings: 144″.)

Cut the 20° angles at each end of the piece. Lay the board on the floor or workbench with the longer edge upward. (This will be the bottom edge.) Lay out and drill the holes for the eye bolts. Remember to leave 16″ clearance between each swing. There will be two holes for the handlebar ropes and one for the rear rope. The two seater will have two eye bolts for each set of handlebars. Another support will be added later for the eye bolt that will support the rear of the double swing. Screw the eye bolts into the holes.

Finally, lay out and cut the four diagonal braces (E) as shown in the pattern.

Figure 3. The ends of the legs are cut at a compound angle. The line is scribed at 70° and the blade on your circular saw is set at 20°.

BILL OF MATERIALS

PART	DESCRIPTION	QTY	THICKNESS	WIDTH OR DIAMETER	LENGTH
A	Legs	4	2″	6″	144″
B	Lower cross brace	2	2″	6″	74″
C	Upper cross brace	2	2″	6″	22½″
D	Leg supports	4	2″	6″	138″
E	Corner braces	4	2″	6″	40½″
F	Rail	2	2″	6″	144″
G	Support	4	2″	2″	11″
H	Double swing support	1	2″	6″	51½″

PART	DESCRIPTION	QTY	THICKNESS	WIDTH OR DIAMETER	LENGTH
J	Cross beam	3	2″	6″	22½″
K	Hex head bolts w/washers	24		½″	4″
L	Lag bolts w/washers	24		⅜″	3″
M	Drywall screws	200		#8	3″
N	Hex head bolts w/washers	4		⅜″	5½″
O	Hex head bolts w/washers	8		⅜″	4″
P	Eye screws	10–14		⅜″	

Final Assembly

The rack is anchored in concrete at each of the four legs. You'll need four 2″ × 4″'s at least 12′ long and a tall ladder to set up the rack. After bringing all of the pieces to the site, measure carefully to find the location of the holes. (You may want to set up the rack, mark the holes, and take it down again to dig the holes, just to be sure.) The holes will have to be large enough to accommodate the angle of the legs. If you make the holes slightly larger at the bottom than at the top, this will help anchor the concrete in the hole. With the holes dug, nail the 2 × 4 temporary braces to the legs so that the two assemblies stand tilting 20° inward, with each leg in its hole.

Then lay the long top pieces, one at a time, in their respective notches. The end of the board will end up flush with the outer surface of the upper cross support. Drill and screw each end with six lag bolts (three into the leg and three into the end grain of the cross support).

With the 2 × 4 braces still in position, cut the 2″ × 6″ leg pieces (D) with a 20° bevel on the top and bottom. Hold these in place to mark the location of the notch which must be cut out to accommodate the bolts from the cross supports (*See exploded view*). Once marked, cut these notches out by making six or eight cuts with a circular saw, and knock out the remaining wood with a hammer. Clamp these legs in place and screw them to their respective legs with #8 × 3″ drywall screws, every 8 inches.

Figure 4. The bottom edge of the notch must be cut at 70° for the long cross piece to sit in it properly. A handsaw will do the job.

Next, hold the diagonal braces in place, making sure that they don't go in front of the eye hooks or they'll interfere with the rope's movement. Put about fifteen #8 × 3″ drywall screws into each brace.

The Double Swing Extension Support

If you're hanging a double swing, you'll need to add another 2″ × 6″ on top of the swing rack to support

the single rope at the rear of the double swing (in the tail). This will be positioned between the two eye screw holes for the handlebars (front and back). Mark its position on top of the beams (F).

Drill the hole in the edge of the 2″ × 6″ for the eye screw and screw it in.

Position the four 2″ × 2″ supports on either side of the 2″ × 6″ (in front of the rack and in the rear), and drill the two ⅜″ holes through all three pieces (fore and aft) and bolt them together with ⅜″ bolts, flat washers and lock washers.

Now position the assembly on top of the rack and clamp the two front supports to the rack, to hold it in place. Drill two ⅜″ holes through the rear supports and the long top piece of the swing rack and bolt them together. Take one clamp off the front supports and drill and bolt it. Remove the last clamp and drill and bolt it.

Filling the Holes with Concrete

The standard mix for concrete is 3:2:1. Three parts gravel, two parts sand, one part cement. Mix the sand and cement first (with a hoe) in a mixing trough or a wheelbarrow. Then add enough water to make it like thick soup. If you make it too wet, it loses strength. Mix it *thoroughly* and then add the gravel. If the soil is dry, you'll want to wet it, so that it won't draw the water out of the concrete before it cures. Make sure the swing is leveled up and shovel the concrete into the holes. Allow one week curing time before the swings are set up and used.

Figure 5. With a scrap of wood under each joint drill three holes all the way through each joint.

Figure 6. 2 × 4s will help support the end assemblies of the rack (at 20° inward from vertical) as you fasten the long top pieces.

256